Cardboa

is an intellectual sport

For thousands of years, sports have glorified physical superiority. But as the human race advances, shouldn't our sports advance as well?

That's why I love Magic. It's a more sophisticated game that rewards careful thought rather than brawn. Magic truly is the intellectual sport of our time.

Wow, that's really ni--

What?! Mana screwed again?! Arrghhh!!!

A collection of comics about the world's most addictive game.

Cardboard Crack is an intellectual sport

Copyright © 2015

Check out these other Cardboard Crack books:
Cardboard Crack
I will never quit Cardboard Crack
Cardboard Crack anytime, anywhere
Cardboard Crack until the day I die
I'm always thinking about Cardboard Crack

This book collects comics that originally appeared online between
March 8, 2015 and August 9, 2015, and can also be viewed at:
cardboard-crack.com
facebook.com/CardboardCrack

For information write:
cardboardcrack.mtg@gmail.com

Printed in the U.S.A.

For Delver of Secrets.
(Maybe it'll flip for me more often if I get on its good side!)

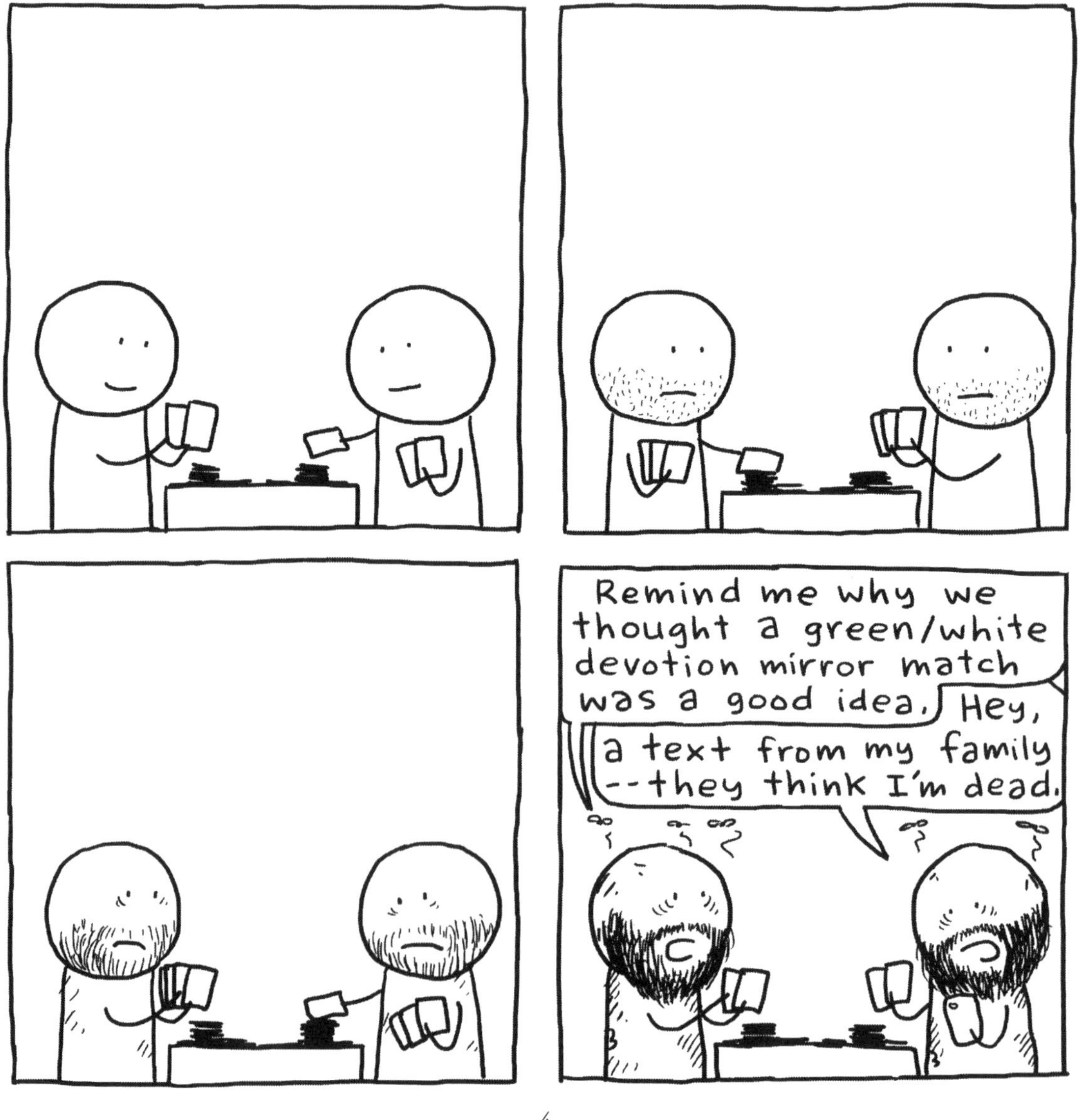
Remind me why we thought a green/white devotion mirror match was a good idea.
Hey, a text from my family --they think I'm dead.

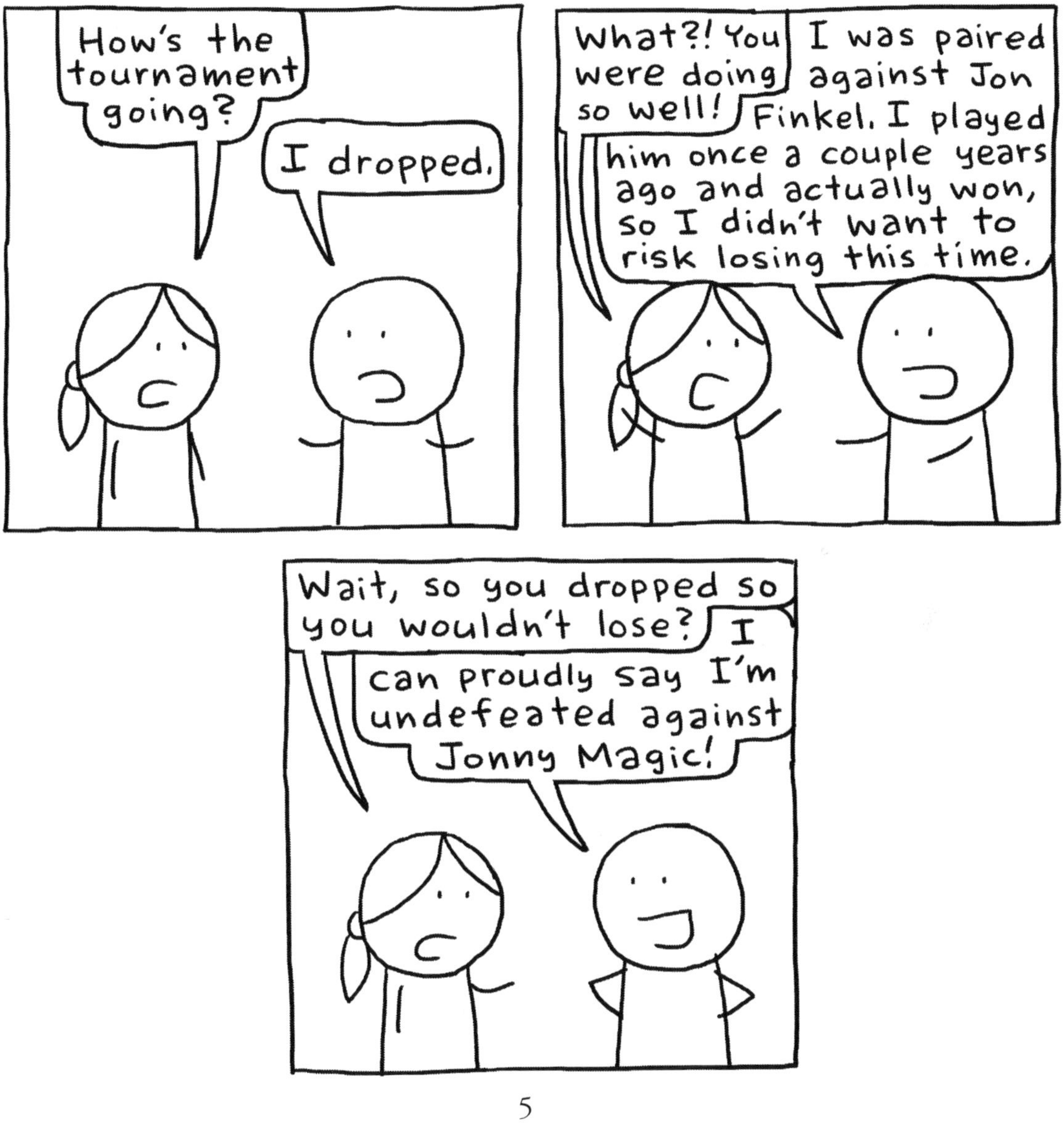
How's the tournament going?
I dropped.
What?! You were doing so well!
I was paired against Jon Finkel. I played him once a couple years ago and actually won, so I didn't want to risk losing this time.
Wait, so you dropped so you wouldn't lose?
I can proudly say I'm undefeated against Jonny Magic!

Something about this just doesn't seem right.

Tasigur in tournaments...

Tasigur in the storyline...

...eek...

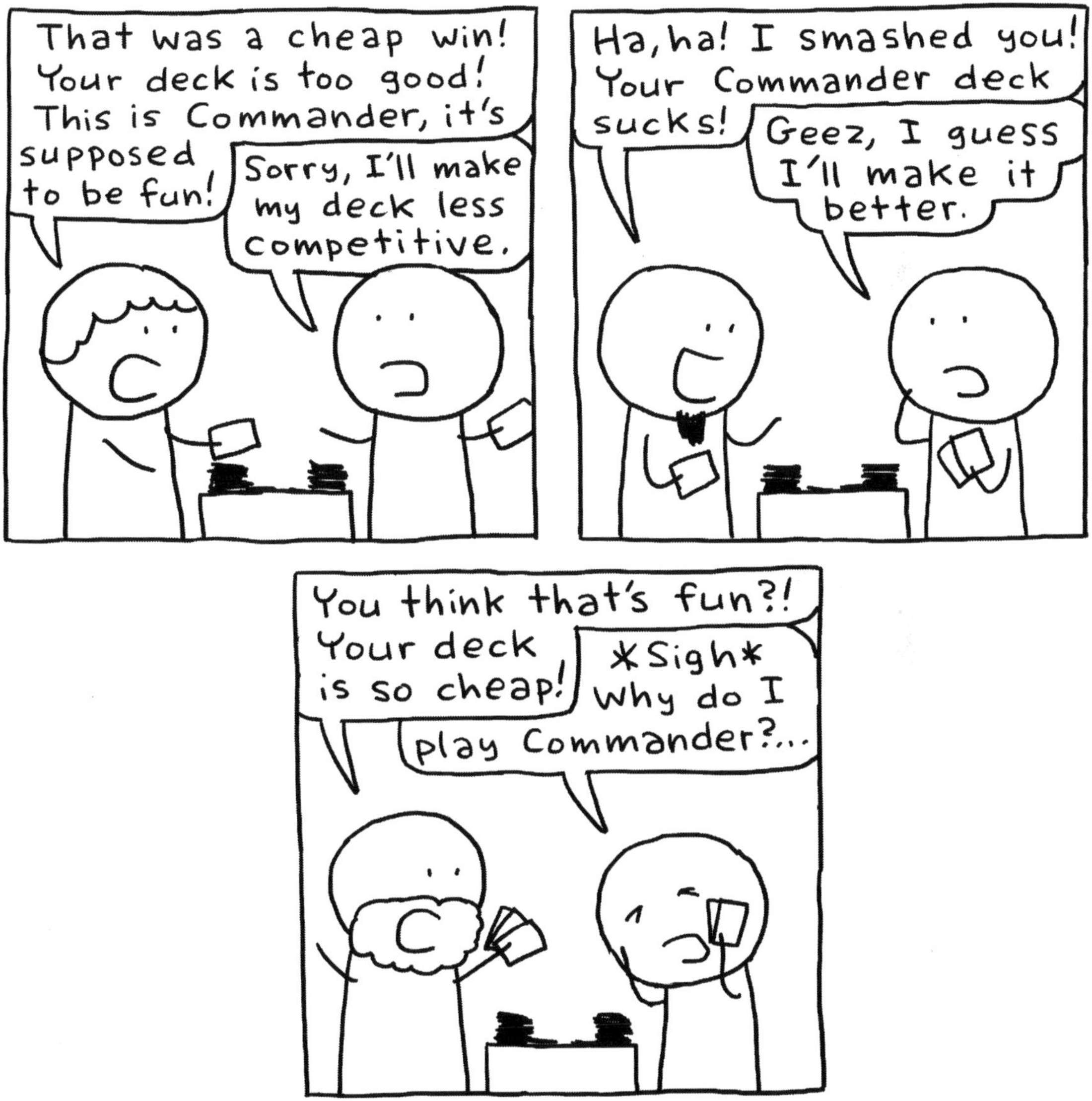
That was a cheap win! Your deck is too good! This is Commander, it's supposed to be fun!
Sorry, I'll make my deck less competitive.
Ha, ha! I smashed you! Your Commander deck sucks!
Geez, I guess I'll make it better.
You think that's fun?! Your deck is so cheap!
Sigh Why do I play Commander?...

Top 5 alternate names that were considered for Megamorph

⑤ Mightymorph

④ Superduperultramegamorph

③ Megamorph because new keywords make us more money

② Underwhelmingmorph

① Morph plus a little extra

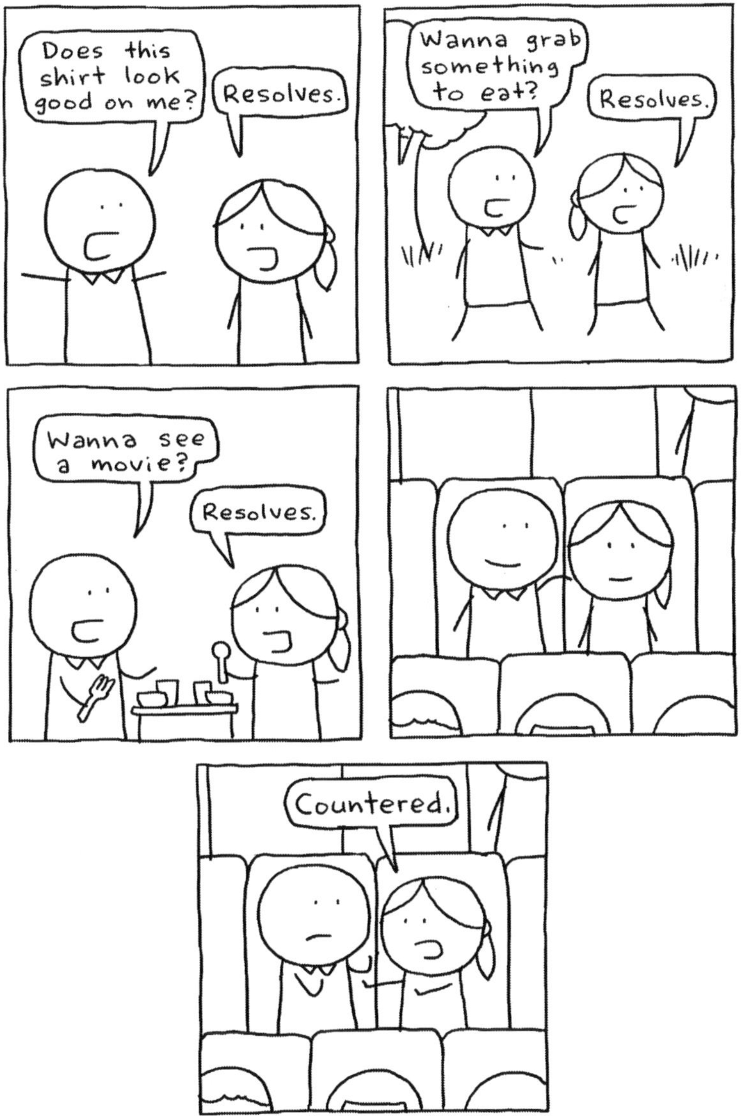

Does this shirt look good on me?
Resolves.
Wanna grab something to eat?
Resolves.
Wanna see a movie?
Resolves.
Countered.

Throughout the past...
This new creature card is awesome!
But does it die to Doom Blade?
These days...
This new removal spell is awesome!
But can it kill Siege Rhino?

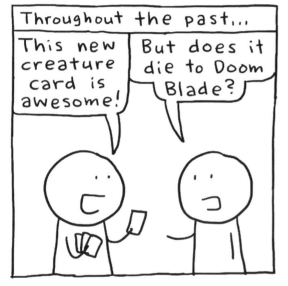

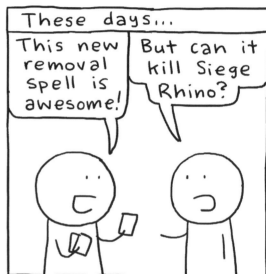

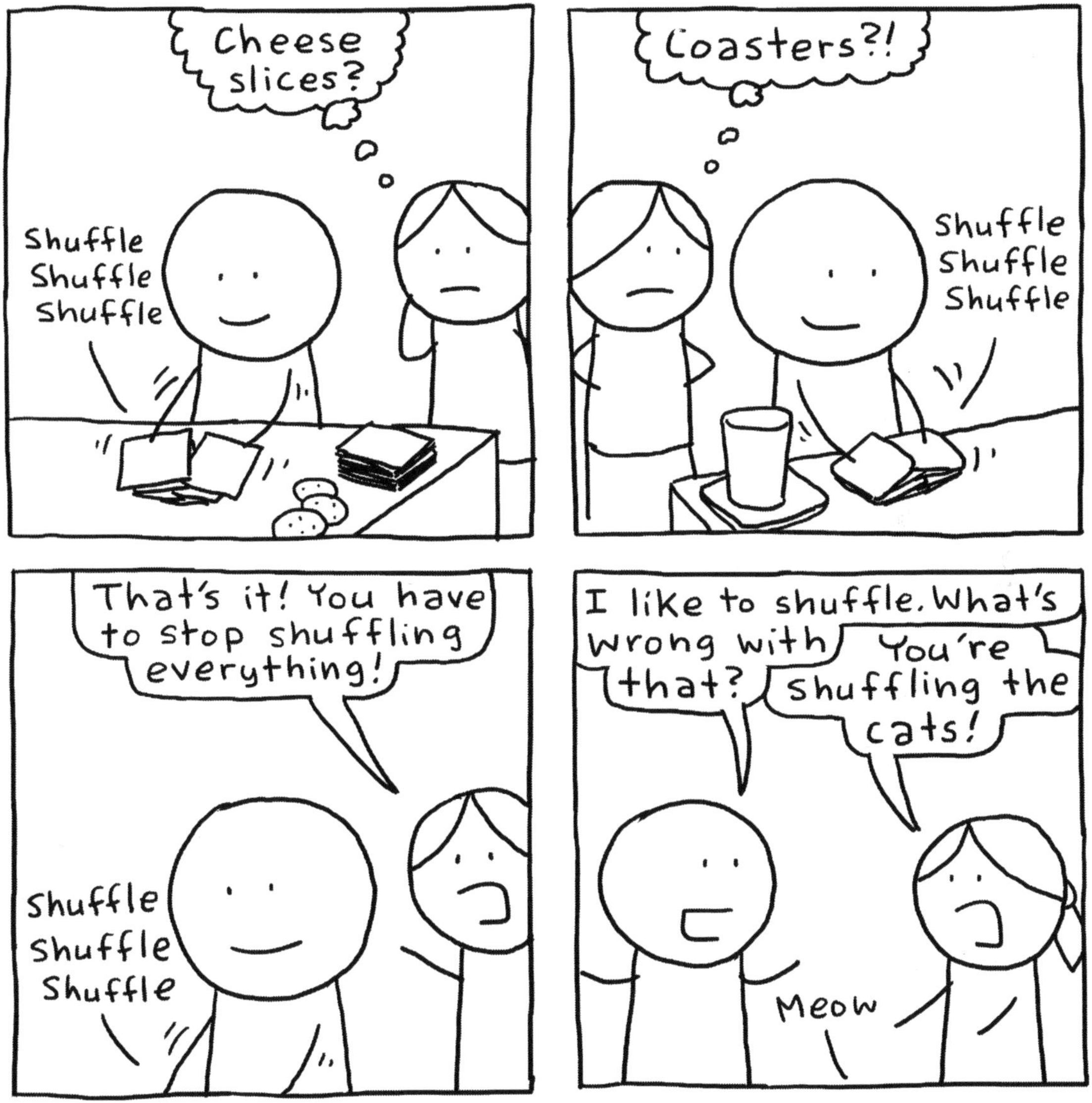
Cheese slices?
Shuffle Shuffle Shuffle
Coasters?!
Shuffle Shuffle Shuffle
That's it! You have to stop shuffling everything!
Shuffle Shuffle Shuffle
I like to shuffle. What's wrong with that?
You're shuffling the cats!
Meow

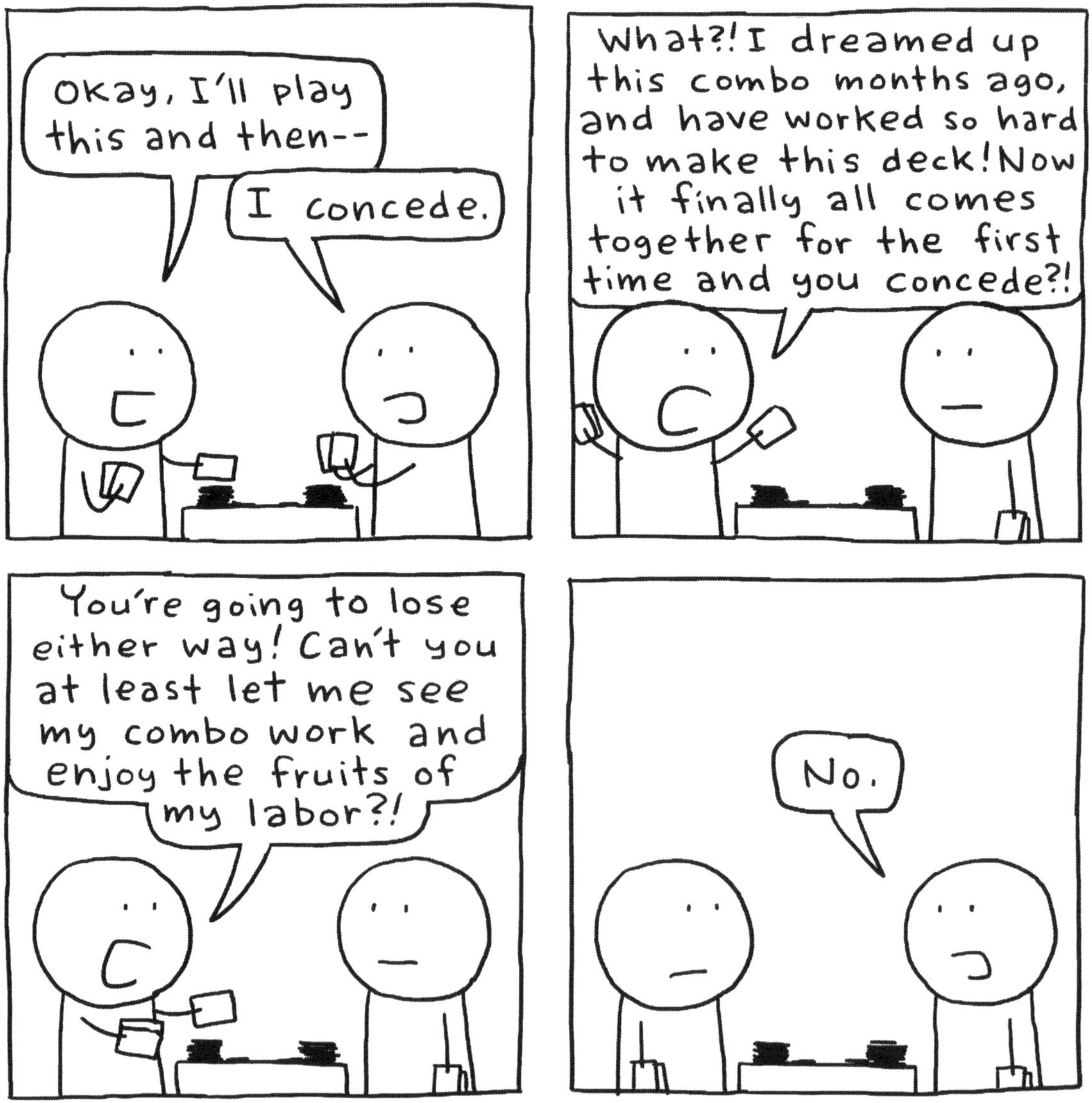
Okay, I'll play this and then--
I concede.
What?! I dreamed up this combo months ago, and have worked so hard to make this deck! Now it finally all comes together for the first time and you concede?!
You're going to lose either way! Can't you at least let me see my combo work and enjoy the fruits of my labor?!
No.

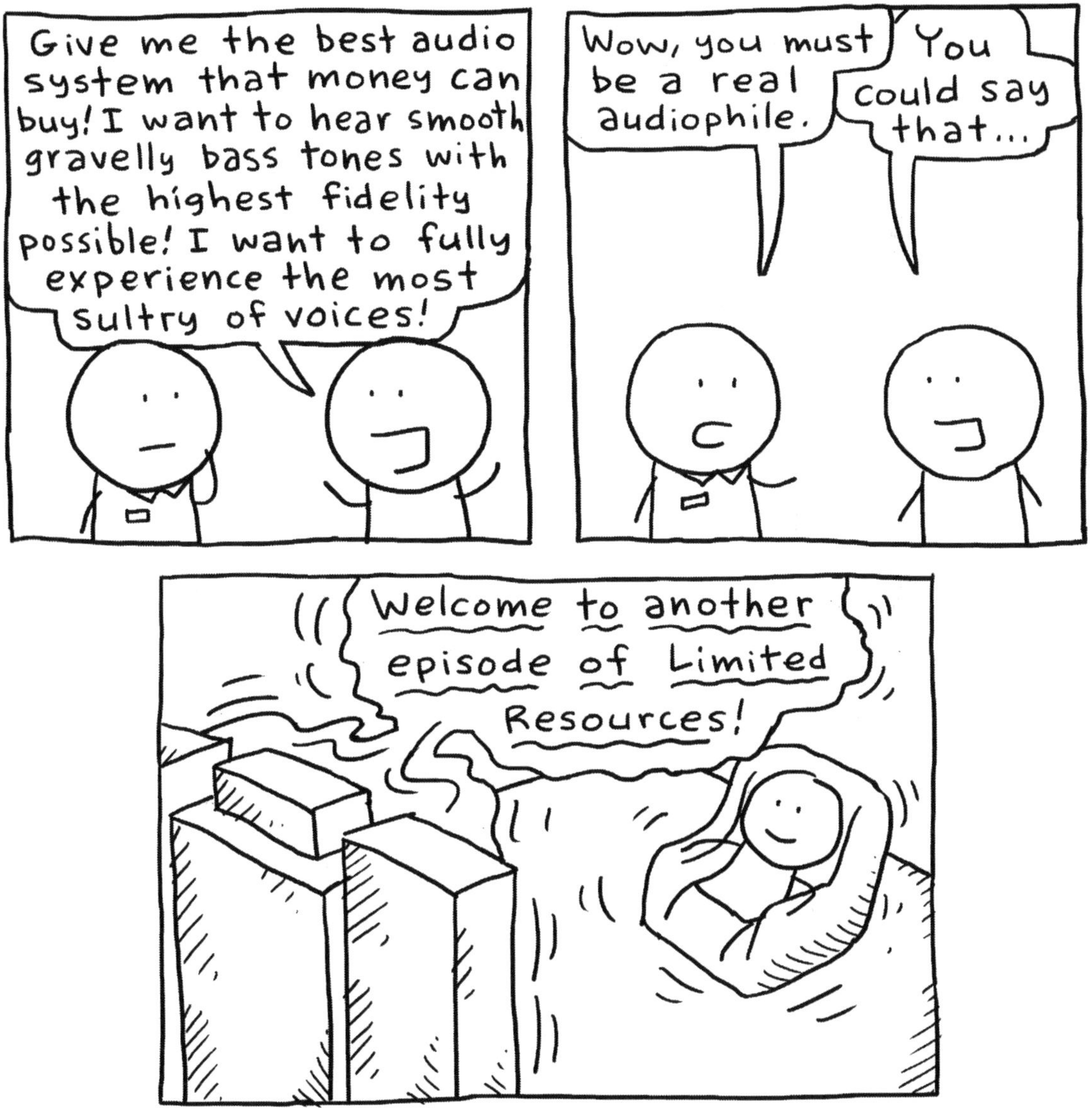
Give me the best audio system that money can buy! I want to hear smooth gravelly bass tones with the highest fidelity possible! I want to fully experience the most sultry of voices!
Wow, you must be a real audiophile.
You could say that...
Welcome to another episode of Limited Resources!

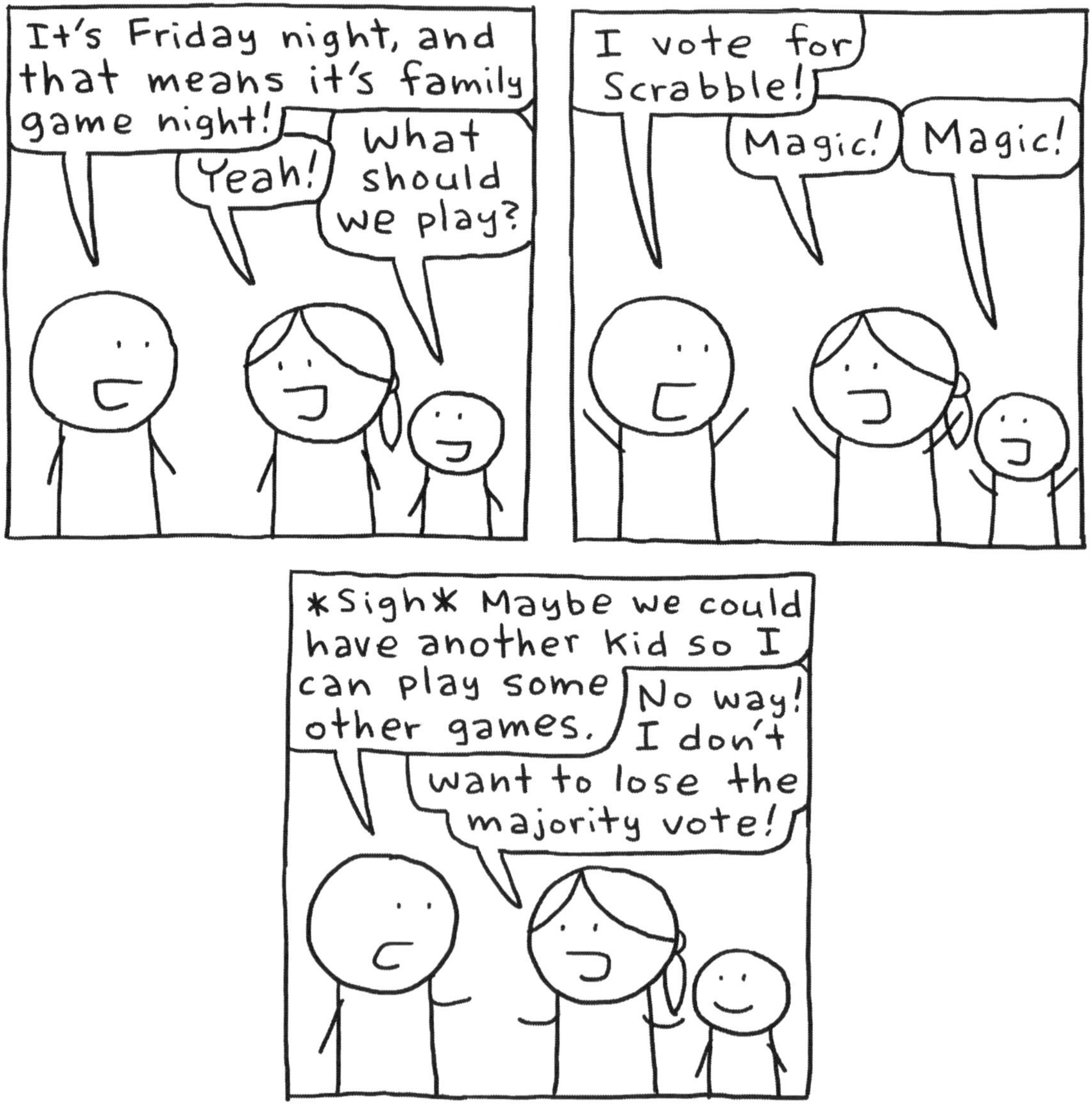
It's Friday night, and that means it's family game night!
Yeah!
What should we play?
I vote for Scrabble!
Magic!
Magic!
Sigh Maybe we could have another kid so I can play some other games.
No way! I don't want to lose the majority vote!

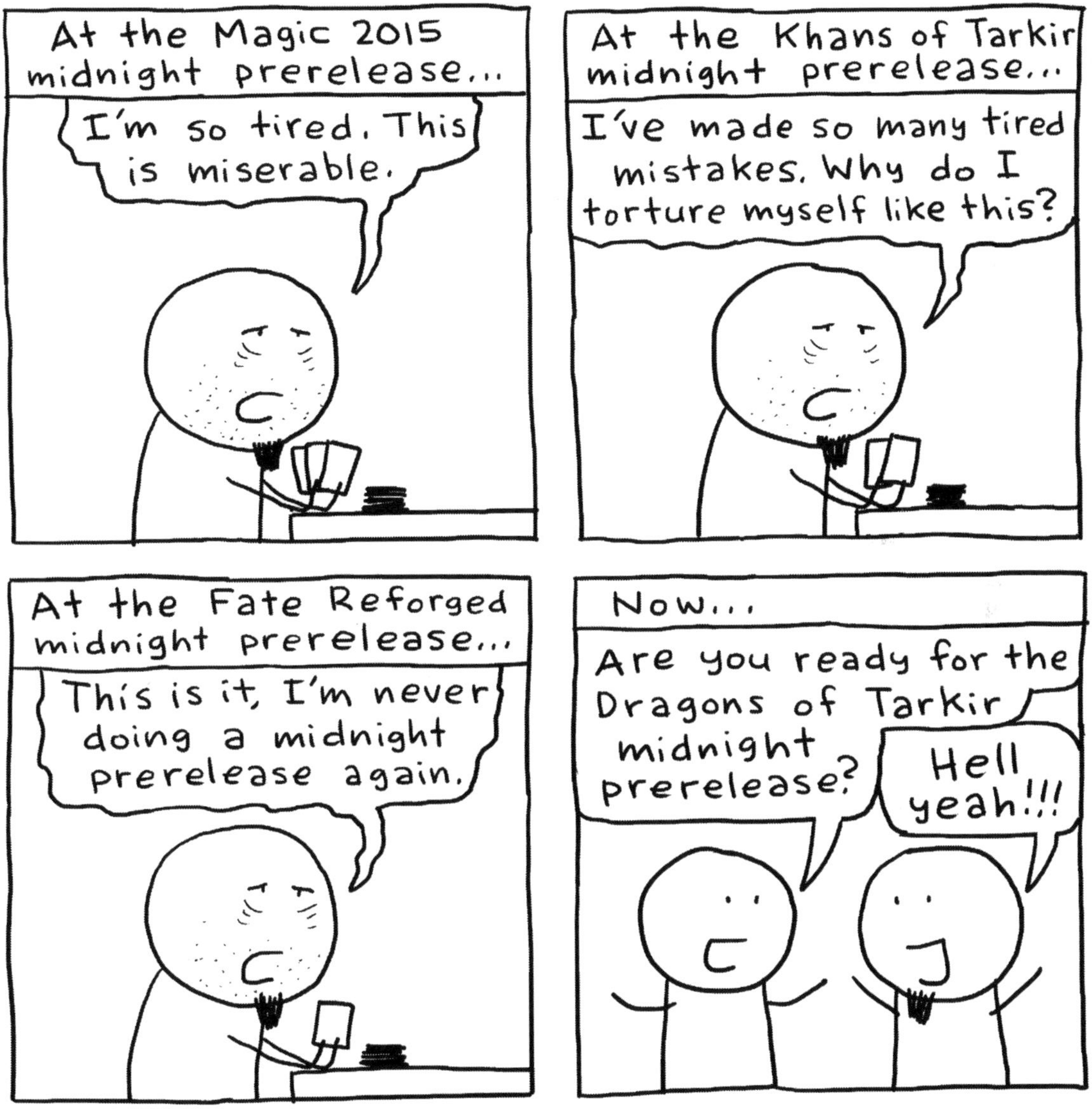
At the Magic 2015 midnight prerelease...
I'm so tired. This is miserable.
At the Khans of Tarkir midnight prerelease...
I've made so many tired mistakes. Why do I torture myself like this?
At the Fate Reforged midnight prerelease...
This is it, I'm never doing a midnight prerelease again.
Now...
Are you ready for the Dragons of Tarkir midnight prerelease?
Hell yeah!!!

Before the tournament...

You're playing a simple aggro deck? That takes like no thought! If you're smart like me, then you play control!

After many, many rounds of playing...

I'm so hungry!

If your deck won fast, you'd have time to get food between rounds--but of course you're smart enough to know that!

munch munch

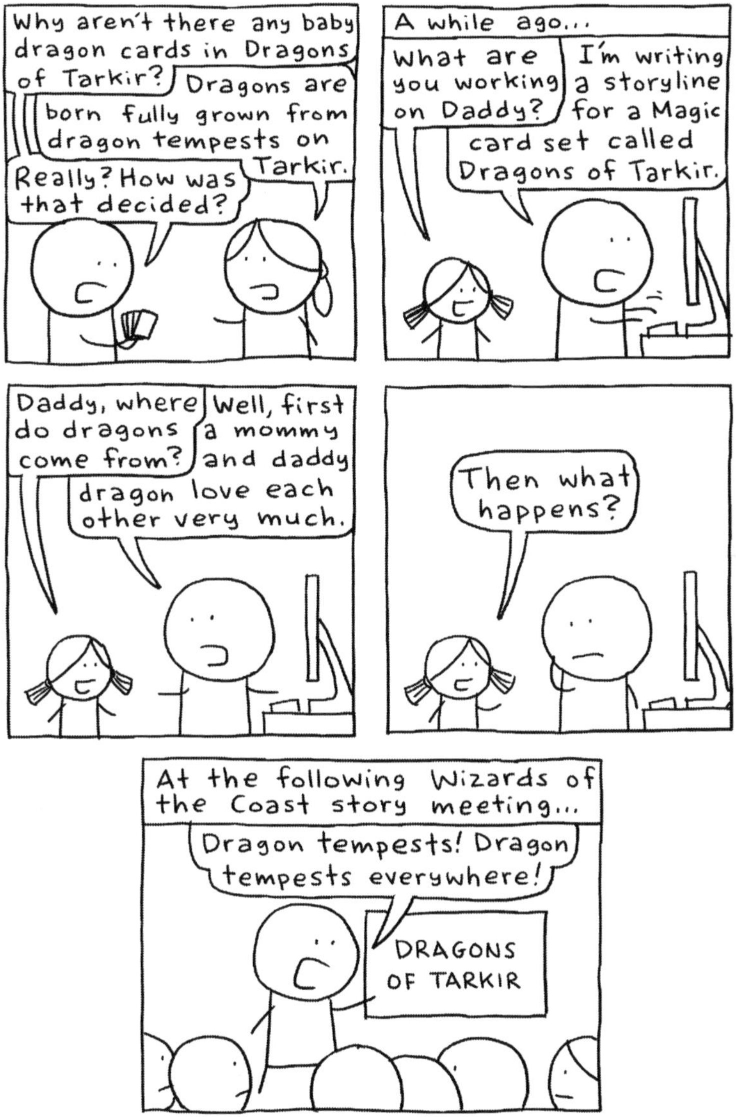
Why aren't there any baby dragon cards in Dragons of Tarkir?
Dragons are born fully grown from dragon tempests on Tarkir.
Really? How was that decided?
A while ago...
What are you working on Daddy?
I'm writing a storyline for a Magic card set called Dragons of Tarkir.
Daddy, where do dragons come from?
Well, first a mommy and daddy dragon love each other very much.
Then what happens?
At the following Wizards of the Coast story meeting...
Dragon tempests! Dragon tempests everywhere!
DRAGONS OF TARKIR

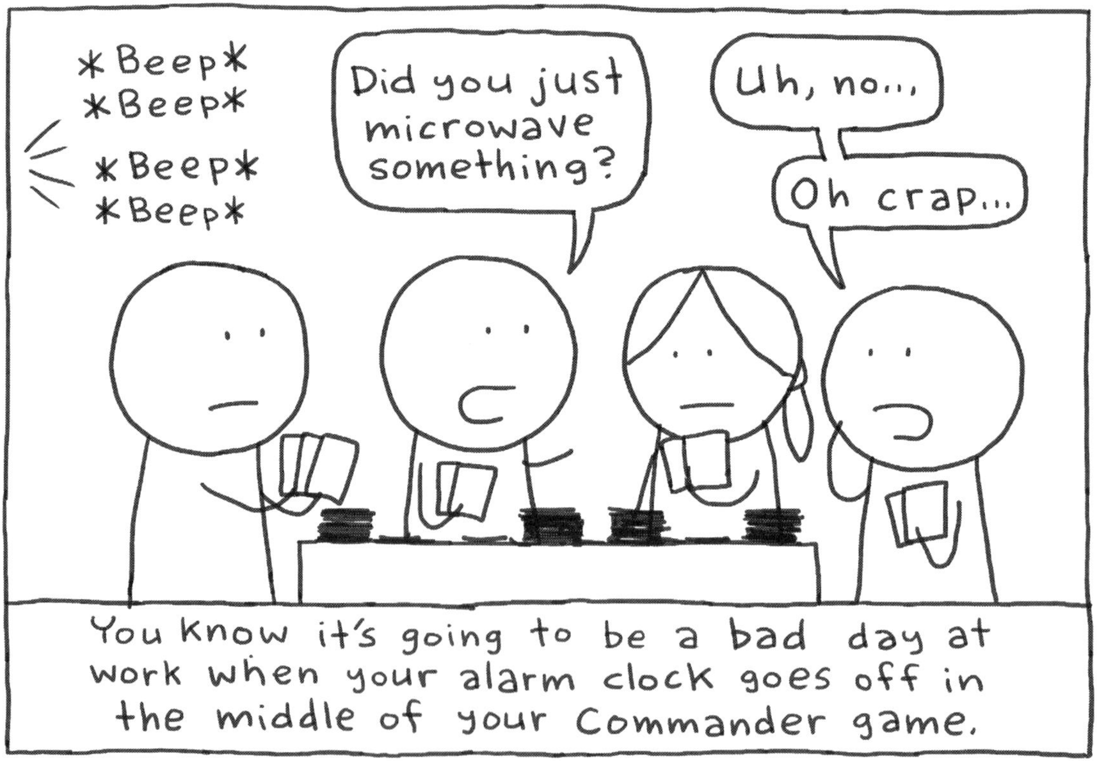
Beep
Beep
Beep
Beep
Did you just microwave something?
Uh, no...,
Oh crap...
You know it's going to be a bad day at work when your alarm clock goes off in the middle of your Commander game.

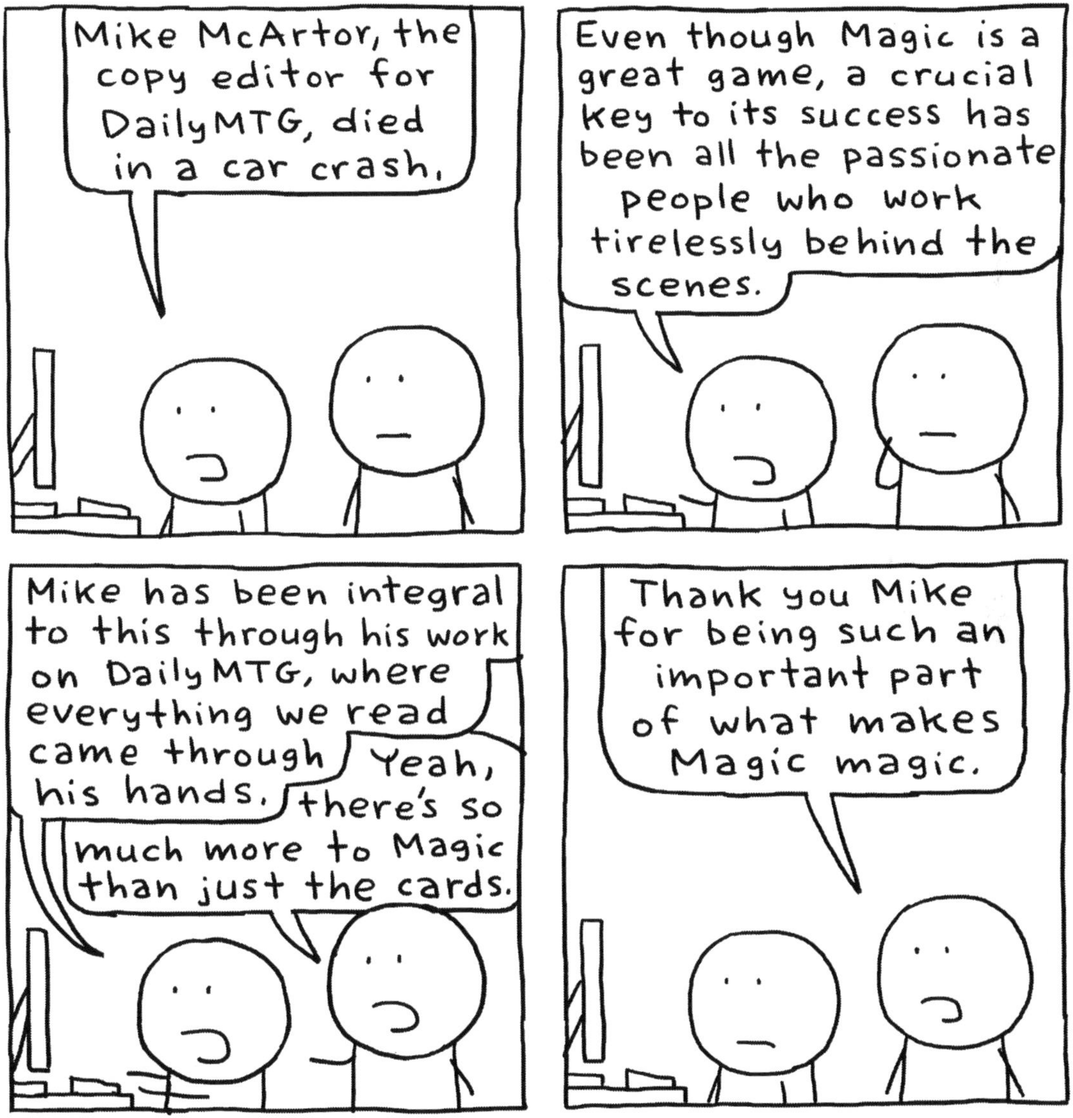
Mike McArtor, the copy editor for DailyMTG, died in a car crash.
Even though Magic is a great game, a crucial key to its success has been all the passionate people who work tirelessly behind the scenes.
Mike has been integral to this through his work on DailyMTG, where everything we read came through his hands.
Yeah, there's so much more to Magic than just the cards.
Thank you Mike for being such an important part of what makes Magic magic.

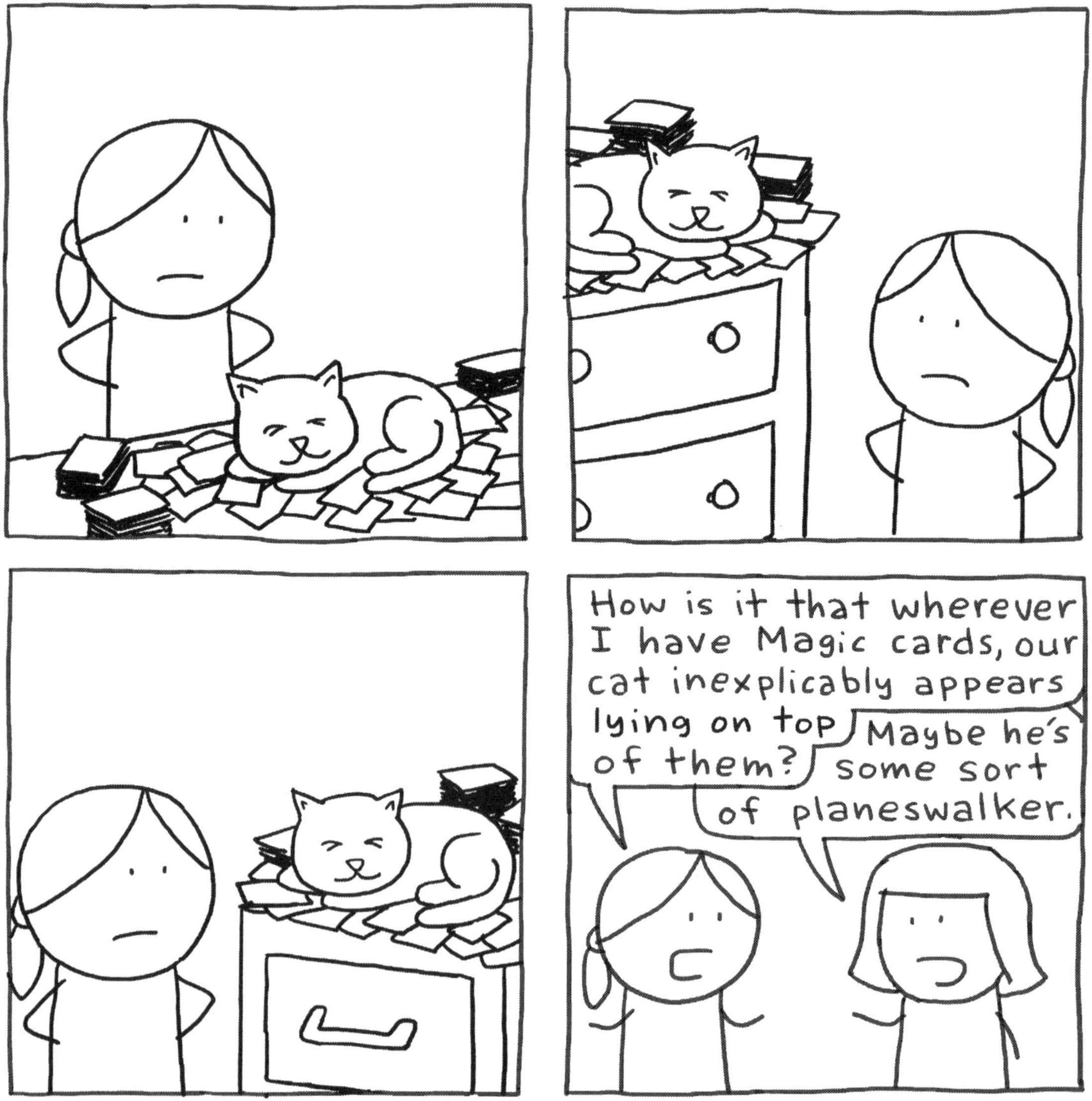
How is it that wherever I have Magic cards, our cat inexplicably appears lying on top of them?
Maybe he's some sort of planeswalker.

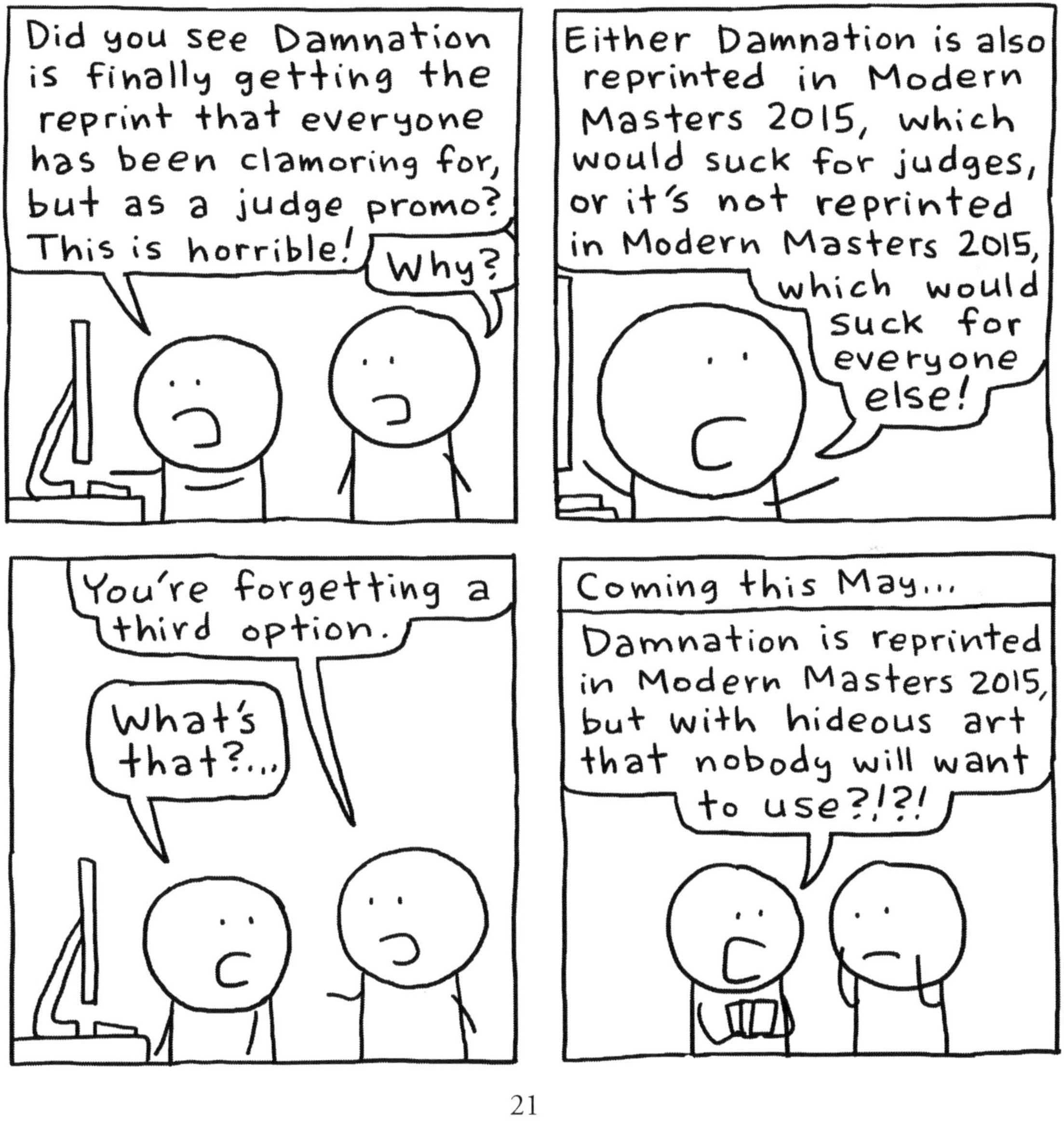
Did you see Damnation is finally getting the reprint that everyone has been clamoring for, but as a judge promo? This is horrible!
Why?
Either Damnation is also reprinted in Modern Masters 2015, which would suck for judges, or it's not reprinted in Modern Masters 2015, which would suck for everyone else!
You're forgetting a third option.
What's that?...
Coming this May...
Damnation is reprinted in Modern Masters 2015, but with hideous art that nobody will want to use?!?!

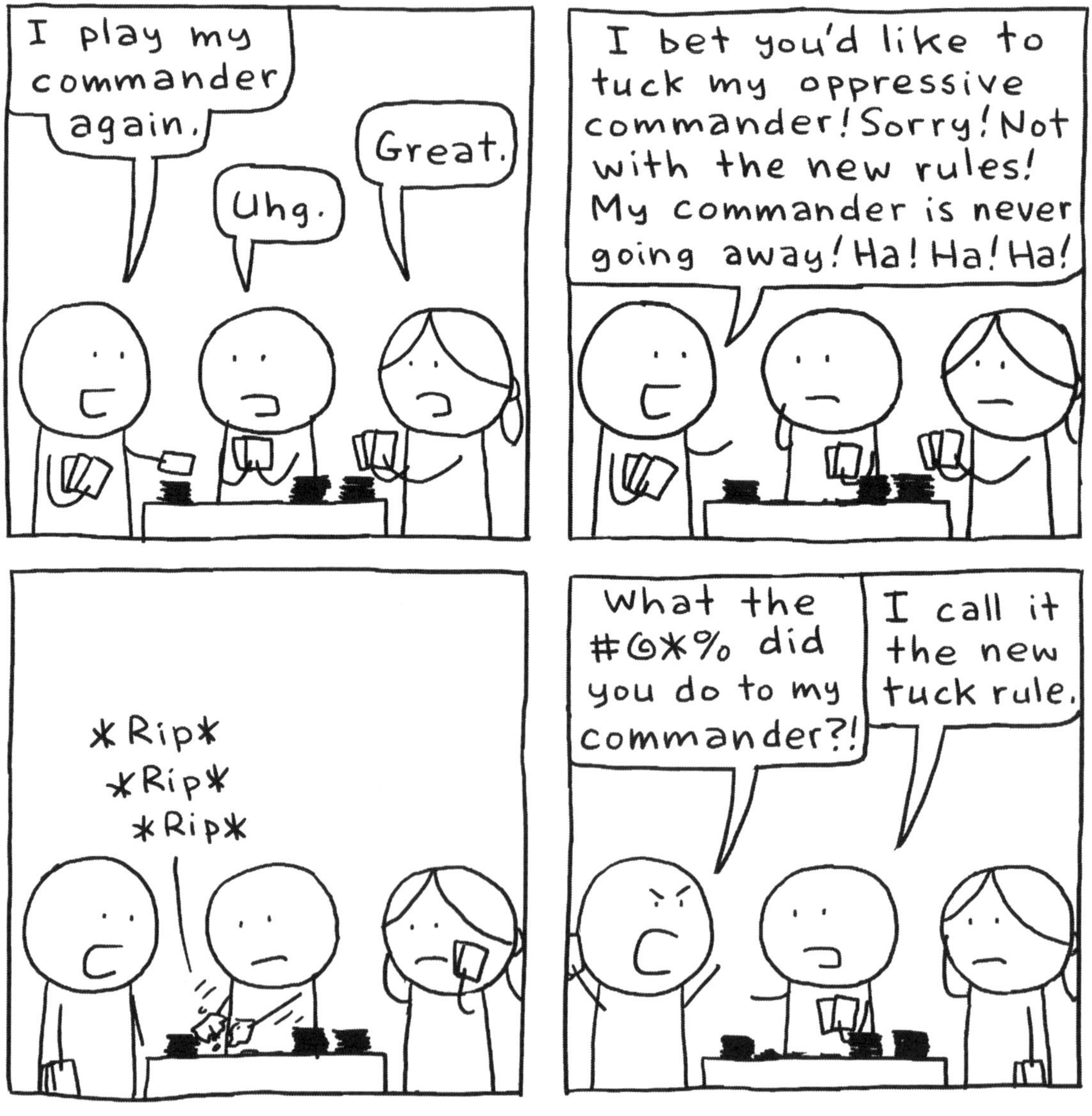
I play my commander again.
Uhg.
Great.
I bet you'd like to tuck my oppressive commander! Sorry! Not with the new rules! My commander is never going away! Ha! Ha! Ha!
Rip
Rip
Rip
What the #@*% did you do to my commander?!
I call it the new tuck rule.

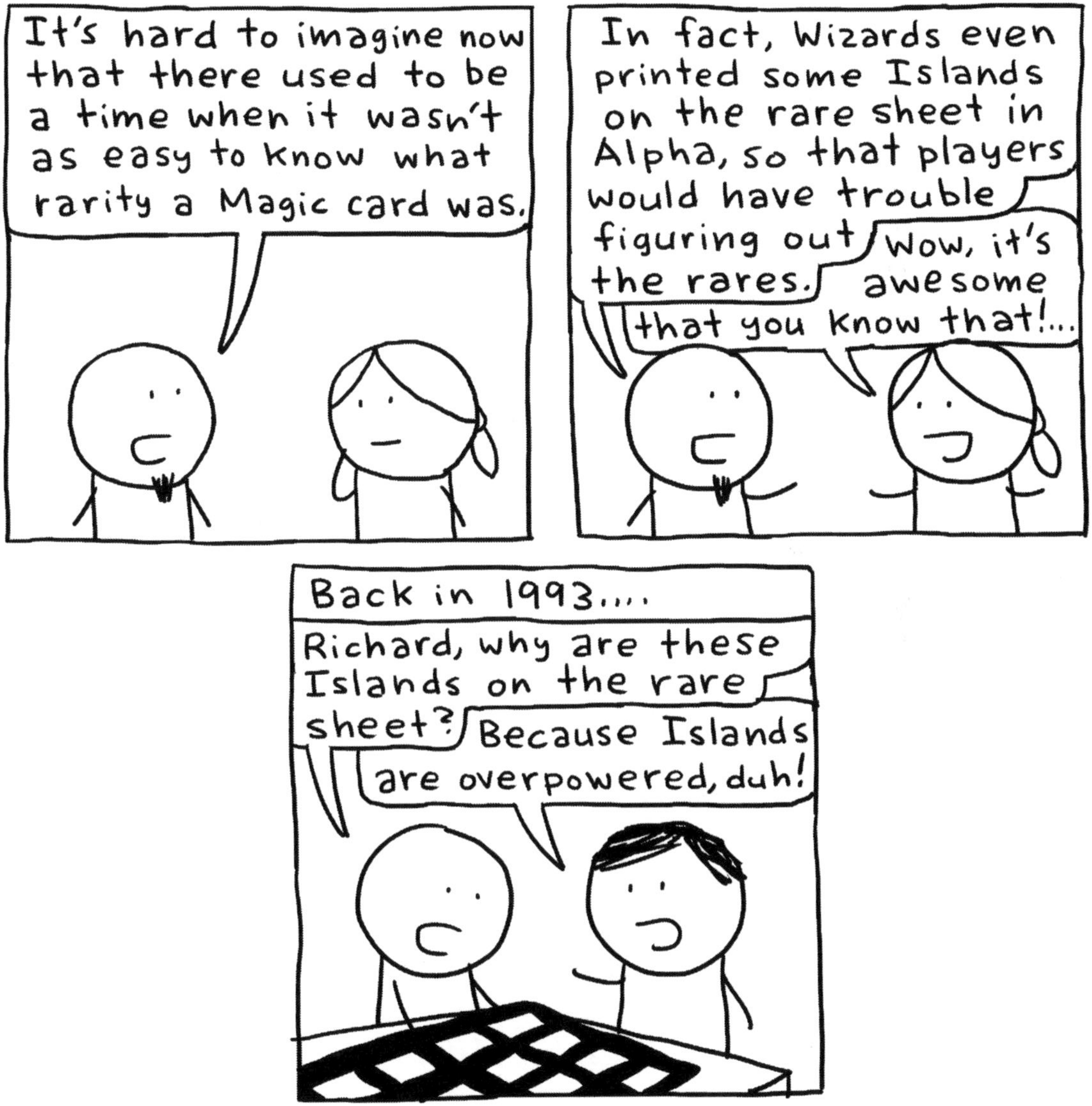
It's hard to imagine now that there used to be a time when it wasn't as easy to know what rarity a Magic card was.
In fact, Wizards even printed some Islands on the rare sheet in Alpha, so that players would have trouble figuring out the rares.
Wow, it's awesome that you know that!...
Back in 1993....
Richard, why are these Islands on the rare sheet?
Because Islands are overpowered, duh!

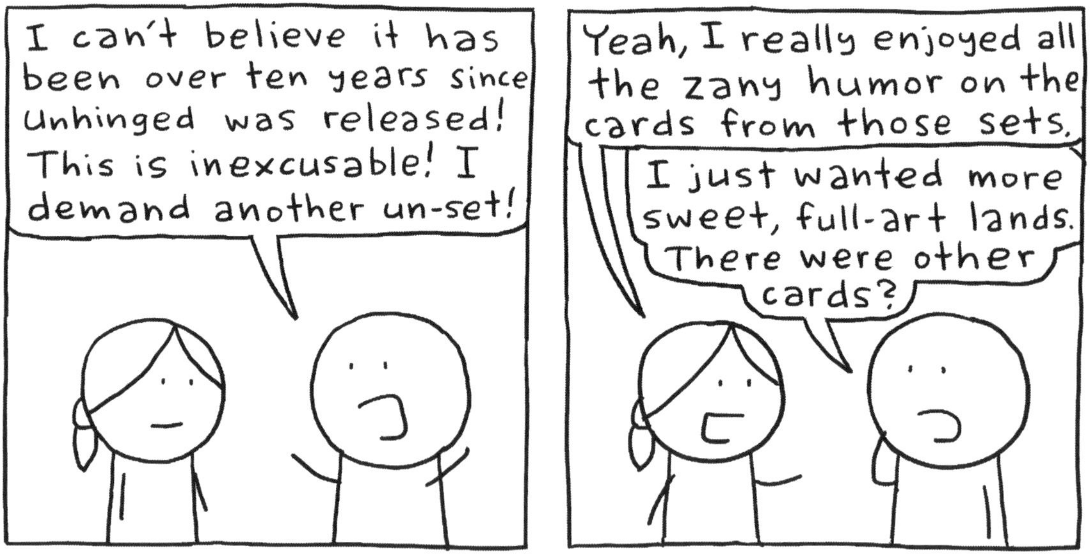
I can't believe it has been over ten years since Unhinged was released! This is inexcusable! I demand another un-set!
Yeah, I really enjoyed all the zany humor on the cards from those sets.
I just wanted more sweet, full-art lands. There were other cards?

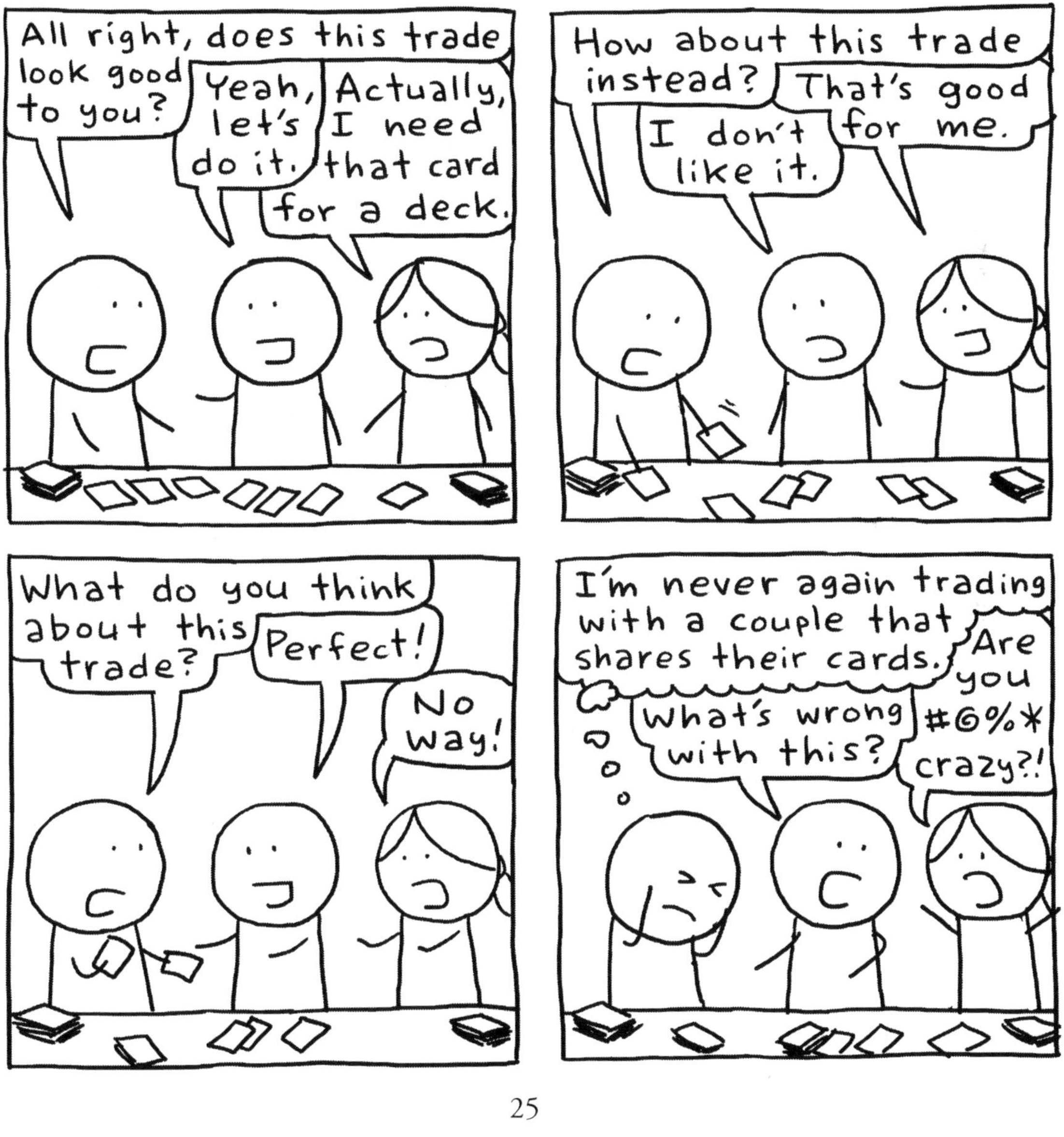
All right, does this trade look good to you?
Yeah, let's do it.
Actually, I need that card for a deck.
How about this trade instead?
I don't like it.
That's good for me.
What do you think about this trade?
Perfect!
No way!
I'm never again trading with a couple that shares their cards.
What's wrong with this?
Are you #6%* crazy?!

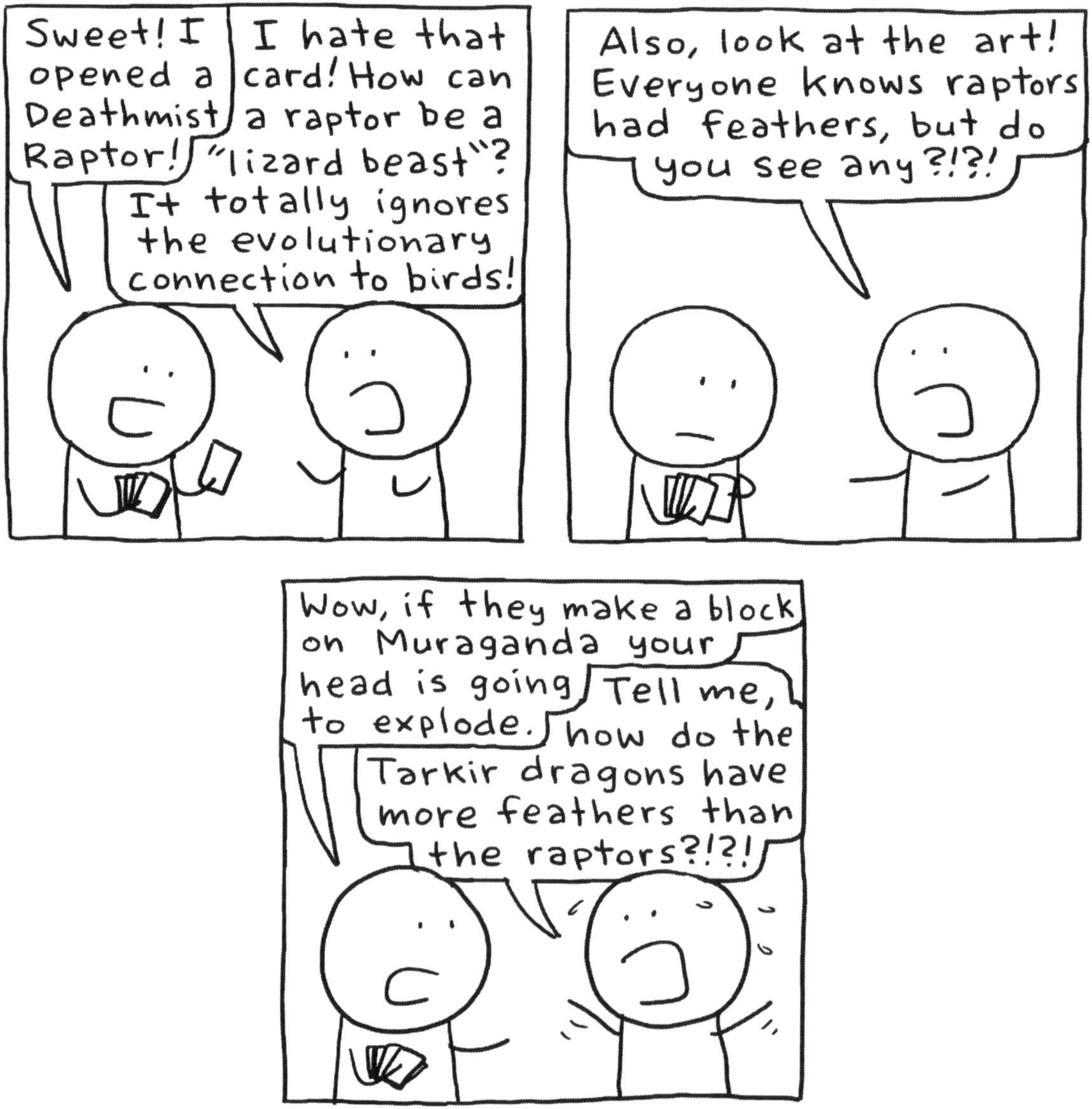
Sweet! I opened a Deathmist Raptor!
I hate that card! How can a raptor be a "lizard beast"? It totally ignores the evolutionary connection to birds!
Also, look at the art! Everyone knows raptors had feathers, but do you see any?!?!
Wow, if they make a block on Muraganda your head is going to explode.
Tell me, how do the Tarkir dragons have more feathers than the raptors?!?!

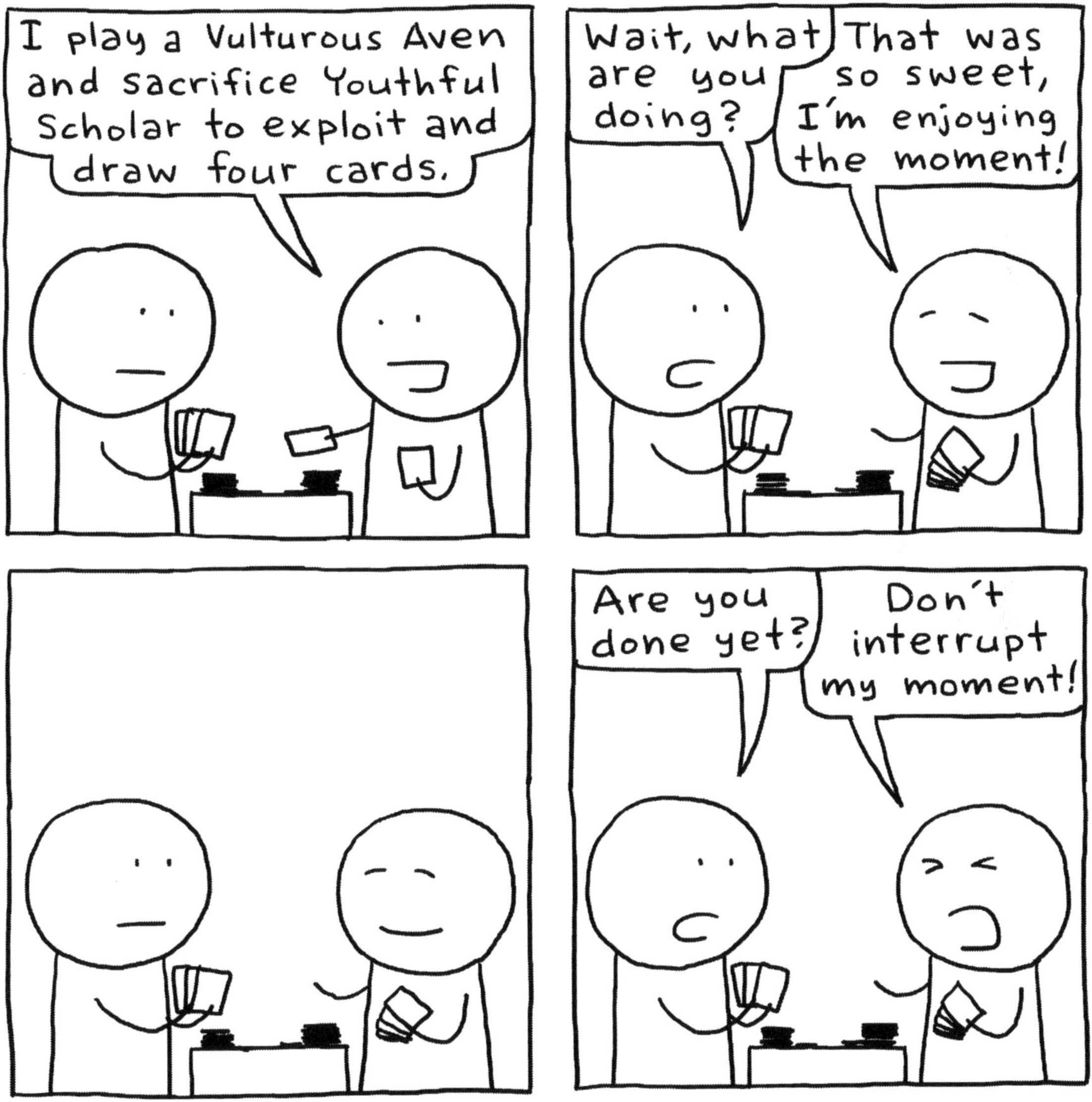
I play a Vulturous Aven and sacrifice Youthful Scholar to exploit and draw four cards.
Wait, what are you doing?
That was so sweet, I'm enjoying the moment!
Are you done yet?
Don't interrupt my moment!

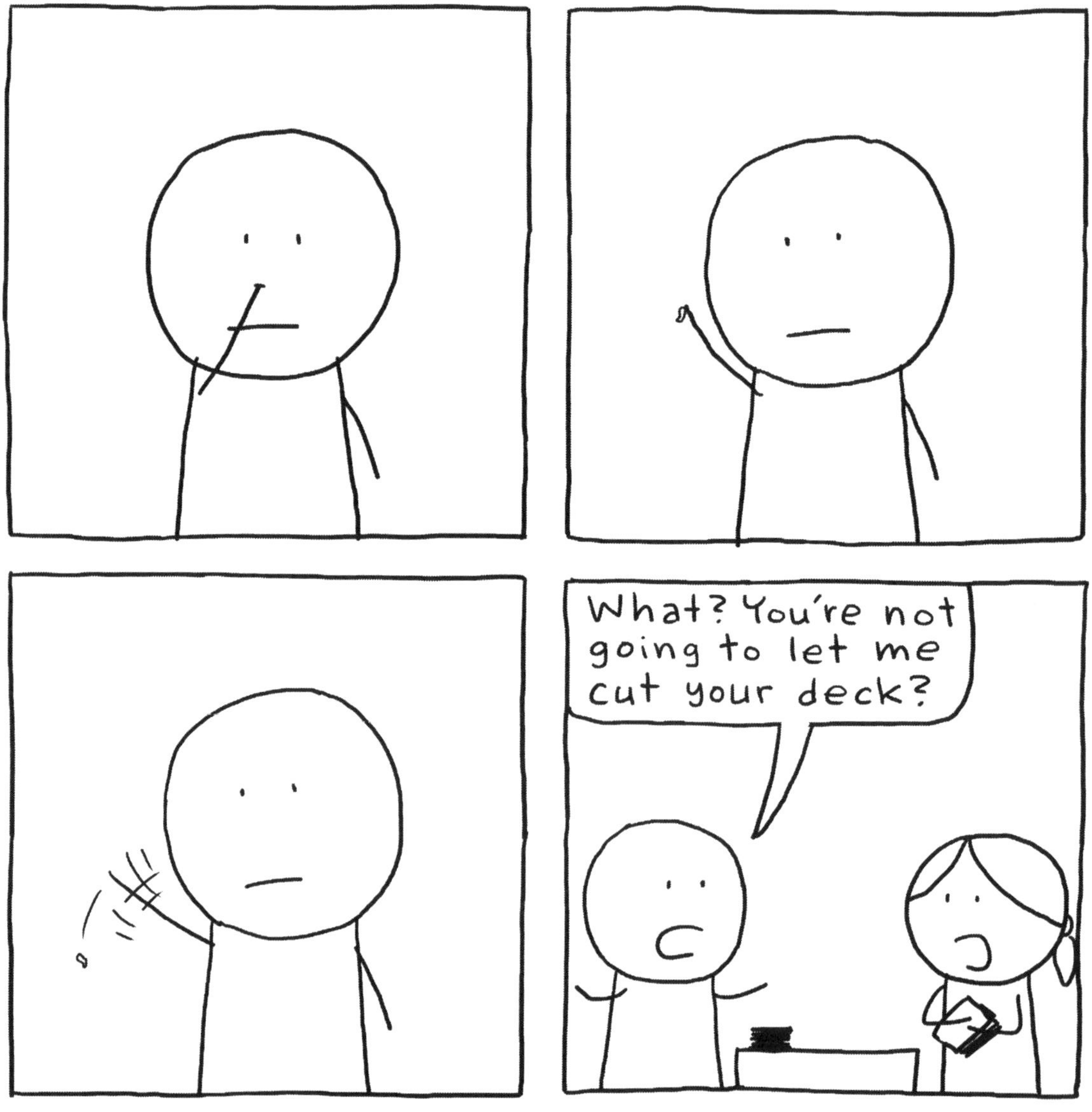
What? You're not going to let me cut your deck?

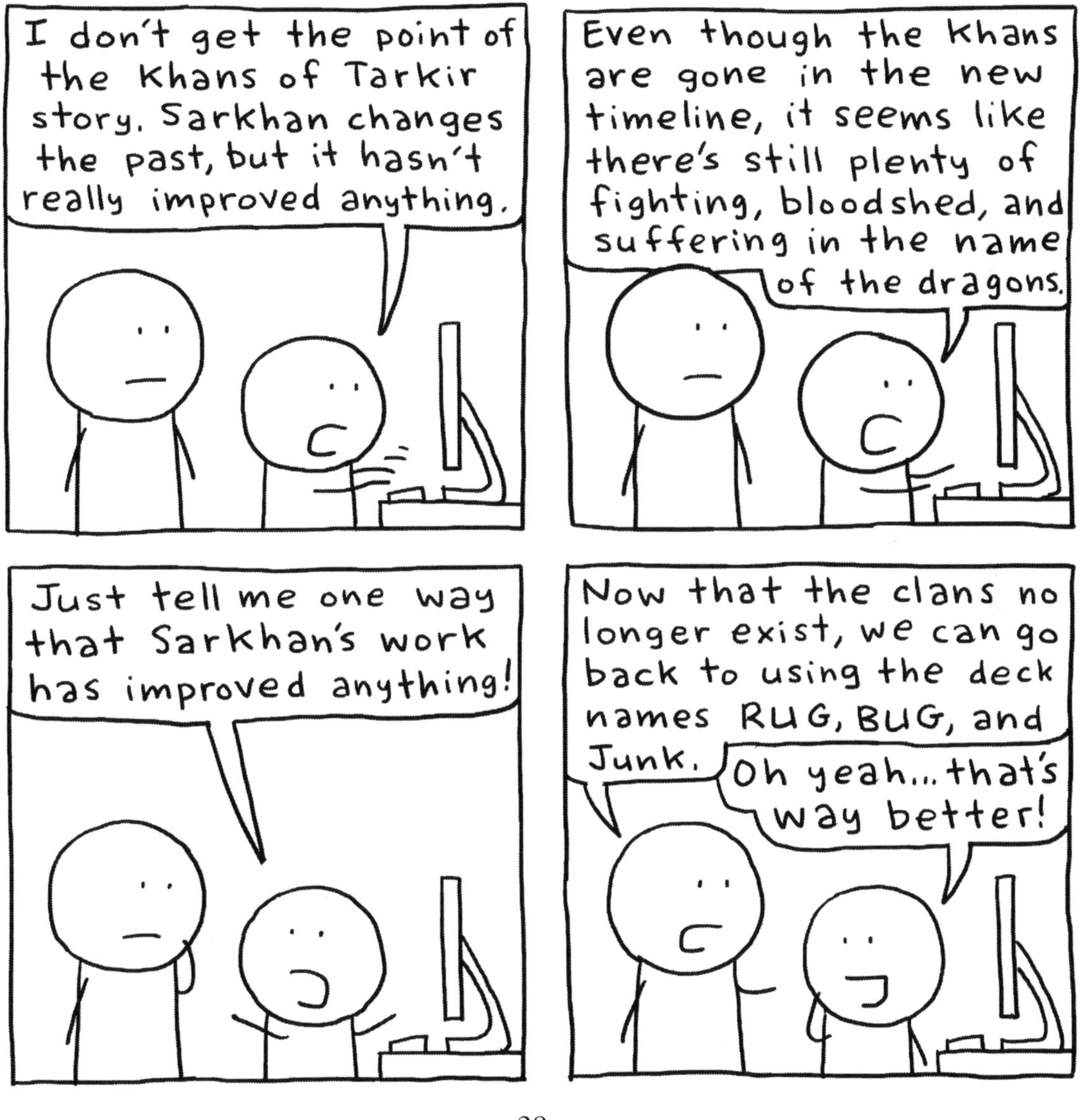
I don't get the point of the Khans of Tarkir story. Sarkhan changes the past, but it hasn't really improved anything.
Even though the Khans are gone in the new timeline, it seems like there's still plenty of fighting, bloodshed, and suffering in the name of the dragons.
Just tell me one way that Sarkhan's work has improved anything!
Now that the clans no longer exist, we can go back to using the deck names RUG, BUG, and Junk.
Oh yeah... that's way better!

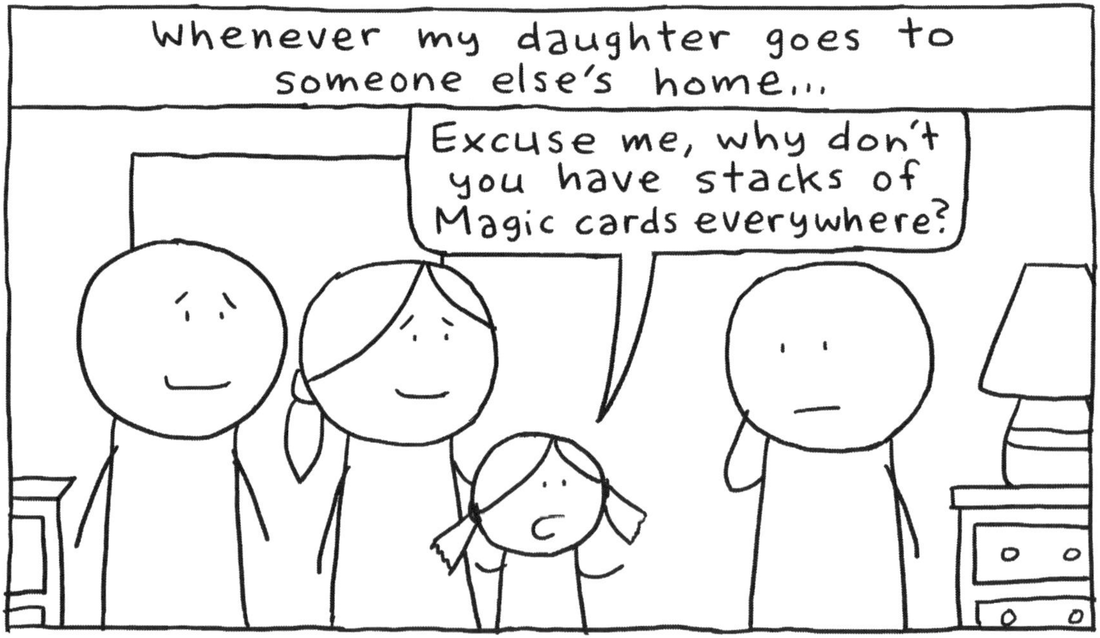
Whenever my daughter goes to someone else's home...
Excuse me, why don't you have stacks of Magic cards everywhere?

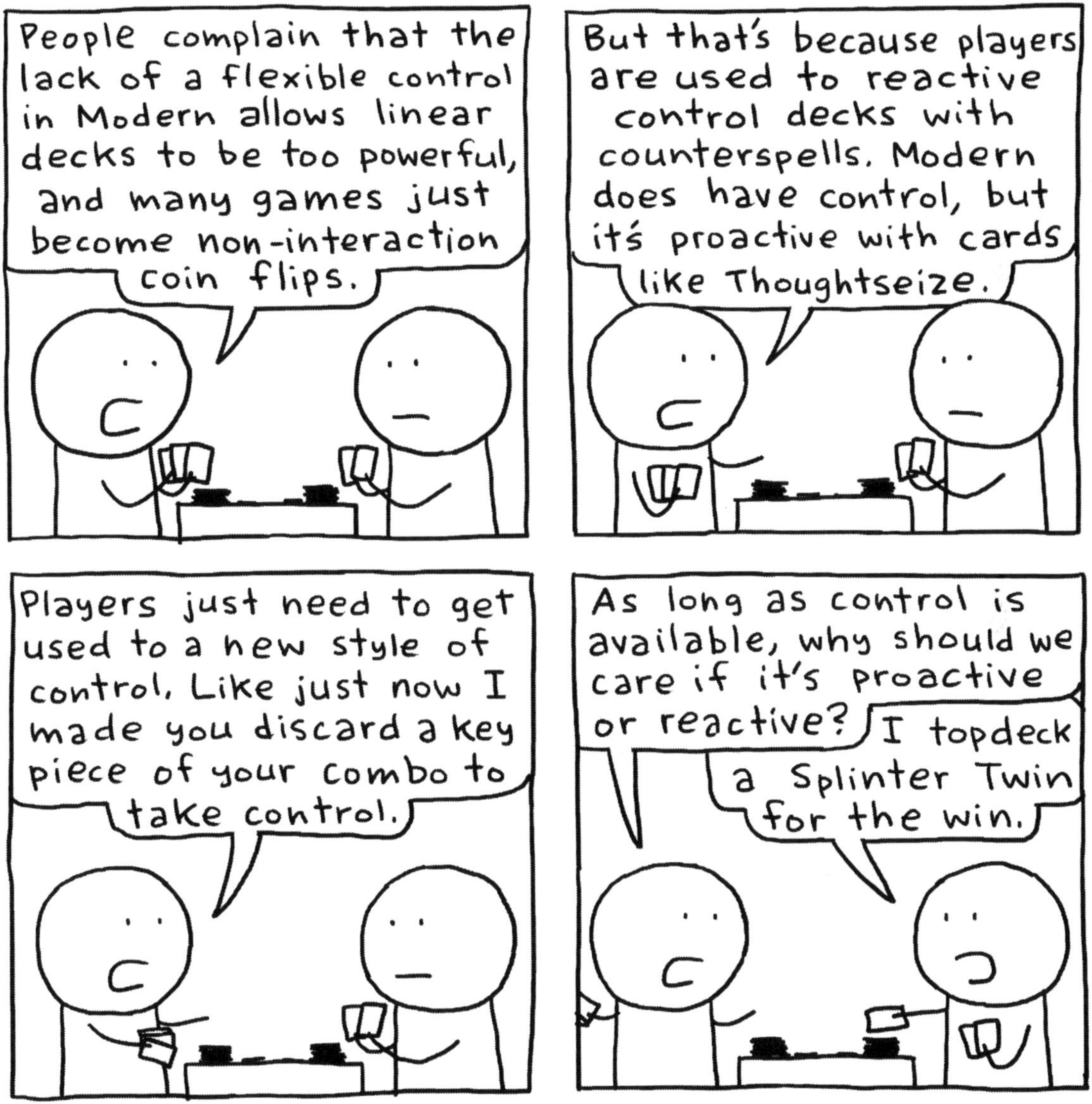
People complain that the lack of a flexible control in Modern allows linear decks to be too powerful, and many games just become non-interaction coin flips.
But that's because players are used to reactive control decks with counterspells. Modern does have control, but it's proactive with cards like Thoughtseize.
Players just need to get used to a new style of control. Like just now I made you discard a key piece of your combo to take control.
As long as control is available, why should we care if it's proactive or reactive?
I topdeck a Splinter Twin for the win.

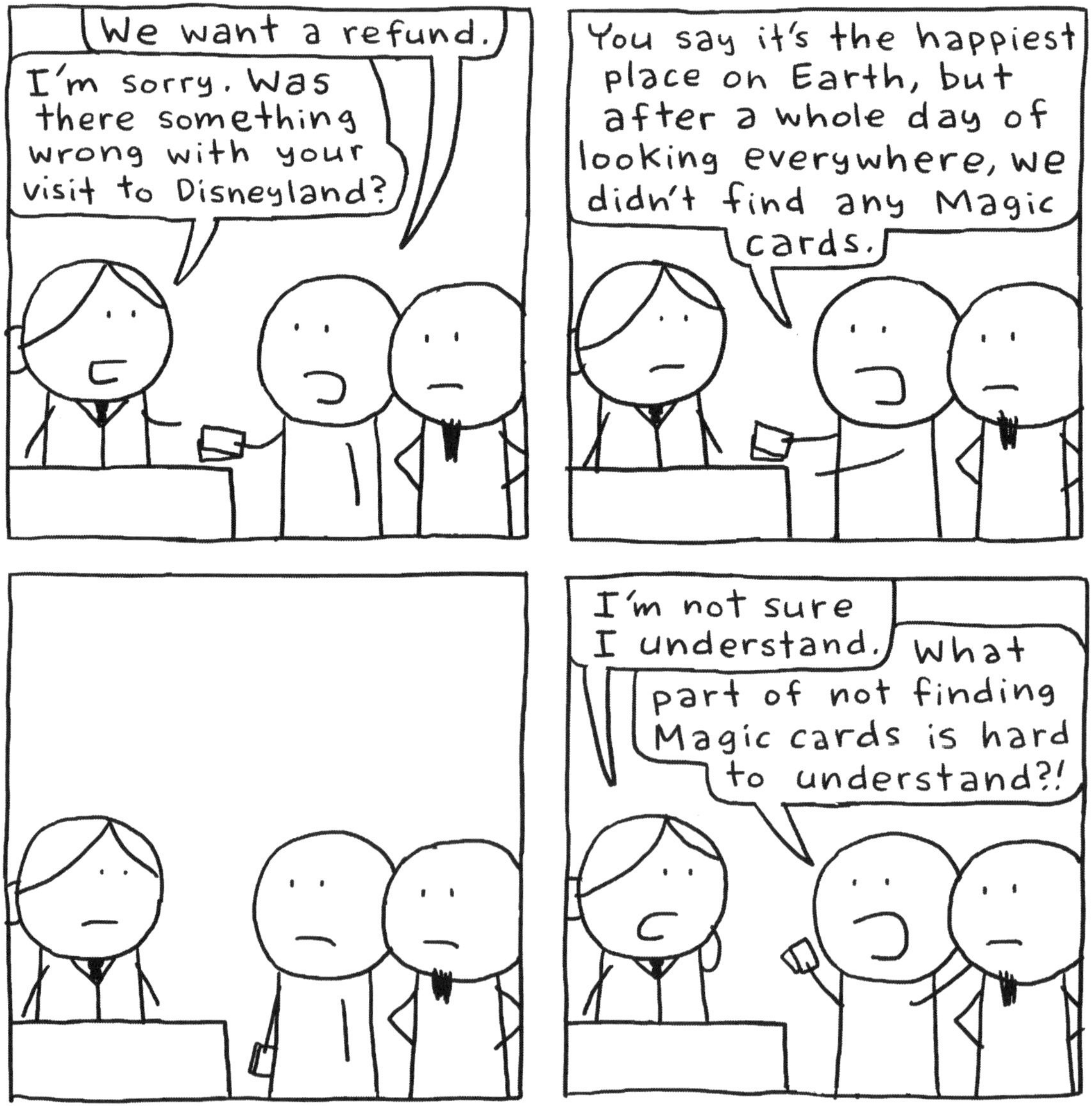
We want a refund.
I'm sorry. Was there something wrong with your visit to Disneyland?
You say it's the happiest place on Earth, but after a whole day of looking everywhere, we didn't find any Magic cards.
I'm not sure I understand.
What part of not finding Magic cards is hard to understand?!

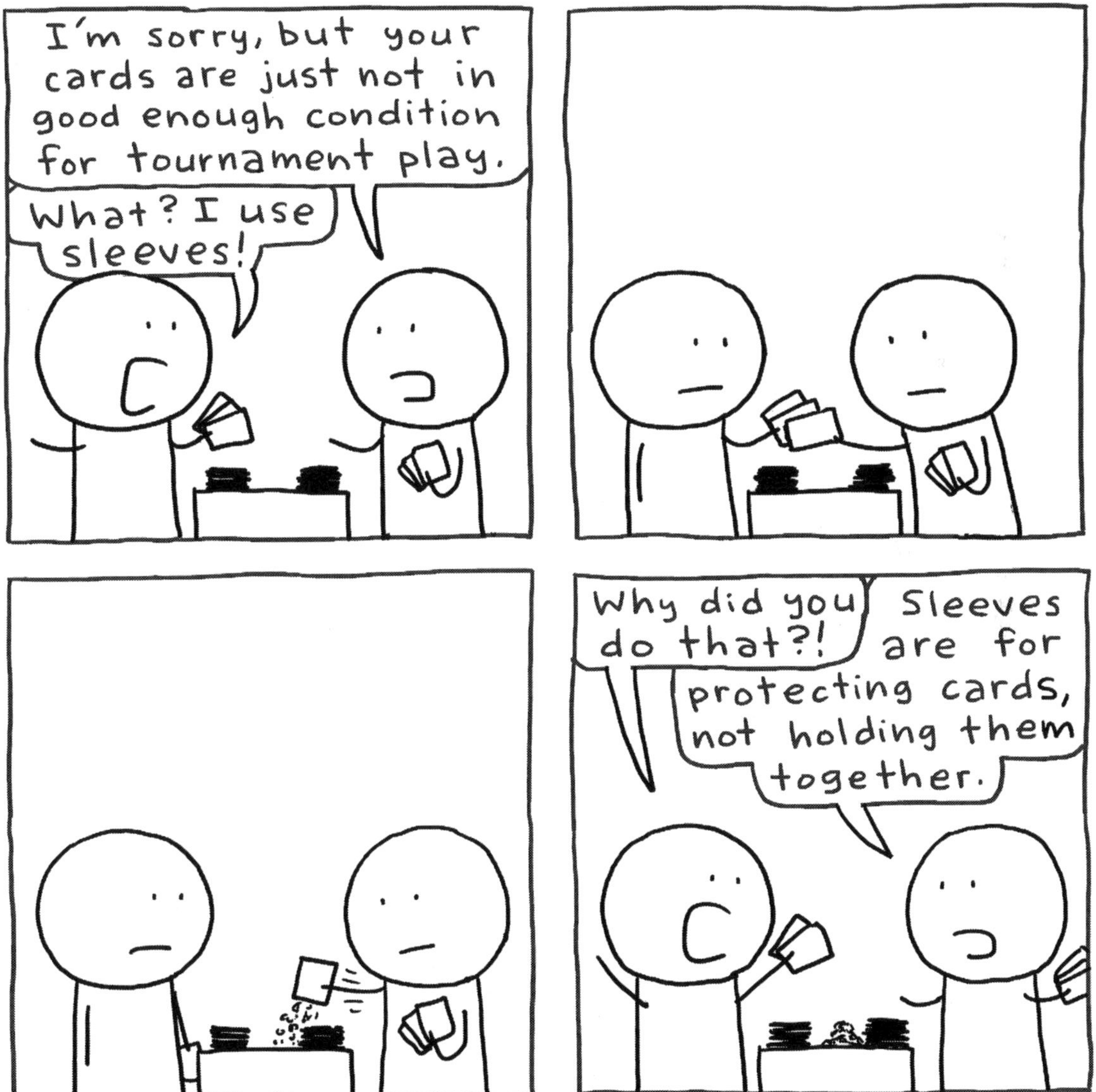
I'm sorry, but your cards are just not in good enough condition for tournament play.
What? I use sleeves!
Why did you do that?!
Sleeves are for protecting cards, not holding them together.

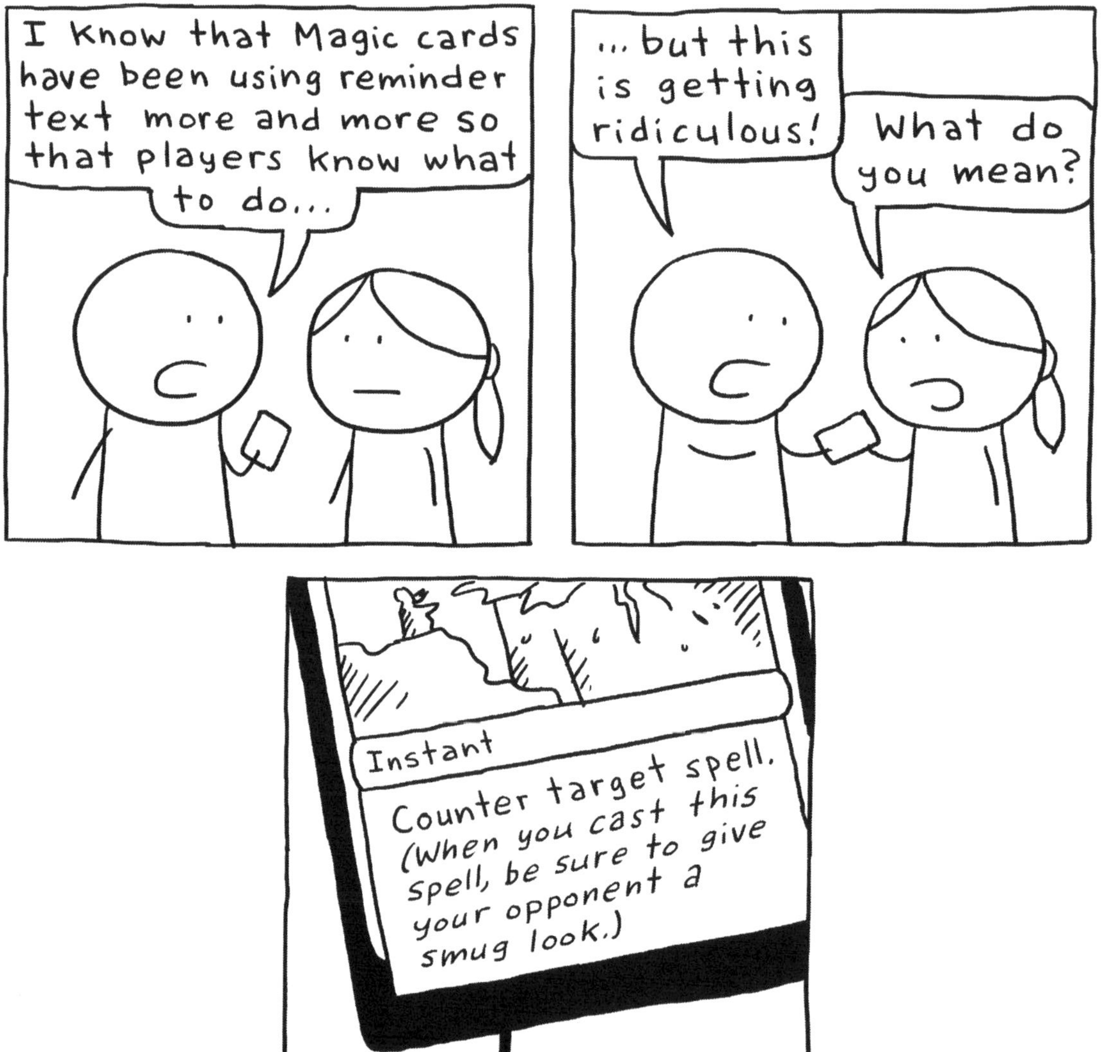
I know that Magic cards have been using reminder text more and more so that players know what to do...
...but this is getting ridiculous!
What do you mean?
Instant
Counter target spell. (When you cast this spell, be sure to give your opponent a smug look.)

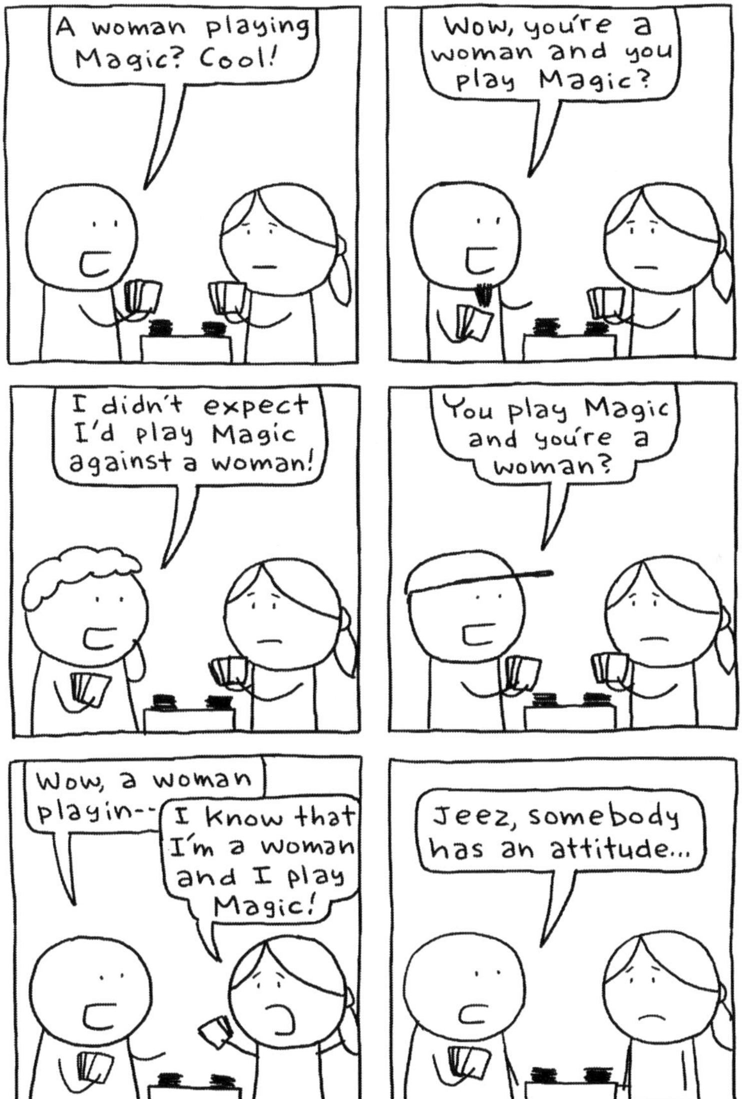
A woman playing Magic? Cool!
Wow, you're a woman and you play Magic?
I didn't expect I'd play Magic against a woman!
You play Magic and you're a woman?
Wow, a woman playin--
I know that I'm a woman and I play Magic!
Jeez, somebody has an attitude...

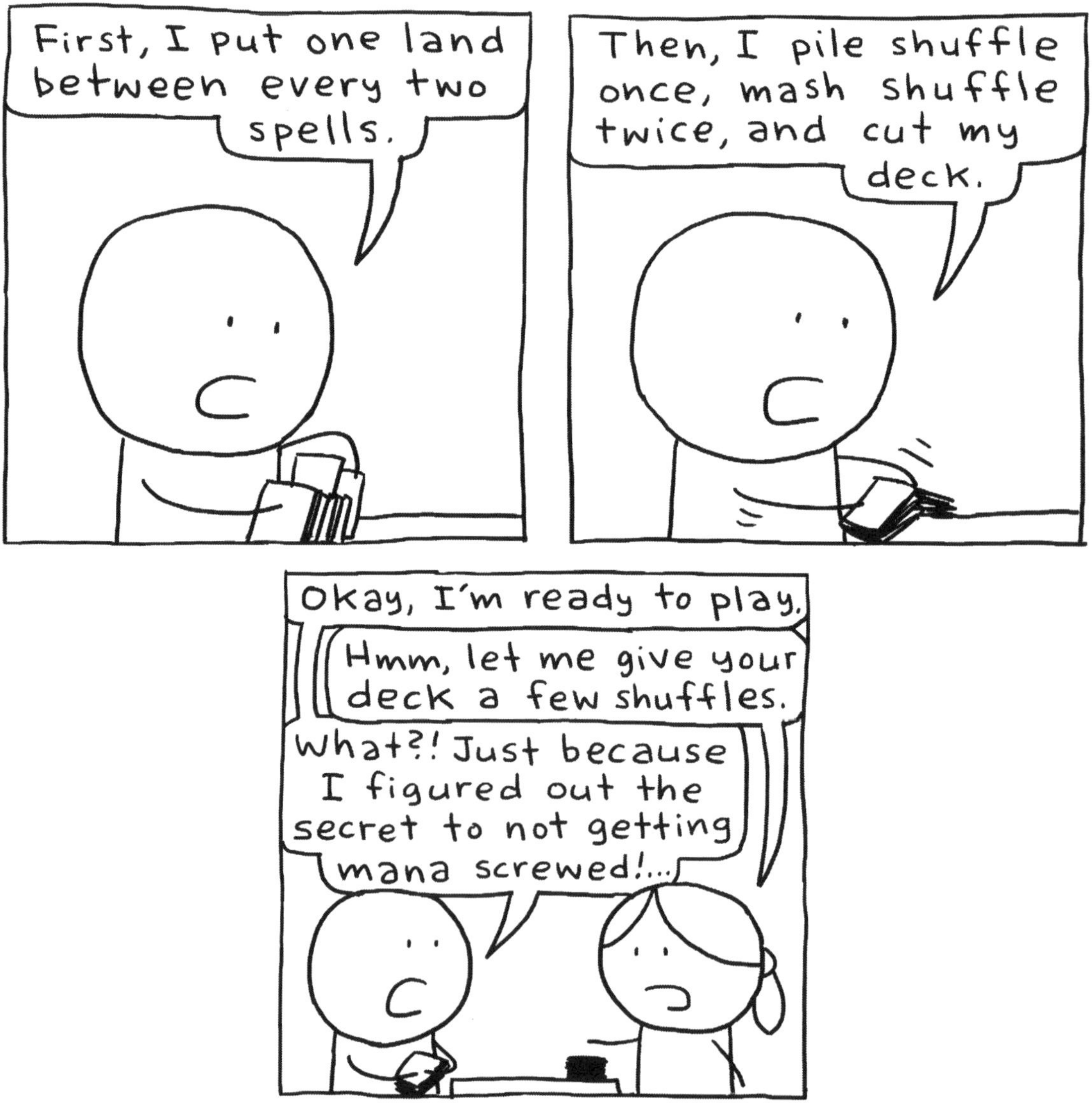
First, I put one land between every two spells.
Then, I pile shuffle once, mash shuffle twice, and cut my deck.
Okay, I'm ready to play.
Hmm, let me give your deck a few shuffles.
What?! Just because I figured out the secret to not getting mana screwed!...

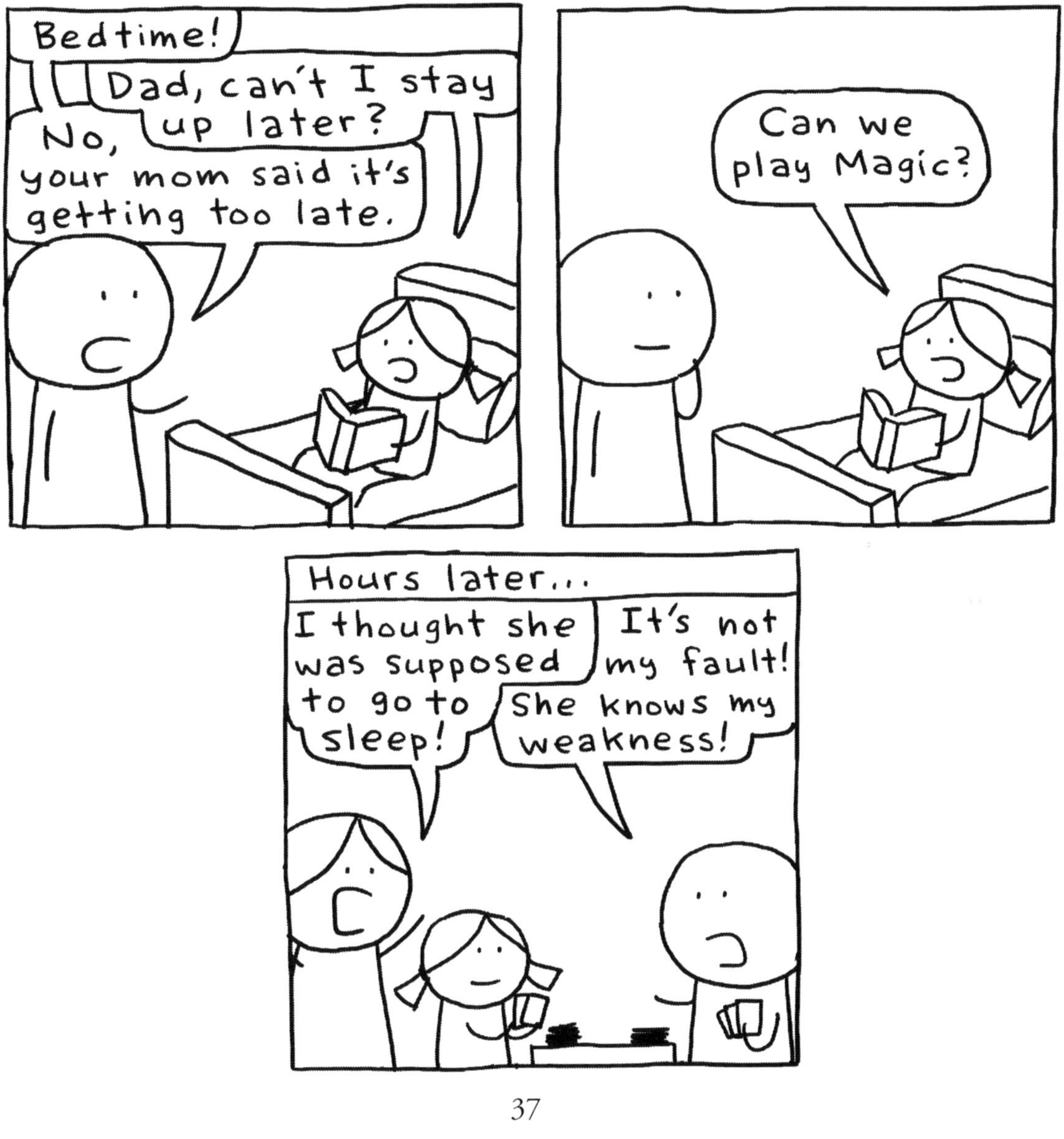
Bedtime!
Dad, can't I stay up later?
No, your mom said it's getting too late.
Can we play Magic?
Hours later...
I thought she was supposed to go to sleep!
It's not my fault! She knows my weakness!

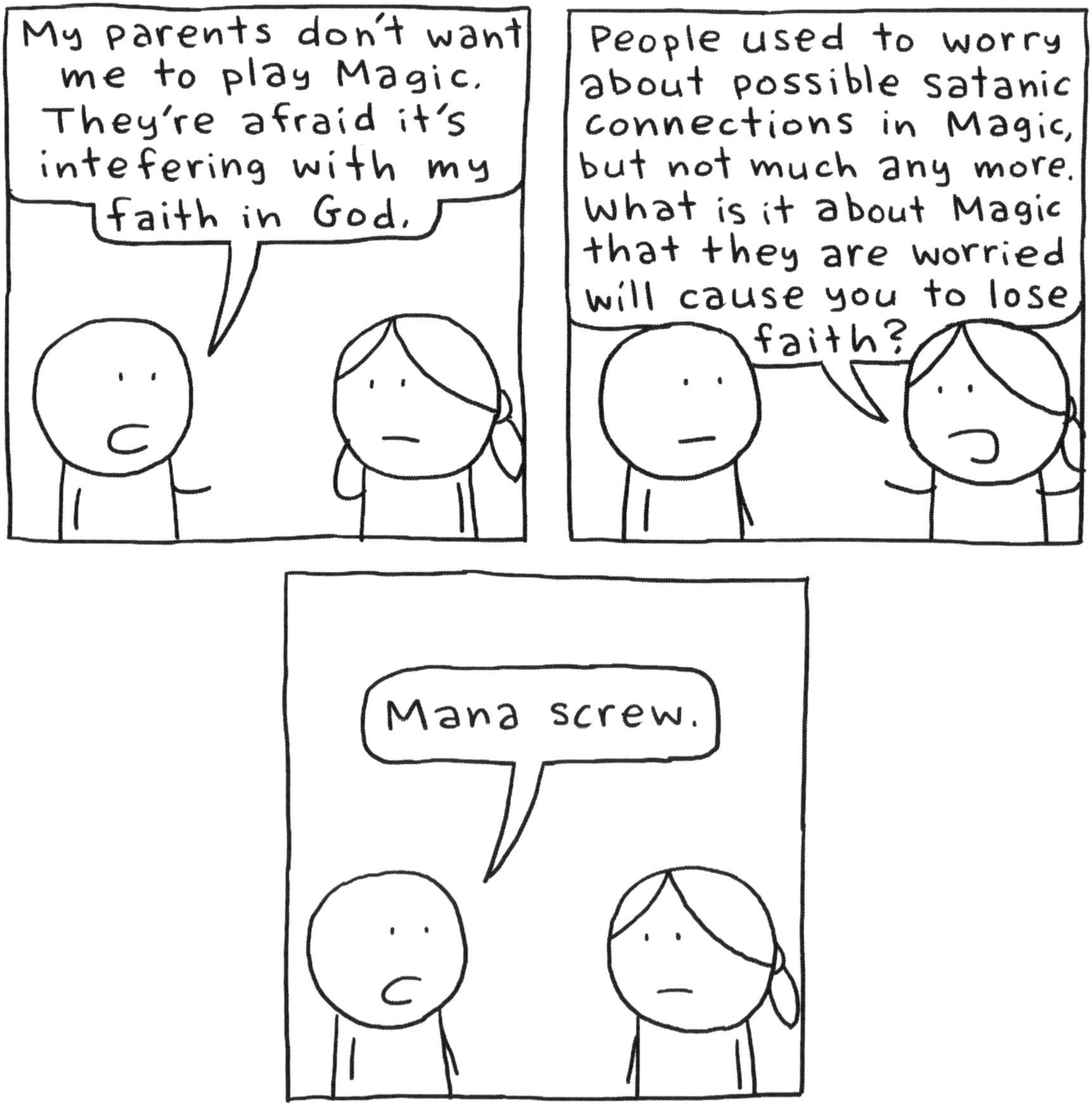
My parents don't want me to play Magic. They're afraid it's intefering with my faith in God.
People used to worry about possible satanic connections in Magic, but not much any more. What is it about Magic that they are worried will cause you to lose faith?
Mana screw.

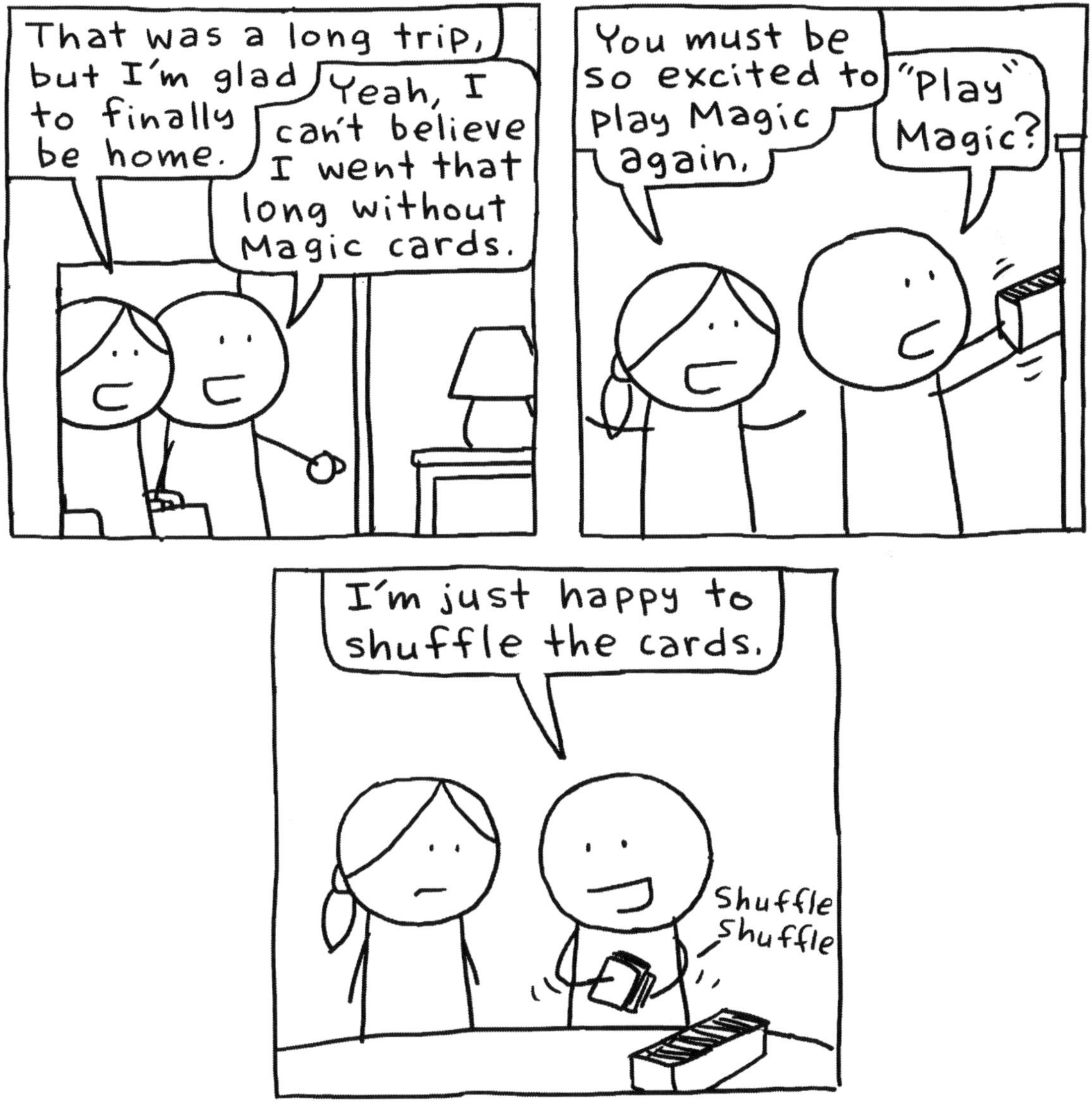
That was a long trip, but I'm glad to finally be home.
Yeah, I can't believe I went that long without Magic cards.
You must be so excited to play Magic again.
"Play" Magic?
I'm just happy to shuffle the cards.
Shuffle Shuffle

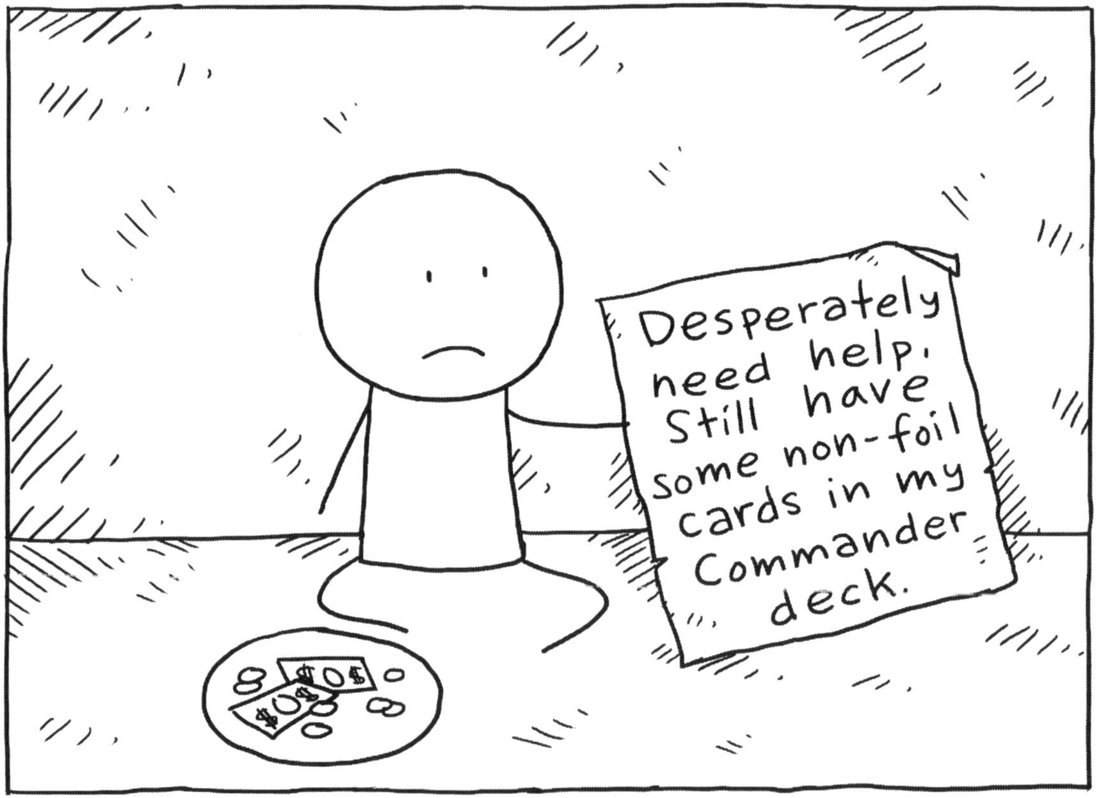
Desperately need help. Still have some non-foil cards in my Commander deck.

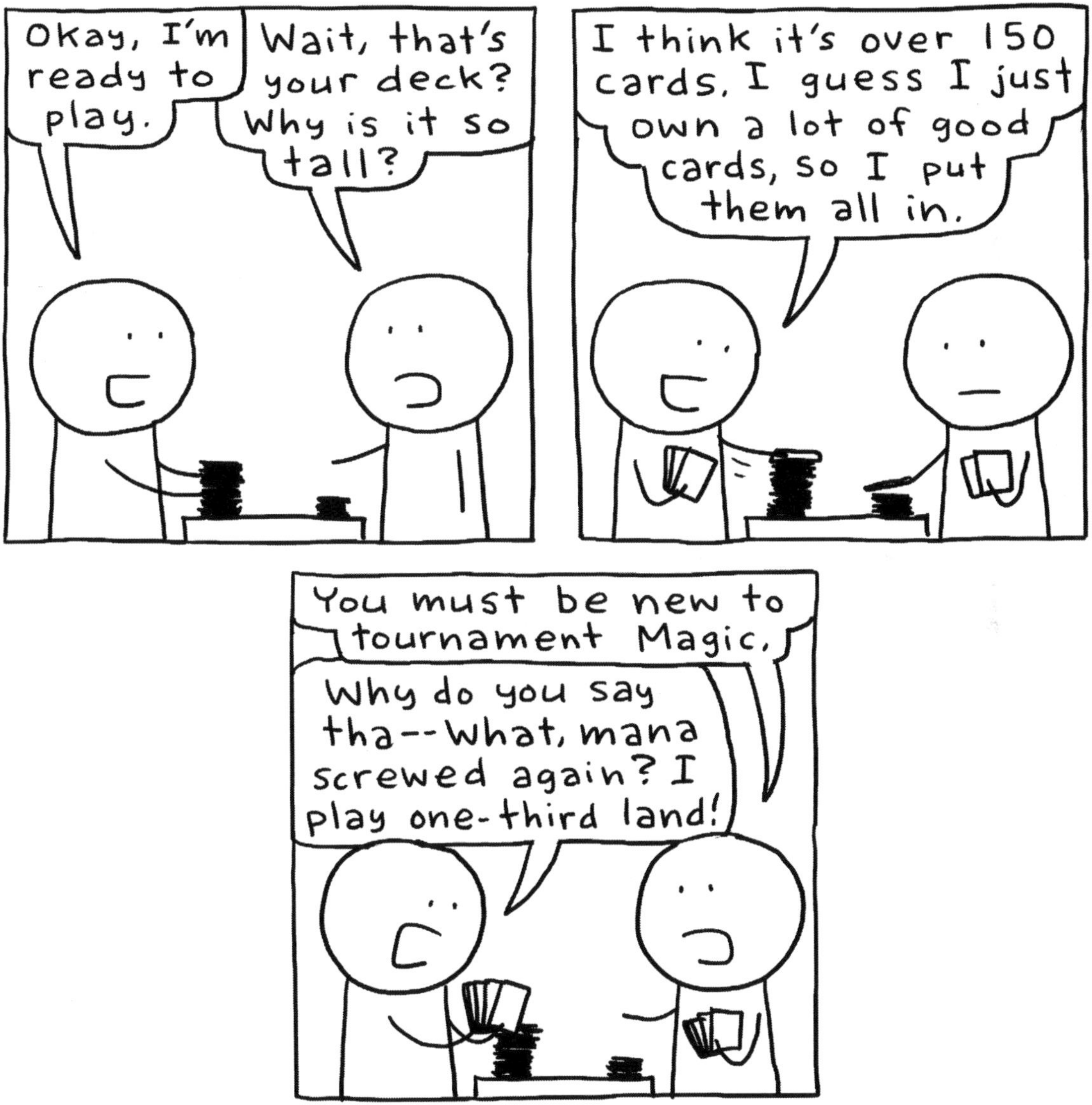

Okay, I'm ready to play.
Wait, that's your deck? Why is it so tall?
I think it's over 150 cards. I guess I just own a lot of good cards, so I put them all in.
You must be new to tournament Magic.
Why do you say tha--What, mana screwed again? I play one-third land!

All right, just got home from work. I have my Magic cards, sleeves, and a crate of energy drinks.
This weekend I'm double sleeving my cube!
You better hurry, it's only about 60 hours until you have to be at work again!

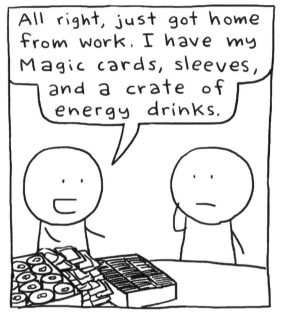

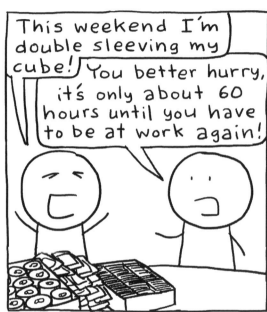

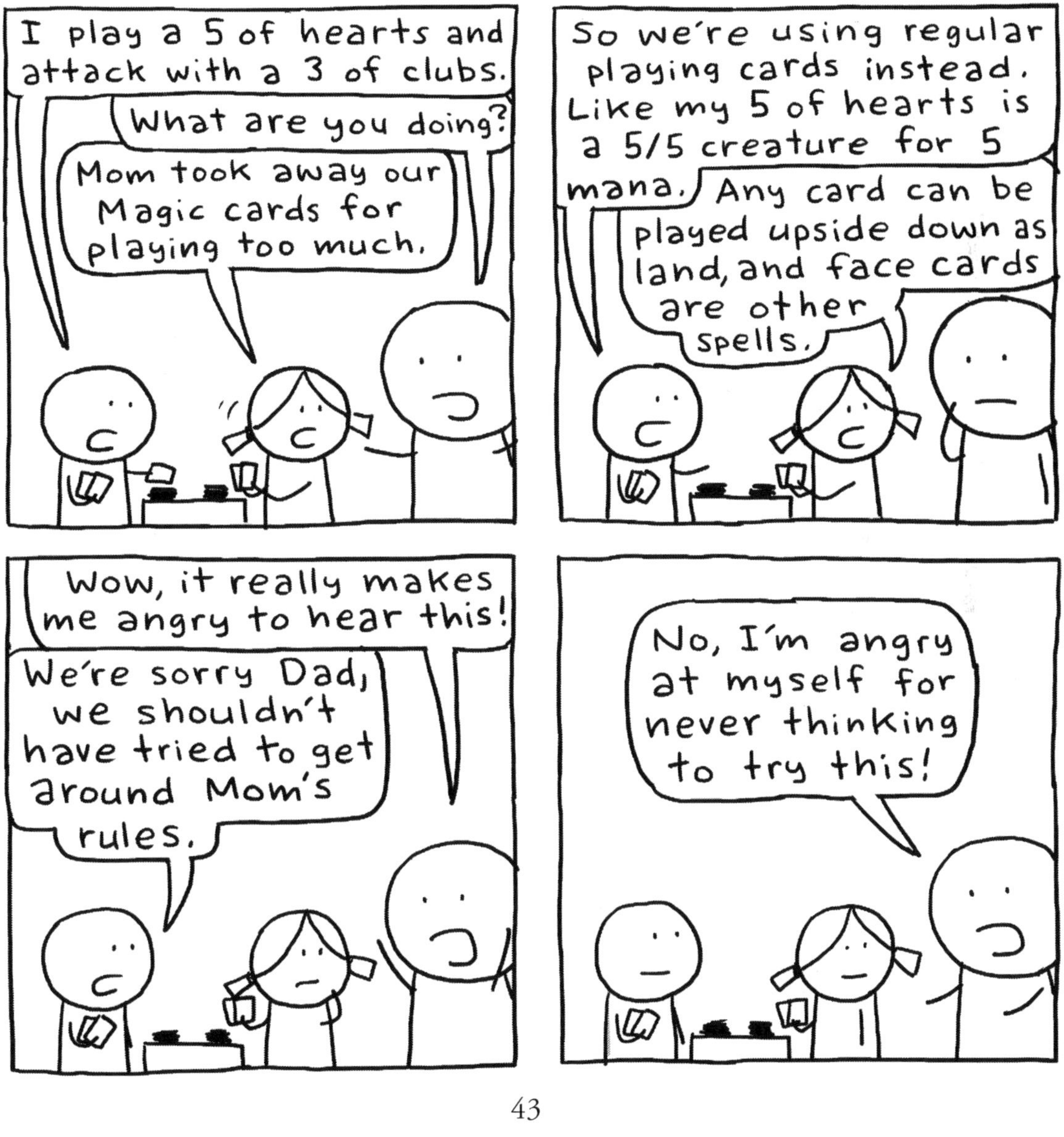
I play a 5 of hearts and attack with a 3 of clubs.
What are you doing?
Mom took away our Magic cards for playing too much.
So we're using regular playing cards instead. Like my 5 of hearts is a 5/5 creature for 5 mana.
Any card can be played upside down as land, and face cards are other spells.
Wow, it really makes me angry to hear this!
We're sorry Dad, we shouldn't have tried to get around Mom's rules.
No, I'm angry at myself for never thinking to try this!

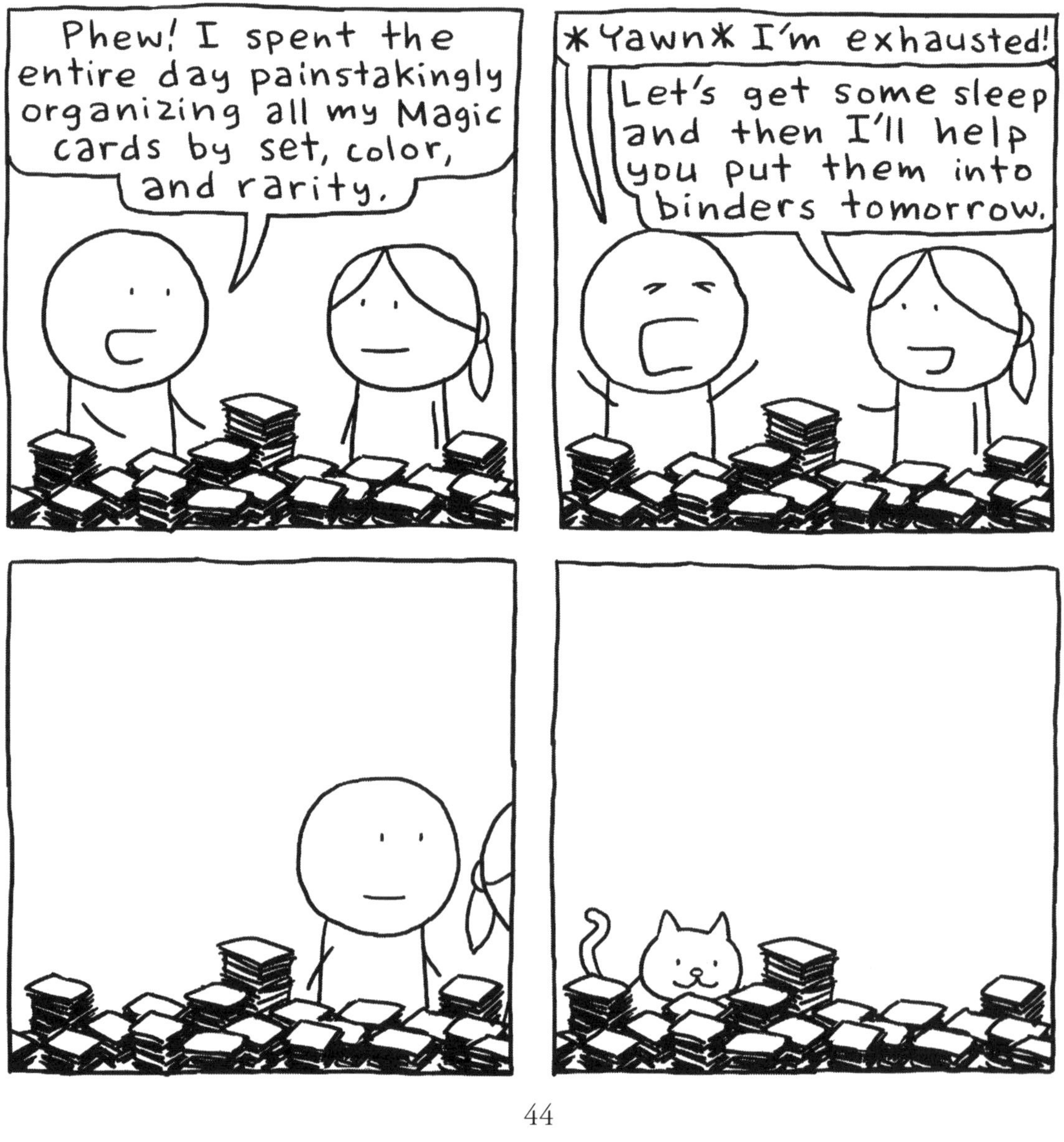
Phew! I spent the entire day painstakingly organizing all my Magic cards by set, color, and rarity.
Yawn I'm exhausted!
Let's get some sleep and then I'll help you put them into binders tomorrow.

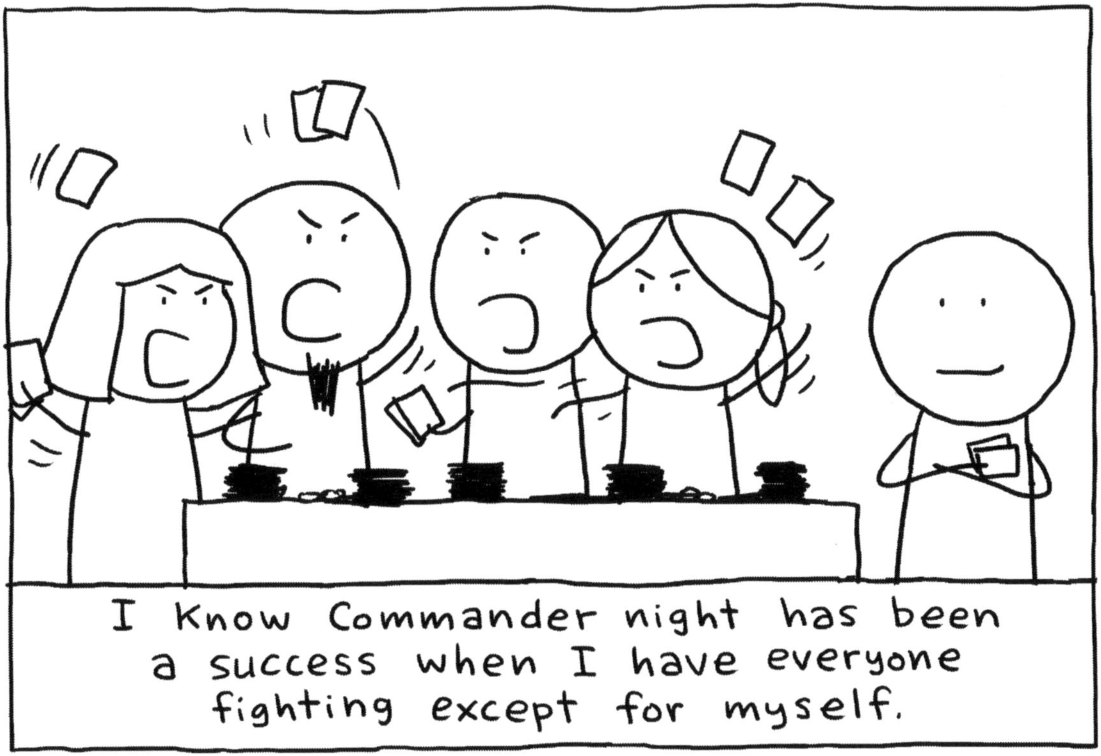
I know Commander night has been a success when I have everyone fighting except for myself.

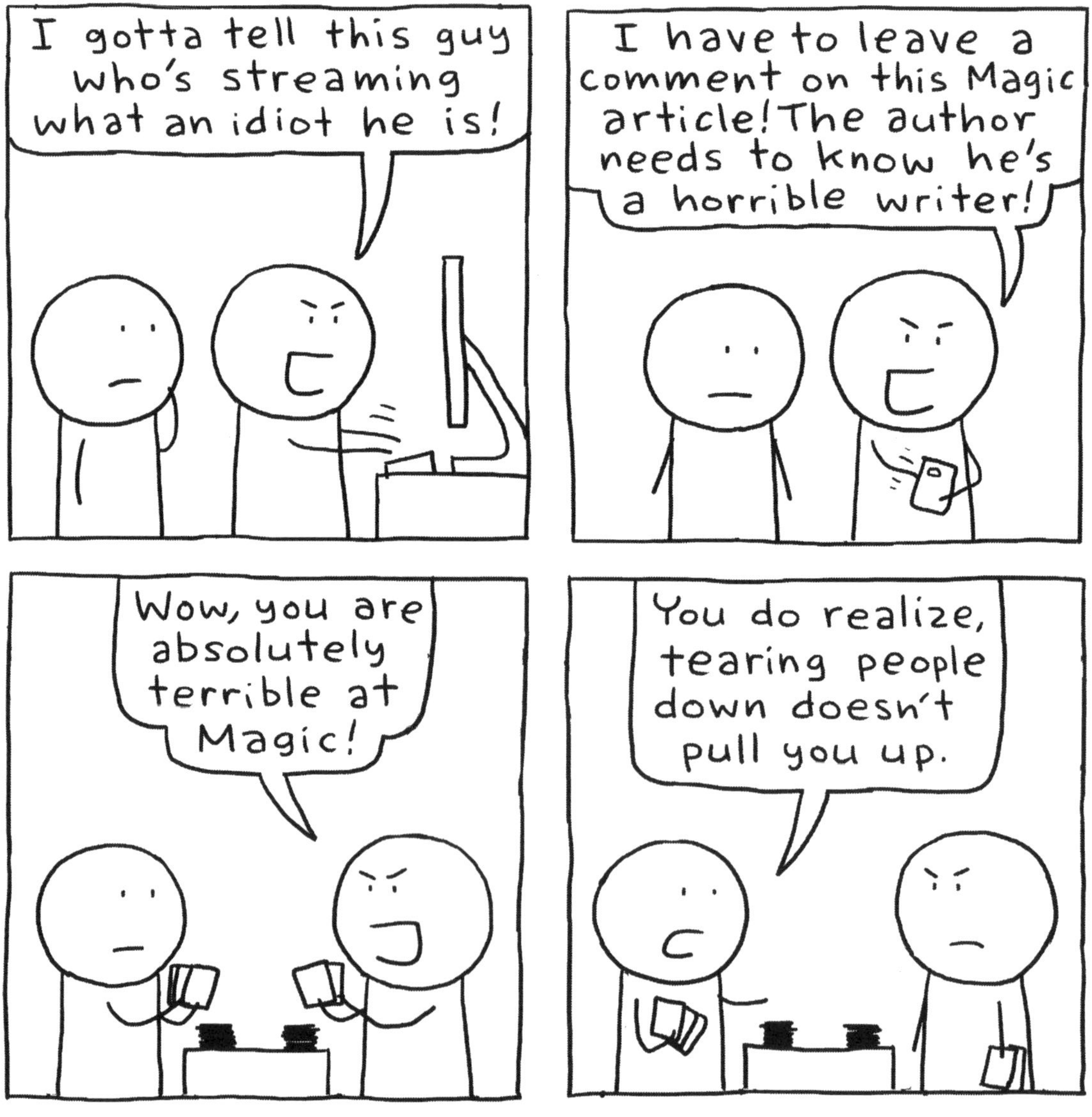
I gotta tell this guy who's streaming what an idiot he is!
I have to leave a comment on this Magic article! The author needs to know he's a horrible writer!
Wow, you are absolutely terrible at Magic!
You do realize, tearing people down doesn't pull you up.

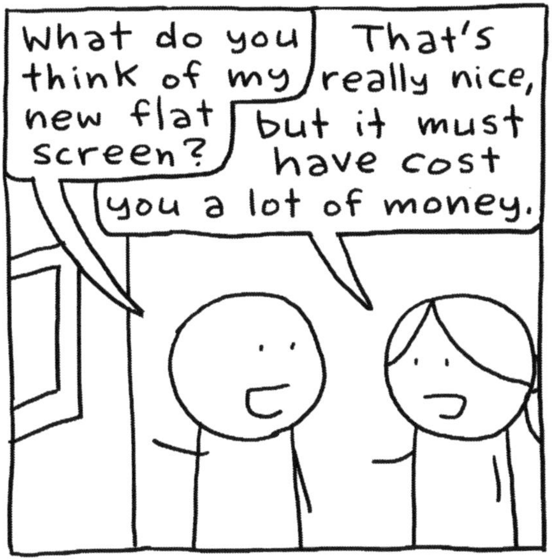
What do you think of my new flat screen?
That's really nice, but it must have cost you a lot of money.

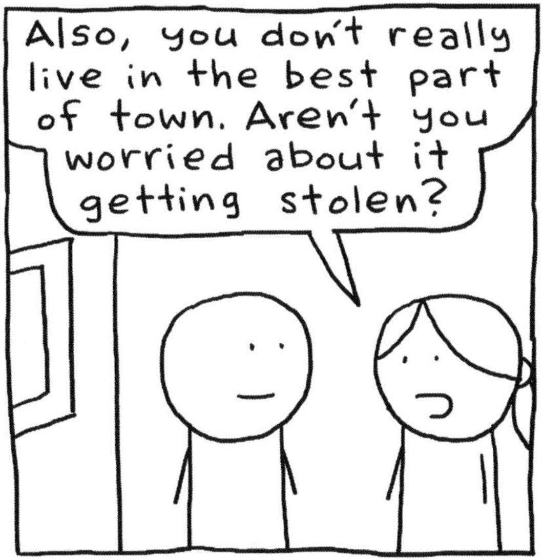
Also, you don't really live in the best part of town. Aren't you worried about it getting stolen?

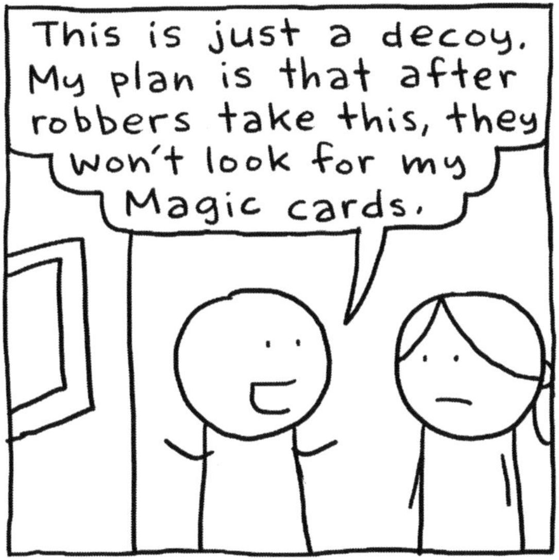
This is just a decoy. My plan is that after robbers take this, they won't look for my Magic cards.

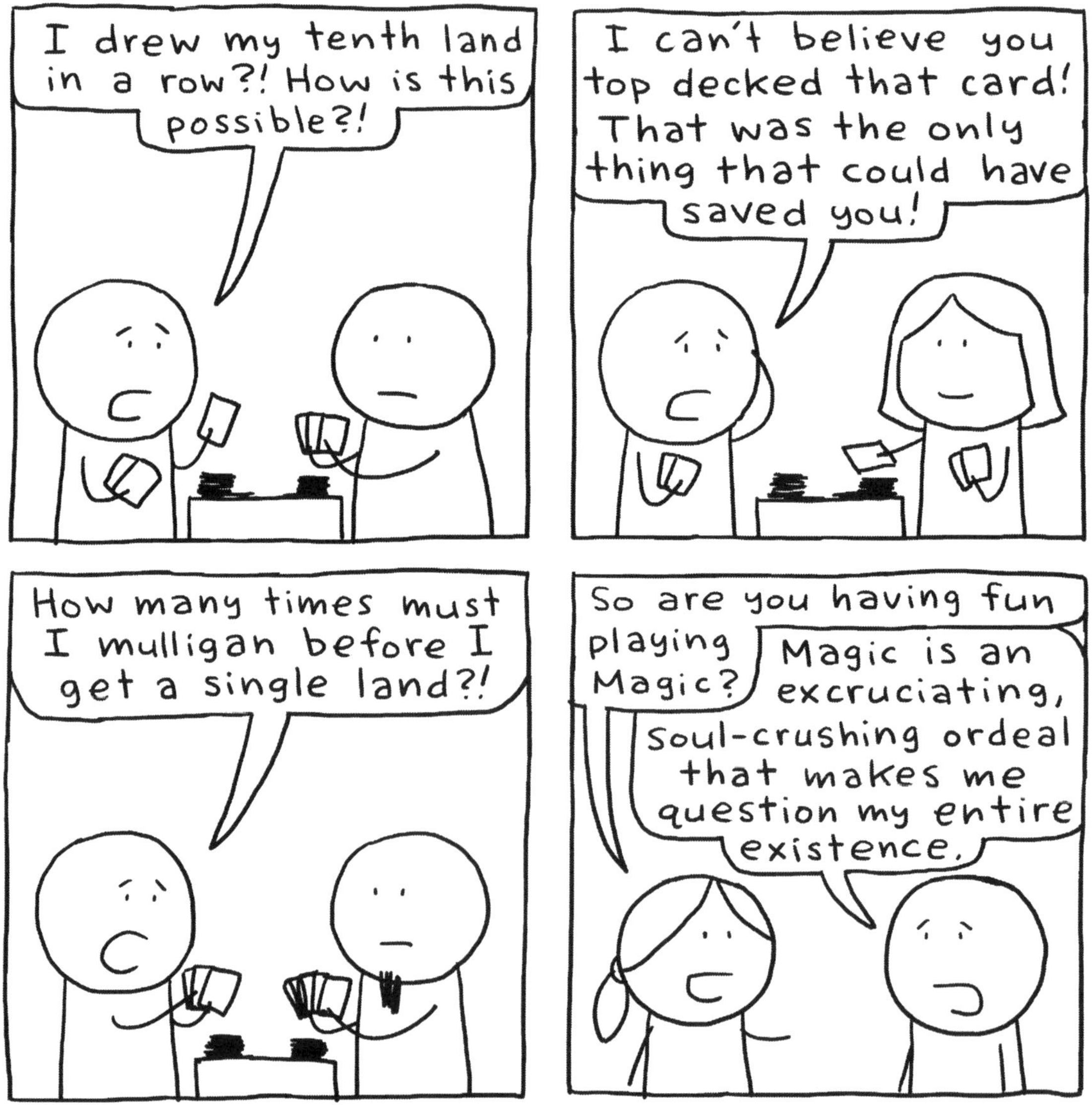
I drew my tenth land in a row?! How is this possible?!
I can't believe you top decked that card! That was the only thing that could have saved you!
How many times must I mulligan before I get a single land?!
So are you having fun playing Magic?
Magic is an excruciating, soul-crushing ordeal that makes me question my entire existence.

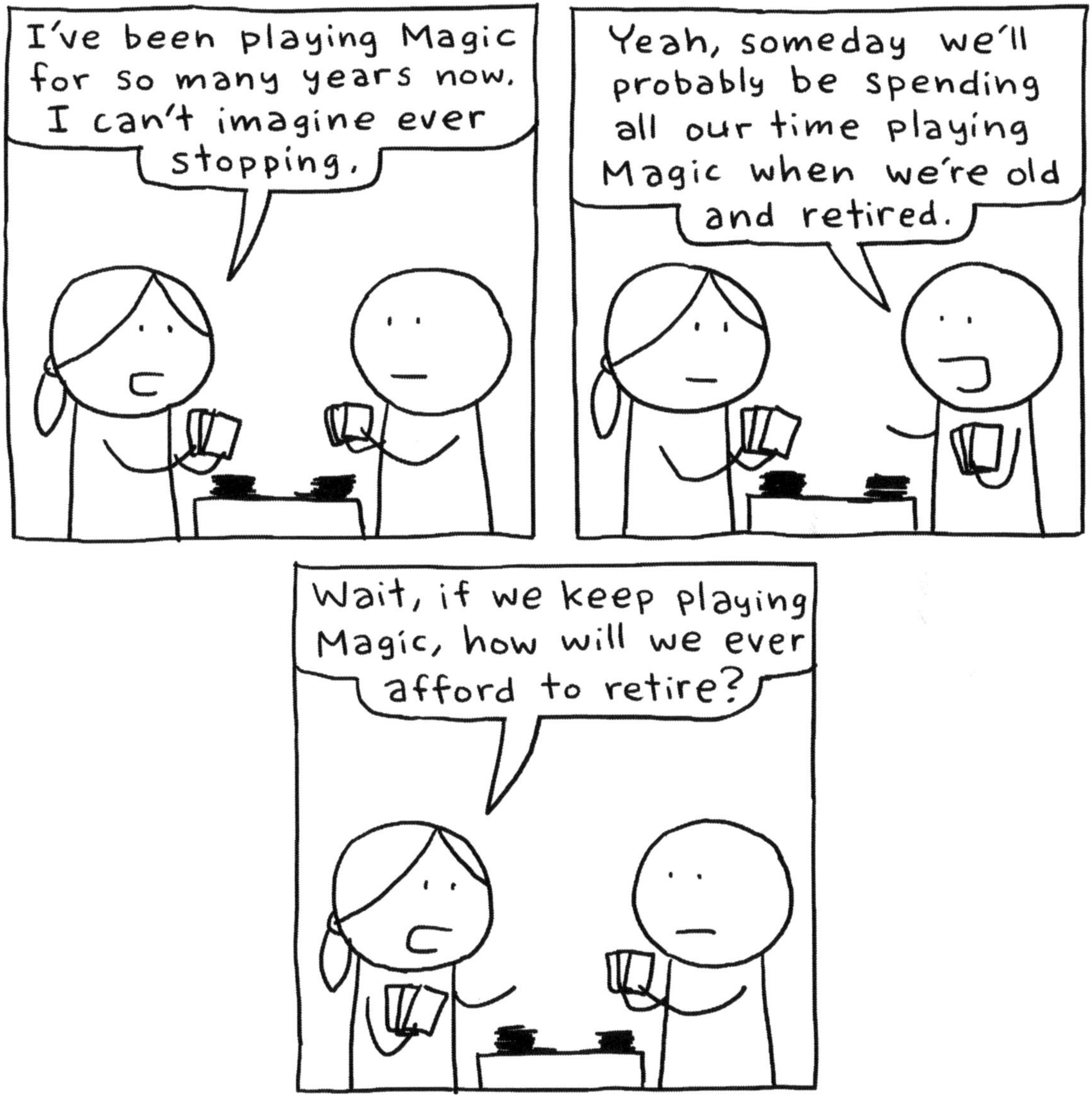
I've been playing Magic for so many years now. I can't imagine ever stopping.
Yeah, someday we'll probably be spending all our time playing Magic when we're old and retired.
Wait, if we keep playing Magic, how will we ever afford to retire?

After losing 3 drafts in a row...
This format is terrible! It's too dependent on luck.
After winning 3 drafts in a row...
This format is awesome! It's so skill intensive.

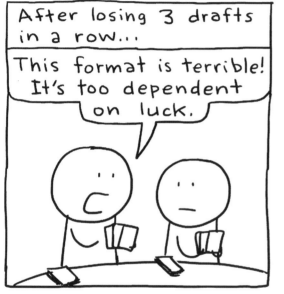

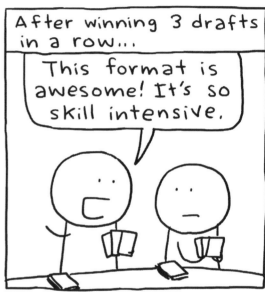

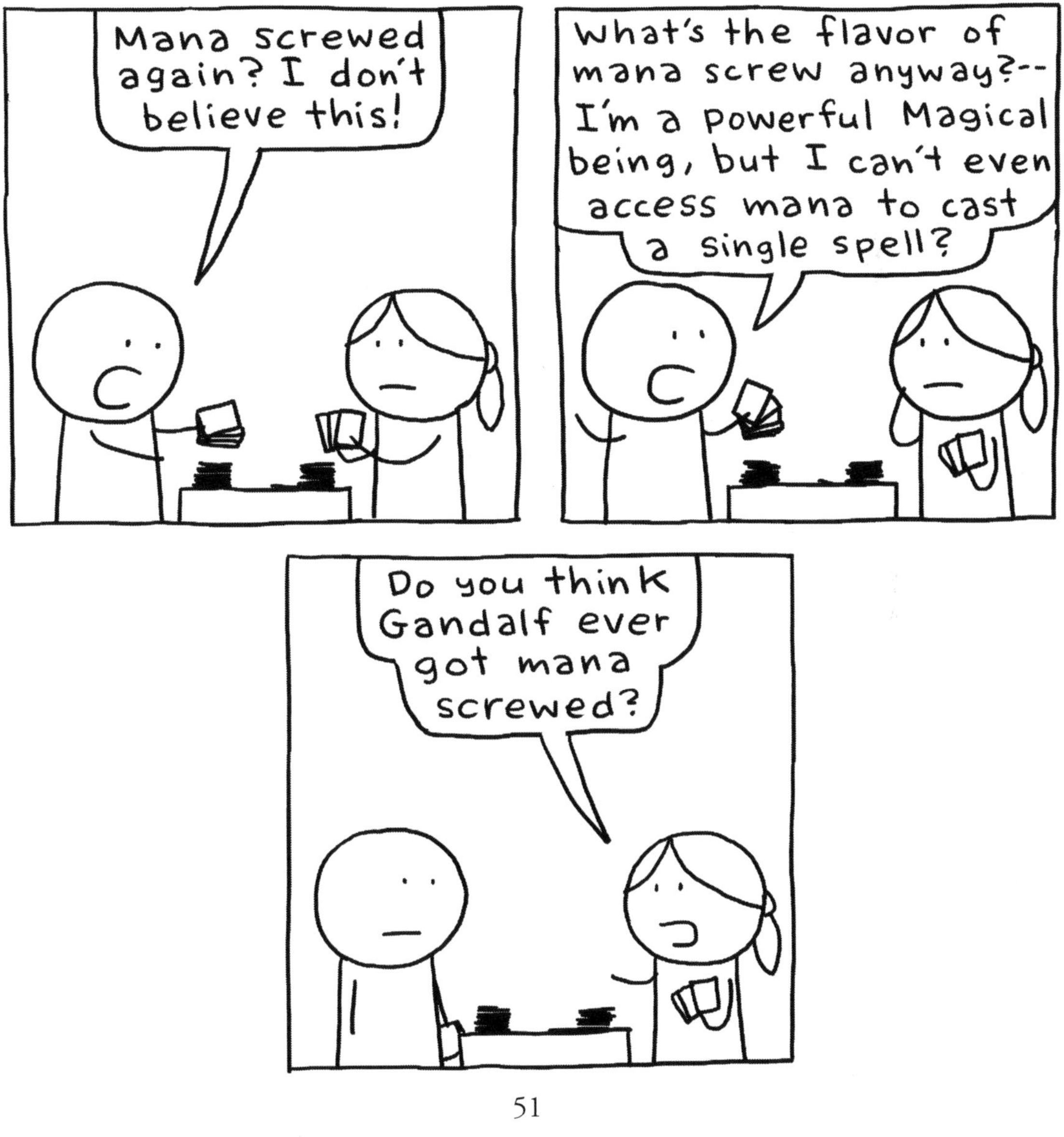
Mana screwed again? I don't believe this!
What's the flavor of mana screw anyway?-- I'm a powerful Magical being, but I can't even access mana to cast a single spell?
Do you think Gandalf ever got mana screwed?

We need to talk. I know your Magic collection is expensive, but this is getting ridiculous.
Can you at least remove the handcuffs before we get romantic together?!
You want me to take this off? I'm not falling for that trick!

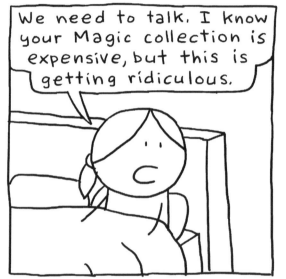

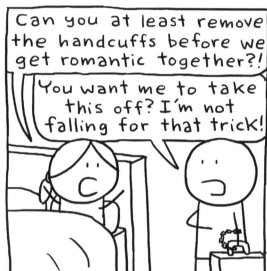

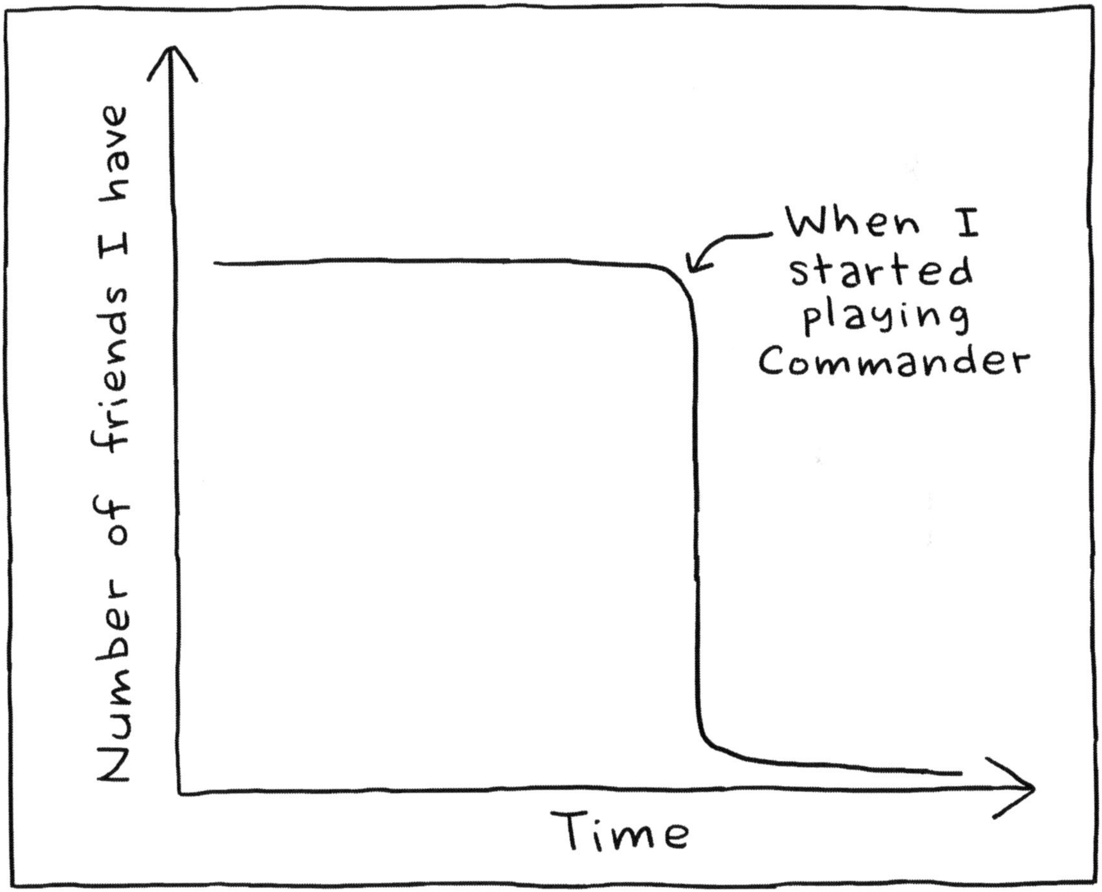
Number of friends I have
When I started playing Commander
Time

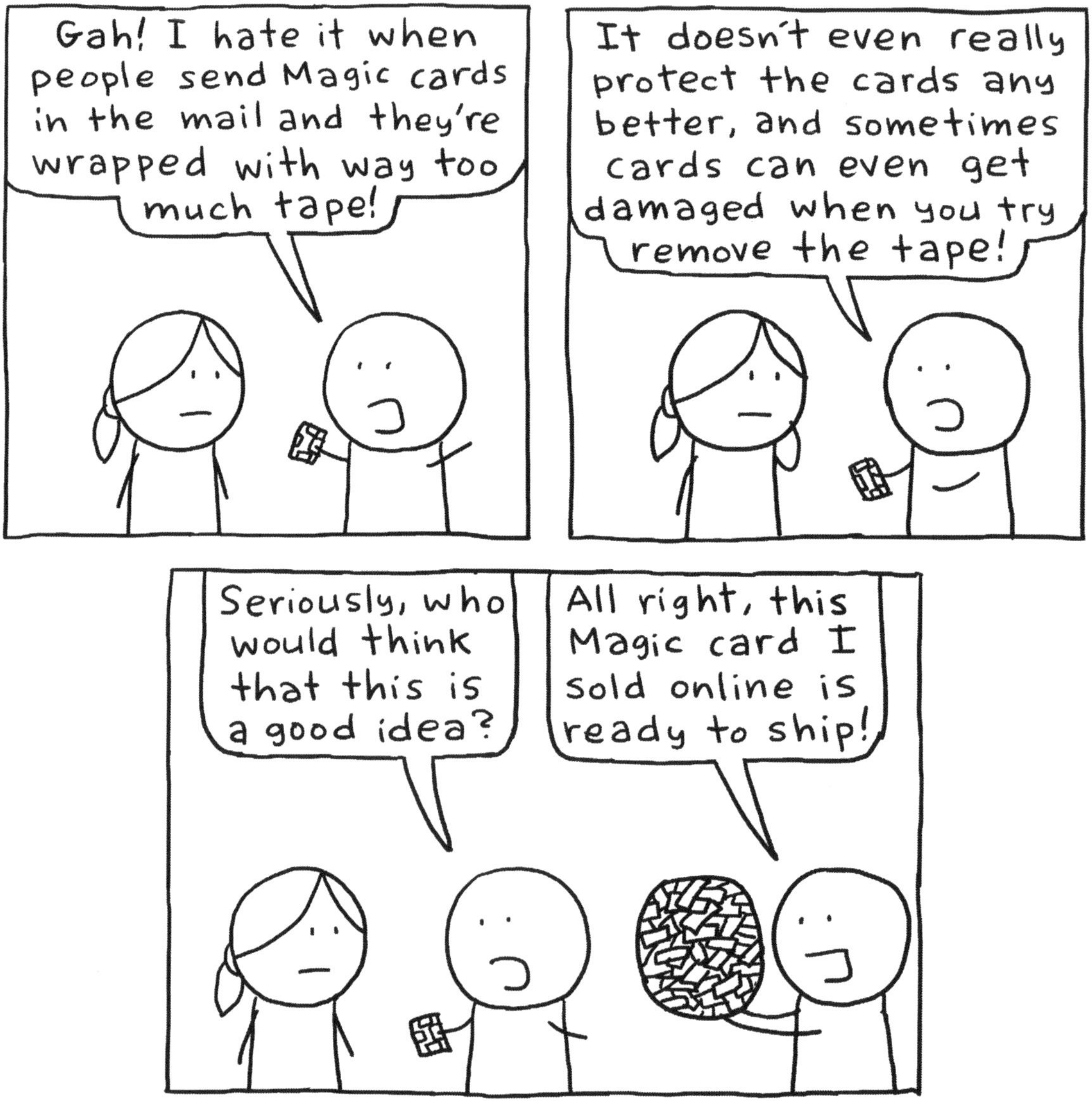
Gah! I hate it when people send Magic cards in the mail and they're wrapped with way too much tape!
It doesn't even really protect the cards any better, and sometimes cards can even get damaged when you try remove the tape!
Seriously, who would think that this is a good idea?
All right, this Magic card I sold online is ready to ship!

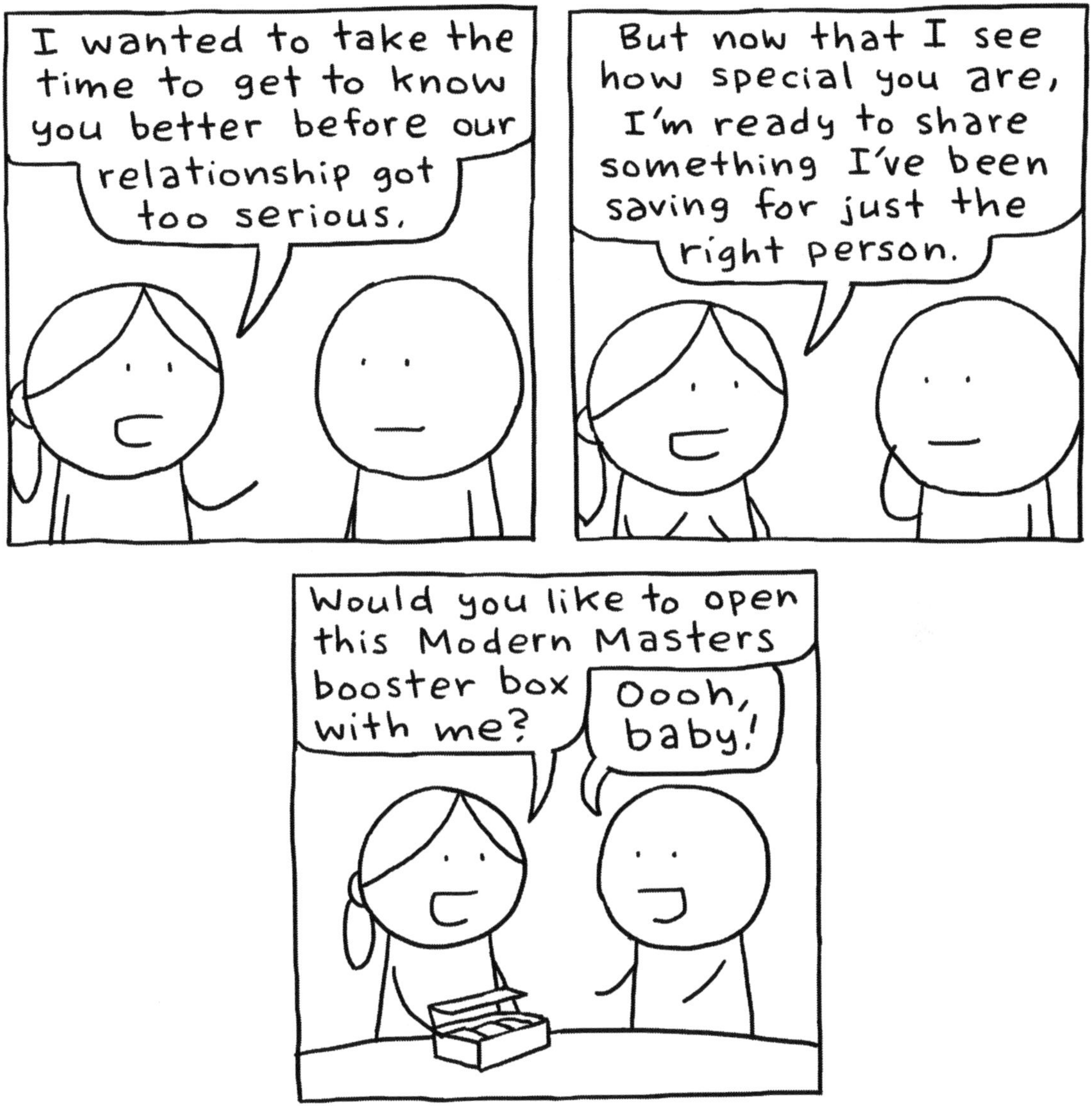
I wanted to take the time to get to know you better before our relationship got too serious.
But now that I see how special you are, I'm ready to share something I've been saving for just the right person.
Would you like to open this Modern Masters booster box with me?
Oooh, baby!

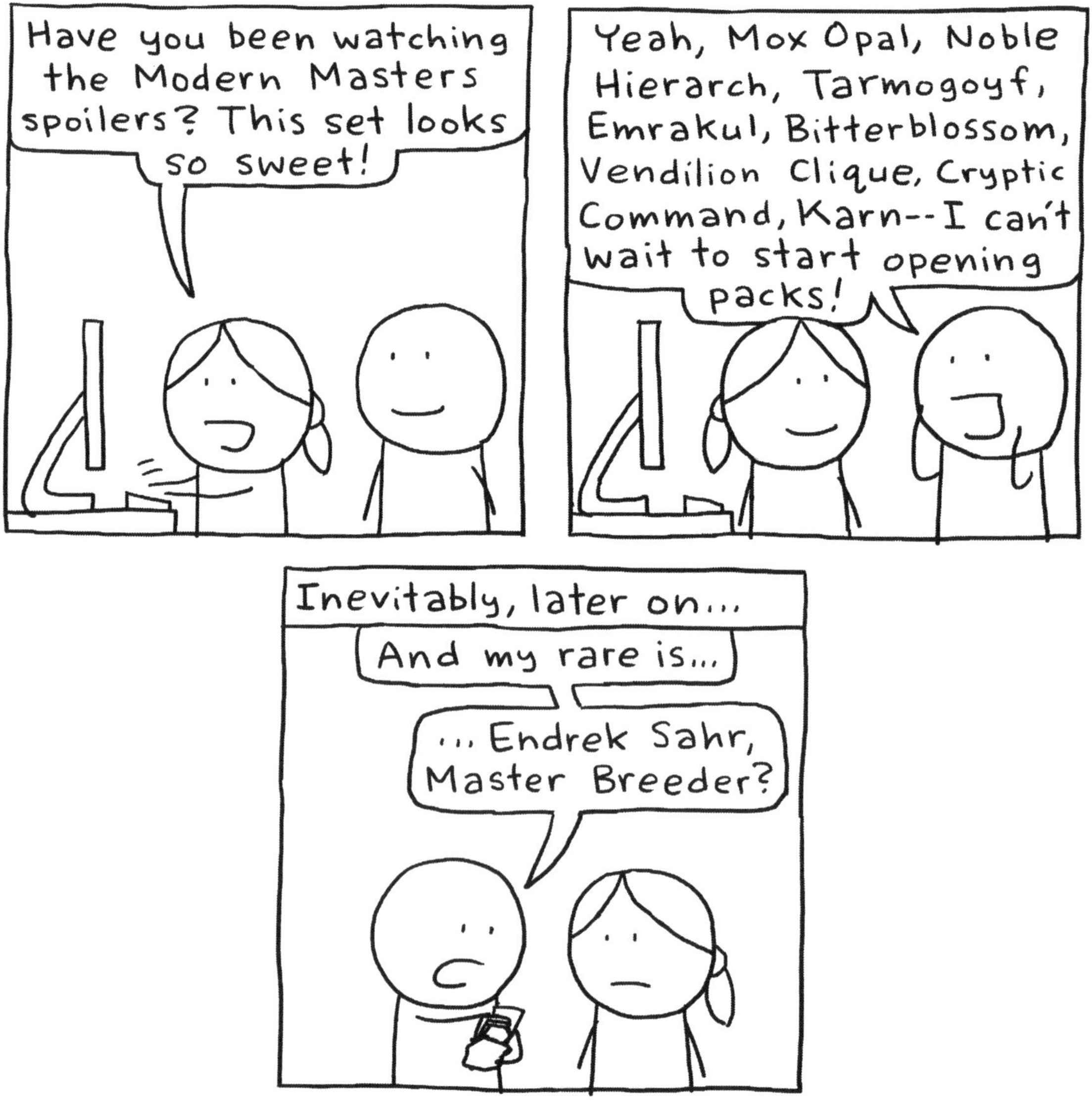
Have you been watching the Modern Masters spoilers? This set looks so sweet!
Yeah, Mox Opal, Noble Hierarch, Tarmogoyf, Emrakul, Bitterblossom, Vendilion Clique, Cryptic Command, Karn--I can't wait to start opening packs!
Inevitably, later on...
And my rare is...
...Endrek Sahr, Master Breeder?

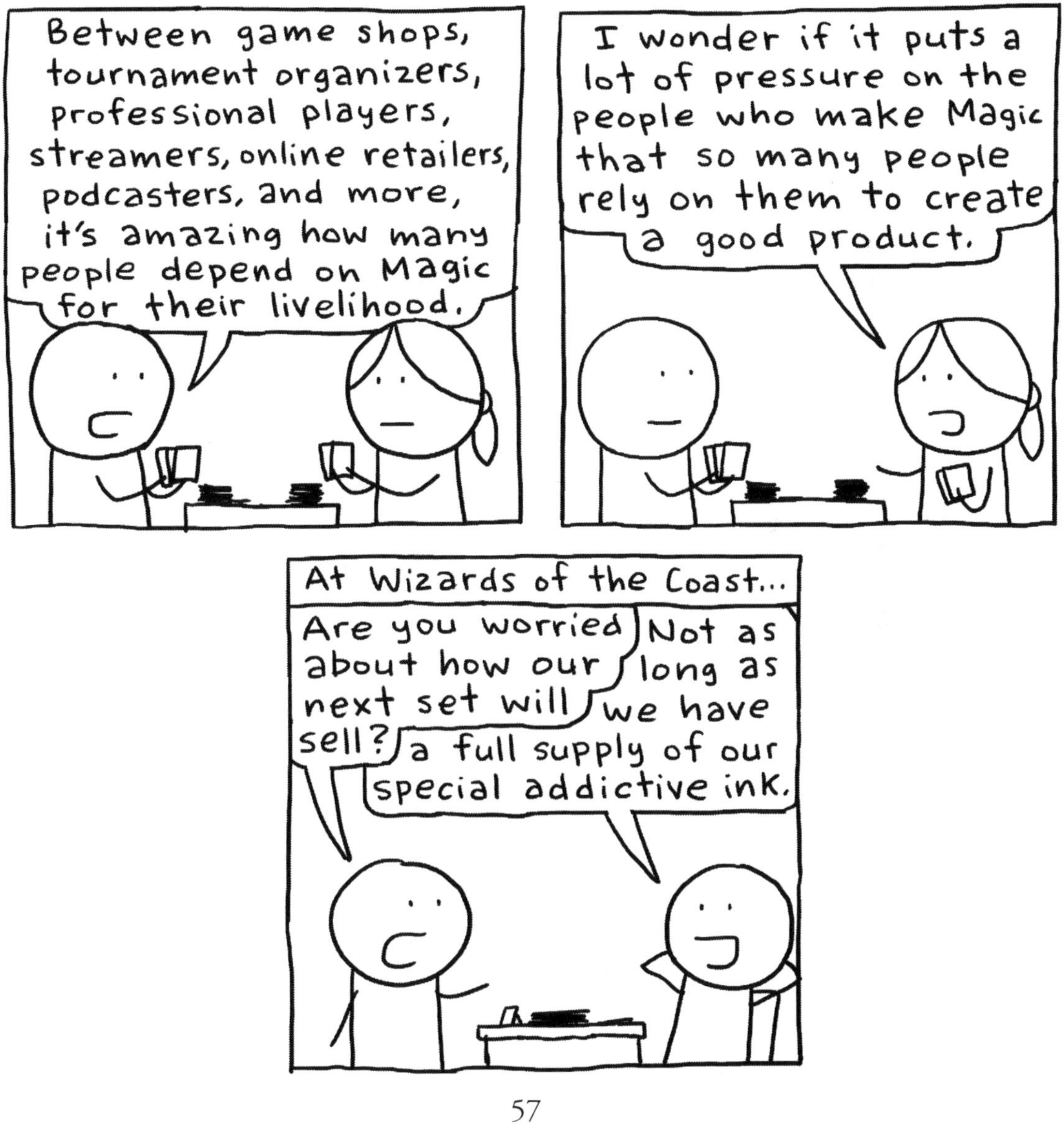
Between game shops, tournament organizers, professional players, streamers, online retailers, podcasters, and more, it's amazing how many people depend on Magic for their livelihood.
I wonder if it puts a lot of pressure on the people who make Magic that so many people rely on them to create a good product.
At Wizards of the Coast...
Are you worried about how our next set will sell?
Not as long as we have a full supply of our special addictive ink.

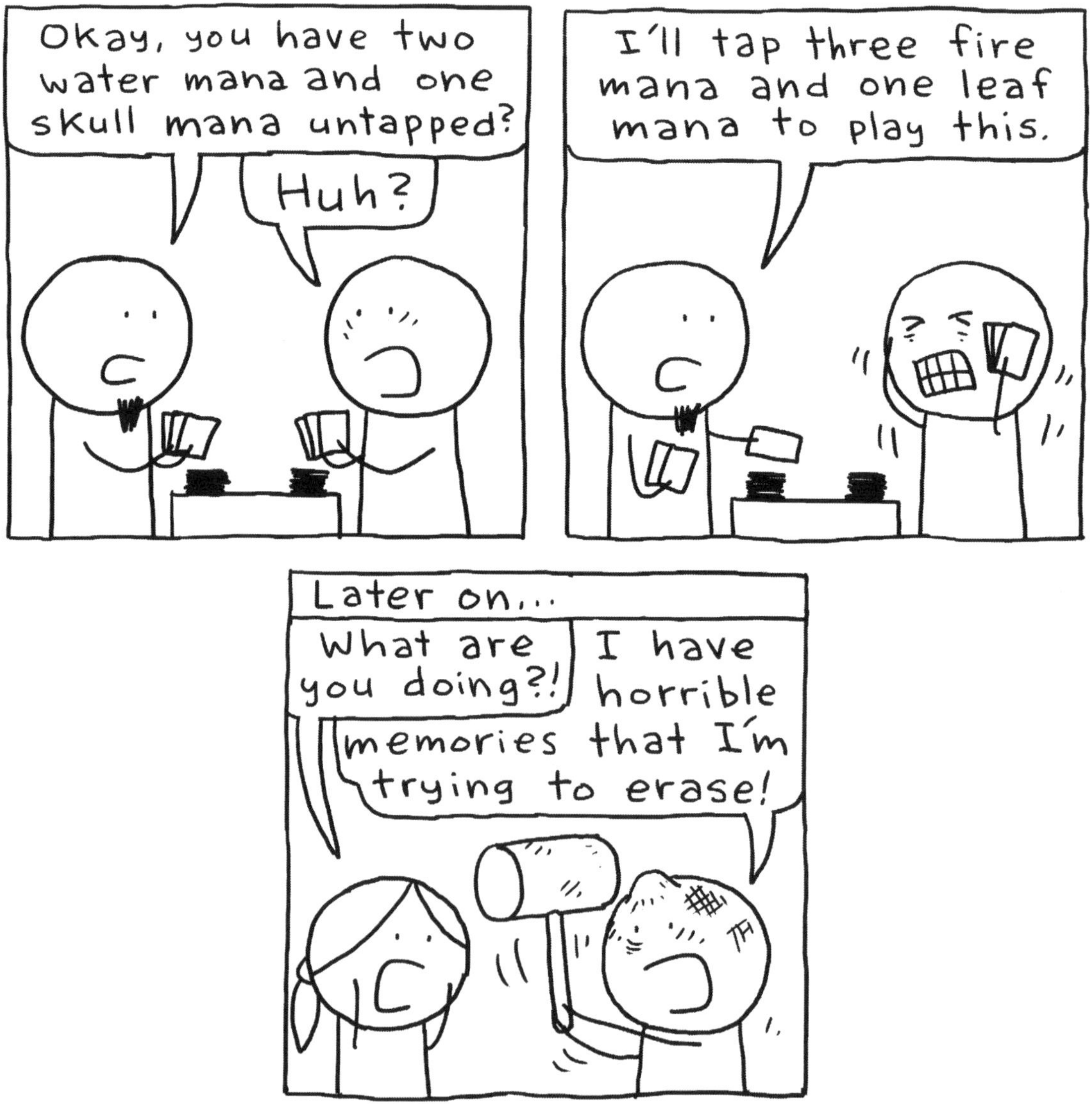
Okay, you have two water mana and one skull mana untapped?
Huh?
I'll tap three fire mana and one leaf mana to play this.
Later on...
What are you doing?!
I have horrible memories that I'm trying to erase!

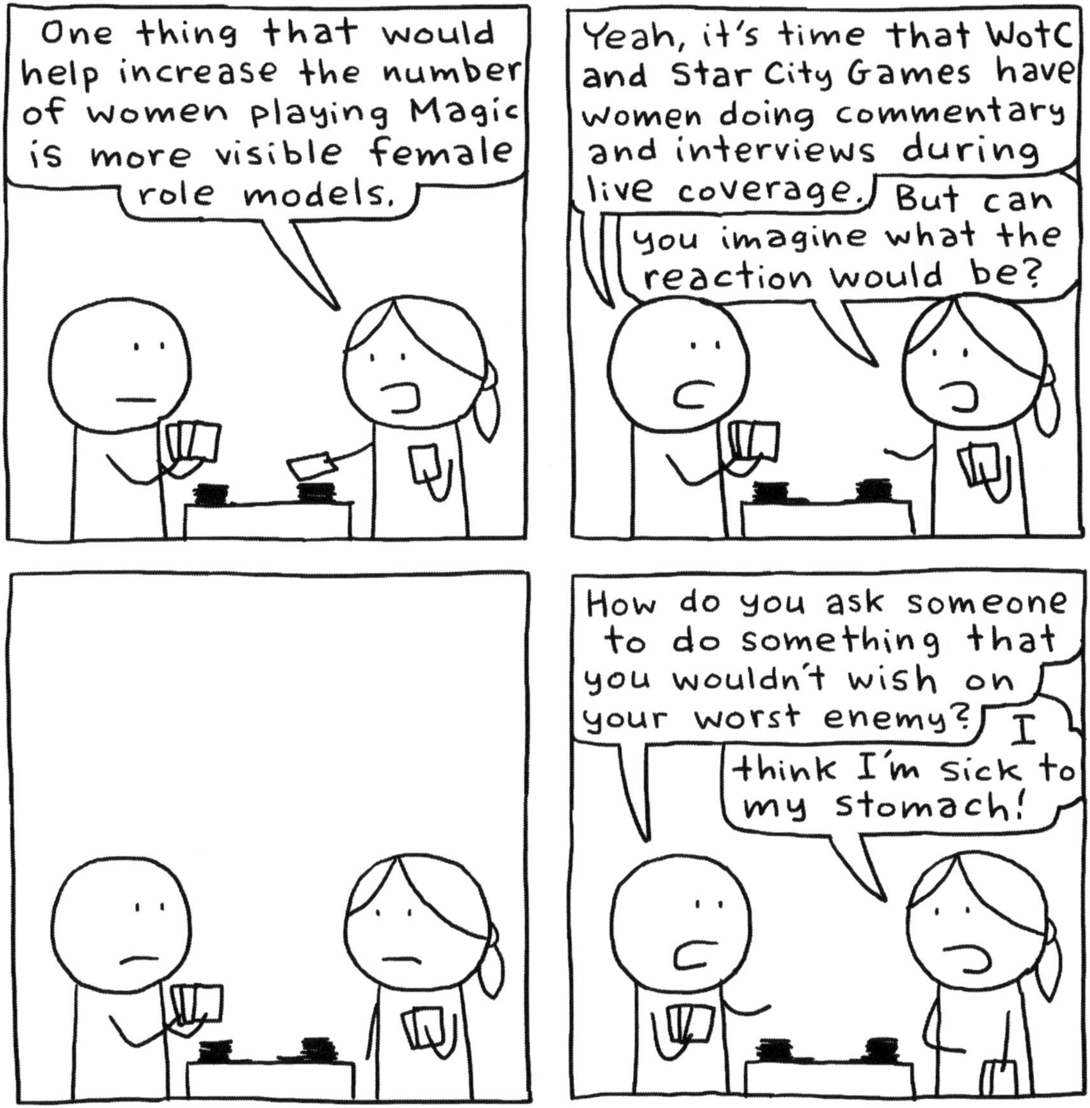
One thing that would help increase the number of women playing Magic is more visible female role models.
Yeah, it's time that WotC and Star City Games have women doing commentary and interviews during live coverage.
But can you imagine what the reaction would be?
How do you ask someone to do something that you wouldn't wish on your worst enemy?
I think I'm sick to my stomach!

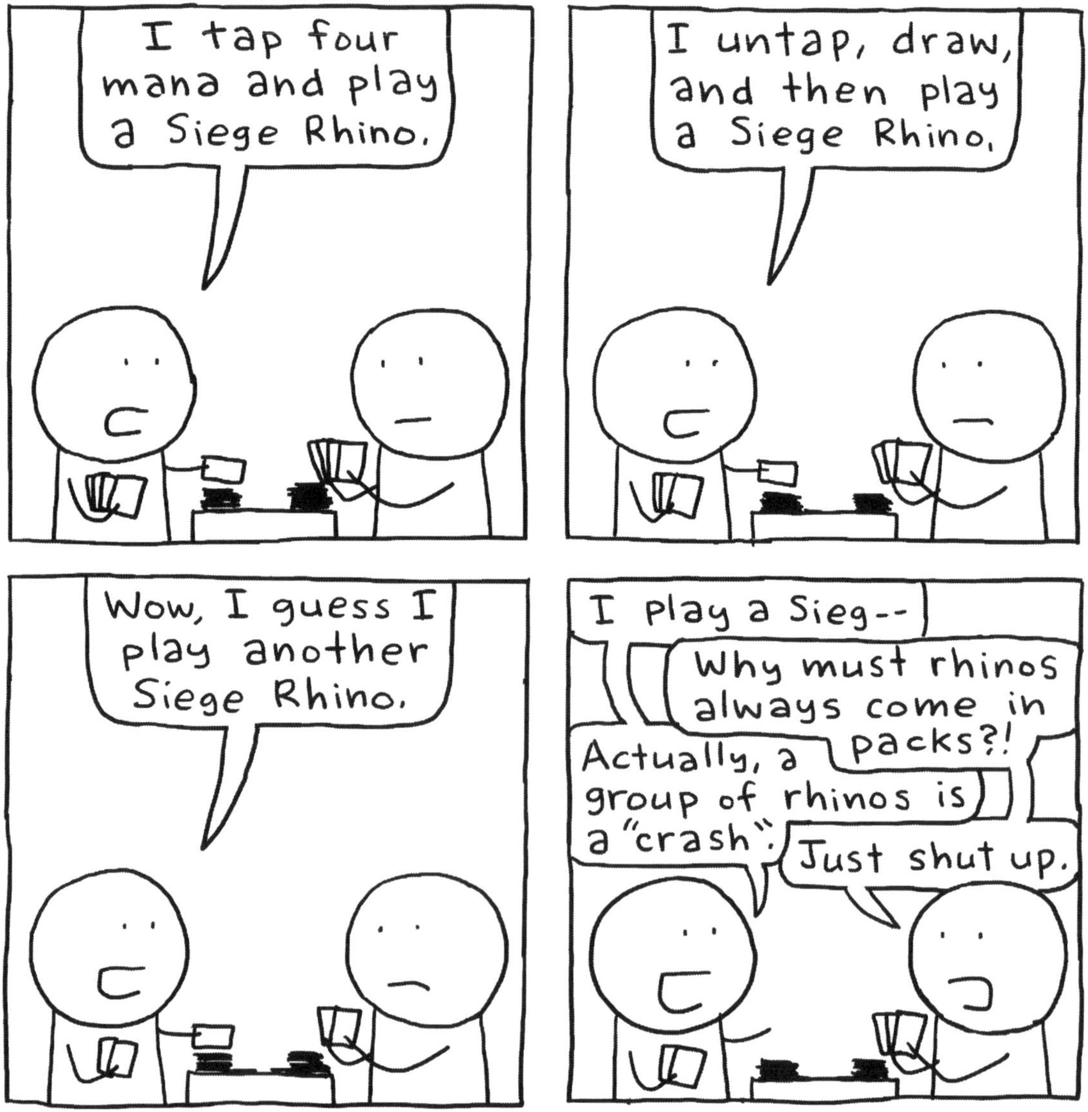
I tap four mana and play a Siege Rhino.
I untap, draw, and then play a Siege Rhino.
Wow, I guess I play another Siege Rhino.
I play a Sieg--
Why must rhinos always come in packs?!
Actually, a group of rhinos is a "crash".
Just shut up.

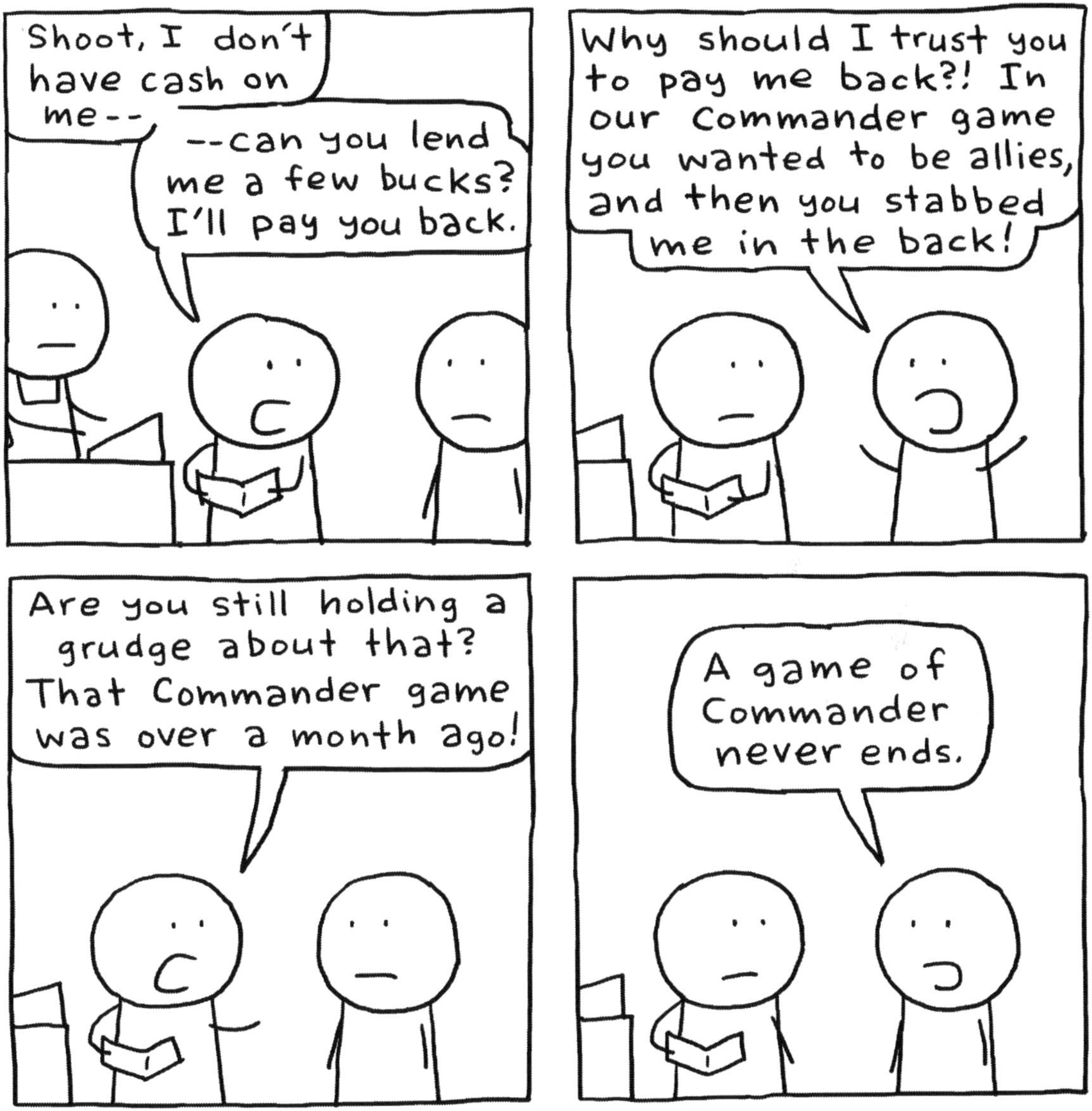
Shoot, I don't have cash on me--
--can you lend me a few bucks? I'll pay you back.
Why should I trust you to pay me back?! In our Commander game you wanted to be allies, and then you stabbed me in the back!
Are you still holding a grudge about that? That Commander game was over a month ago!
A game of Commander never ends.

My typical drafting experience
Win 2 drafts in a row...
I'm the boss of this format! Bow down to me!
Then lose 12 in a row...
I'm hopeless! I know nothing!

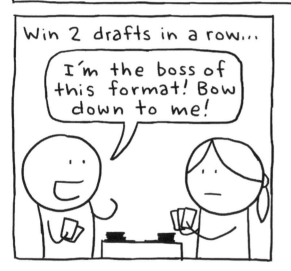

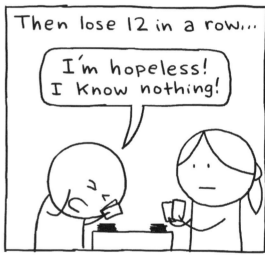

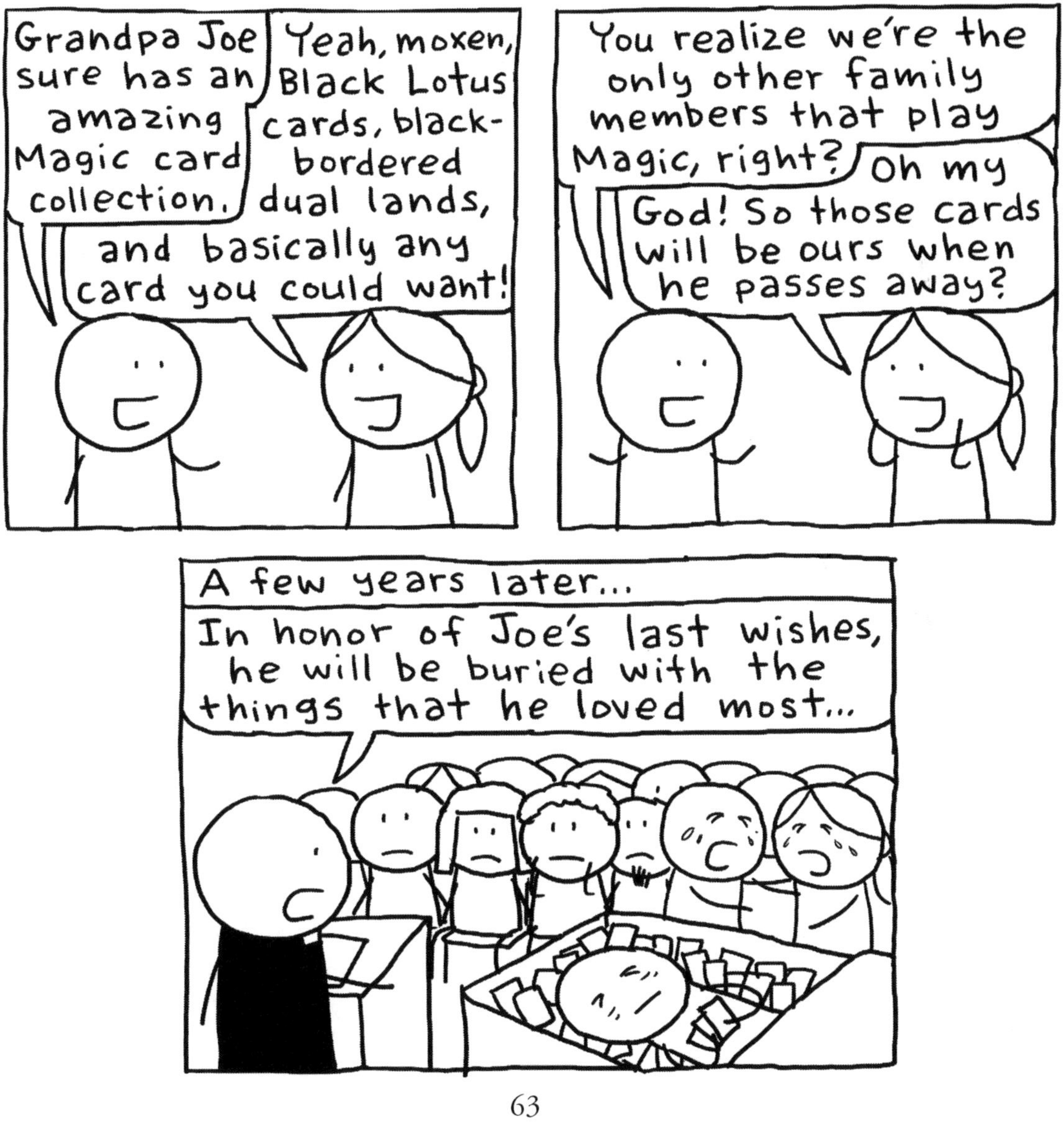
Grandpa Joe sure has an amazing Magic card collection.
Yeah, moxen, Black Lotus cards, black-bordered dual lands, and basically any card you could want!
You realize we're the only other family members that play Magic, right?
Oh my God! So those cards will be ours when he passes away?
A few years later...
In honor of Joe's last wishes, he will be buried with the things that he loved most...

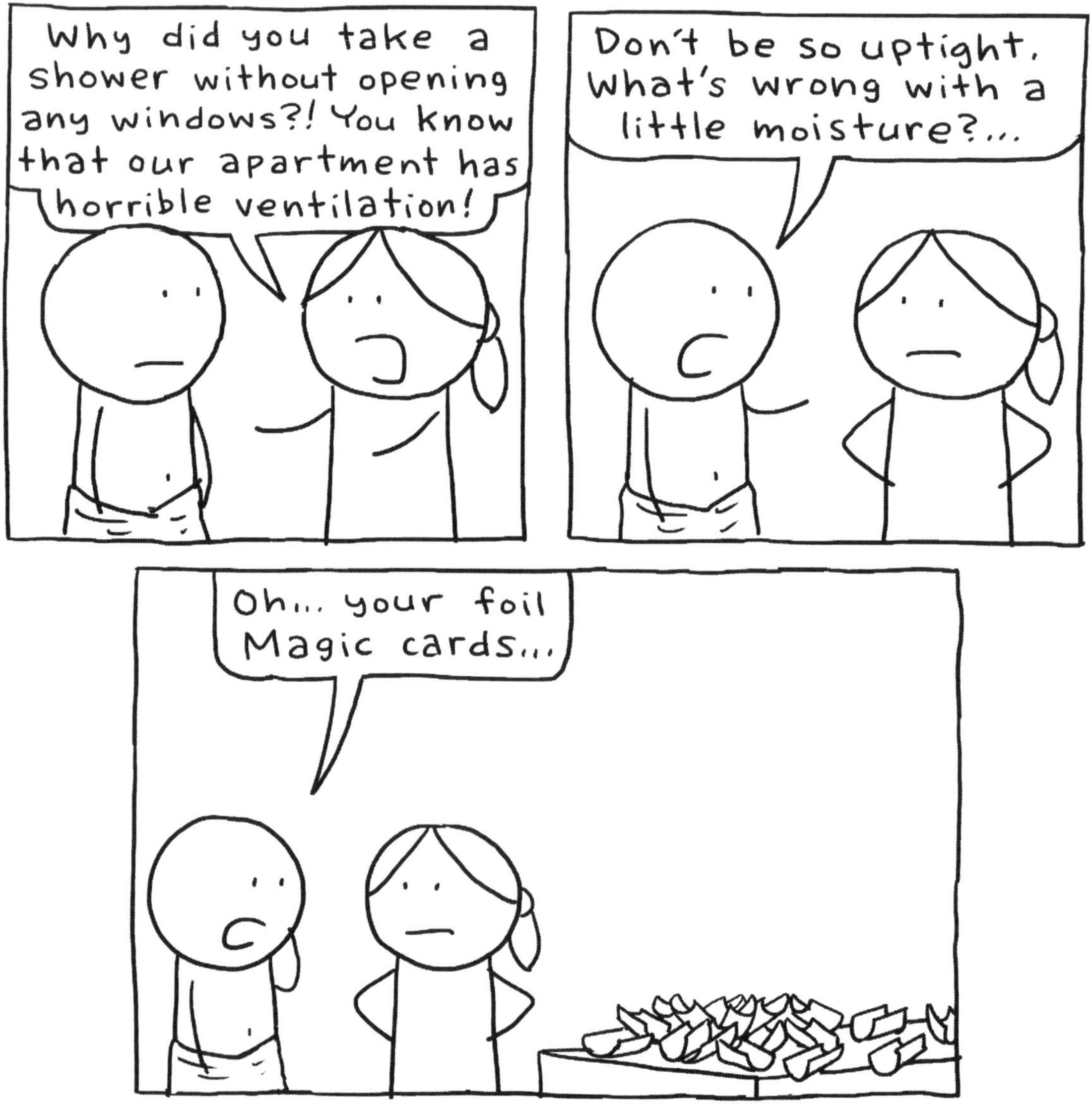
Why did you take a shower without opening any windows?! You know that our apartment has horrible ventilation!
Don't be so uptight. What's wrong with a little moisture?...
Oh... your foil Magic cards...

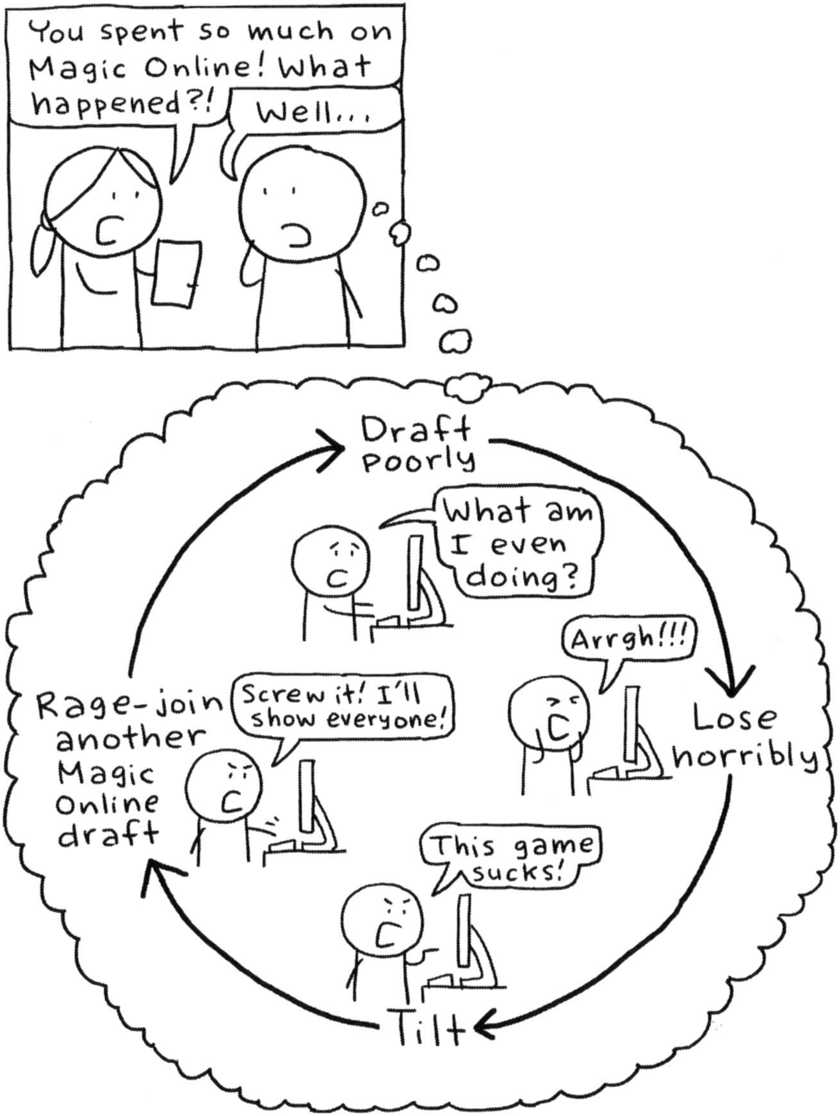
You spent so much on Magic Online! What happened?!
Well...
Draft poorly
What am I even doing?
Arrgh!!!
Lose horribly
This game sucks!
Tilt
Screw it! I'll show everyone!
Rage-join another Magic Online draft

Modern players...
Please reprint Serum Visions! A staple common shouldn't cost so much!
Legacy players...
Modern players pay that much for that effect?! Ha! Ha! Ha!

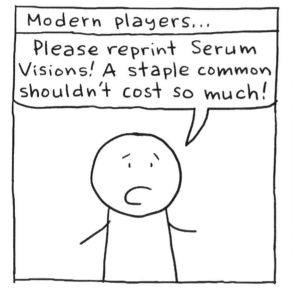

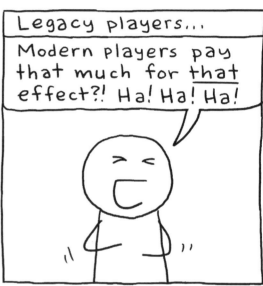

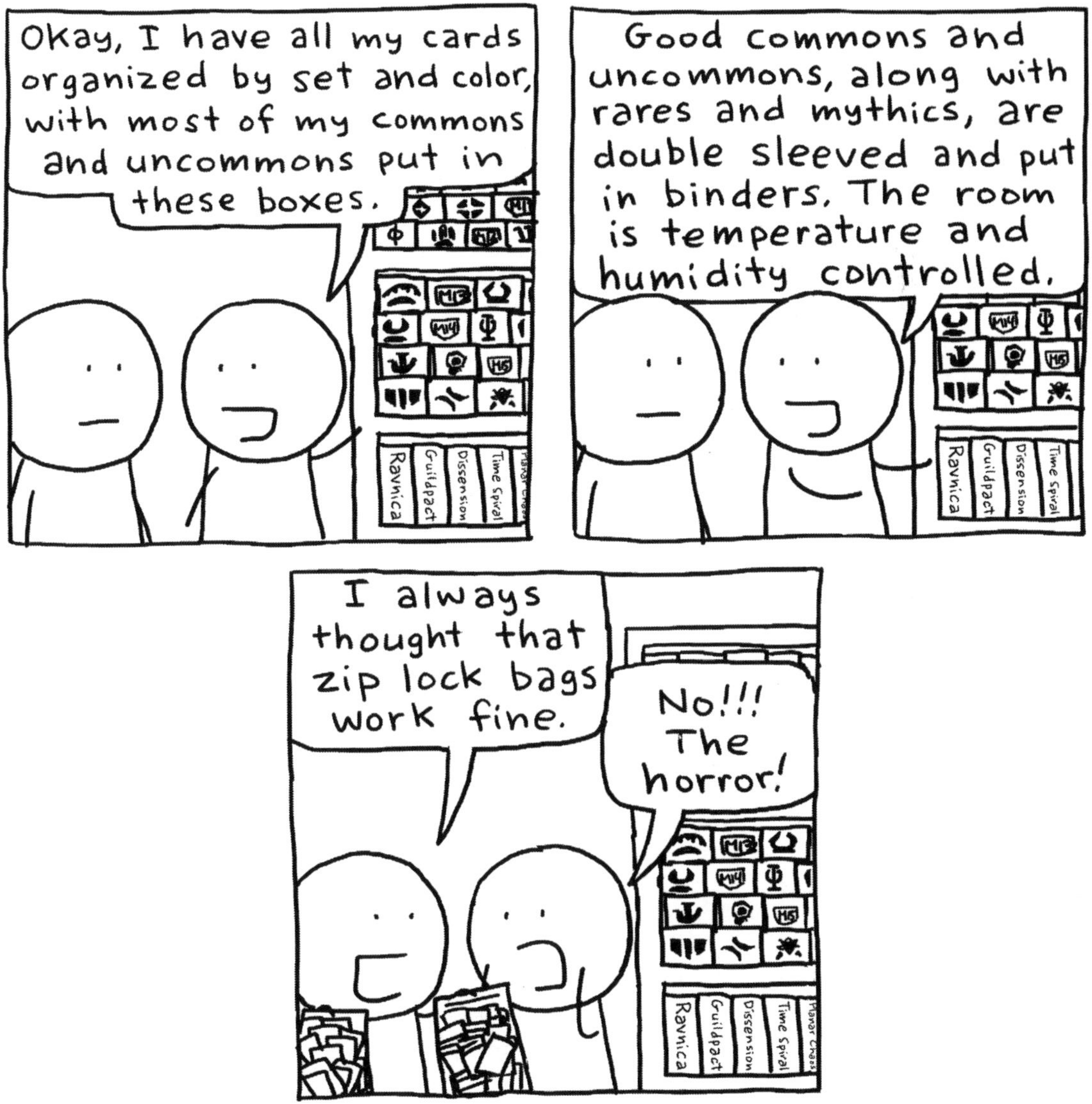
Okay, I have all my cards organized by set and color, with most of my commons and uncommons put in these boxes.
Ravnica
Guildpact
Dissension
Time Spiral
Good commons and uncommons, along with rares and mythics, are double sleeved and put in binders. The room is temperature and humidity controlled.
I always thought that zip lock bags work fine.
No!!! The horror!

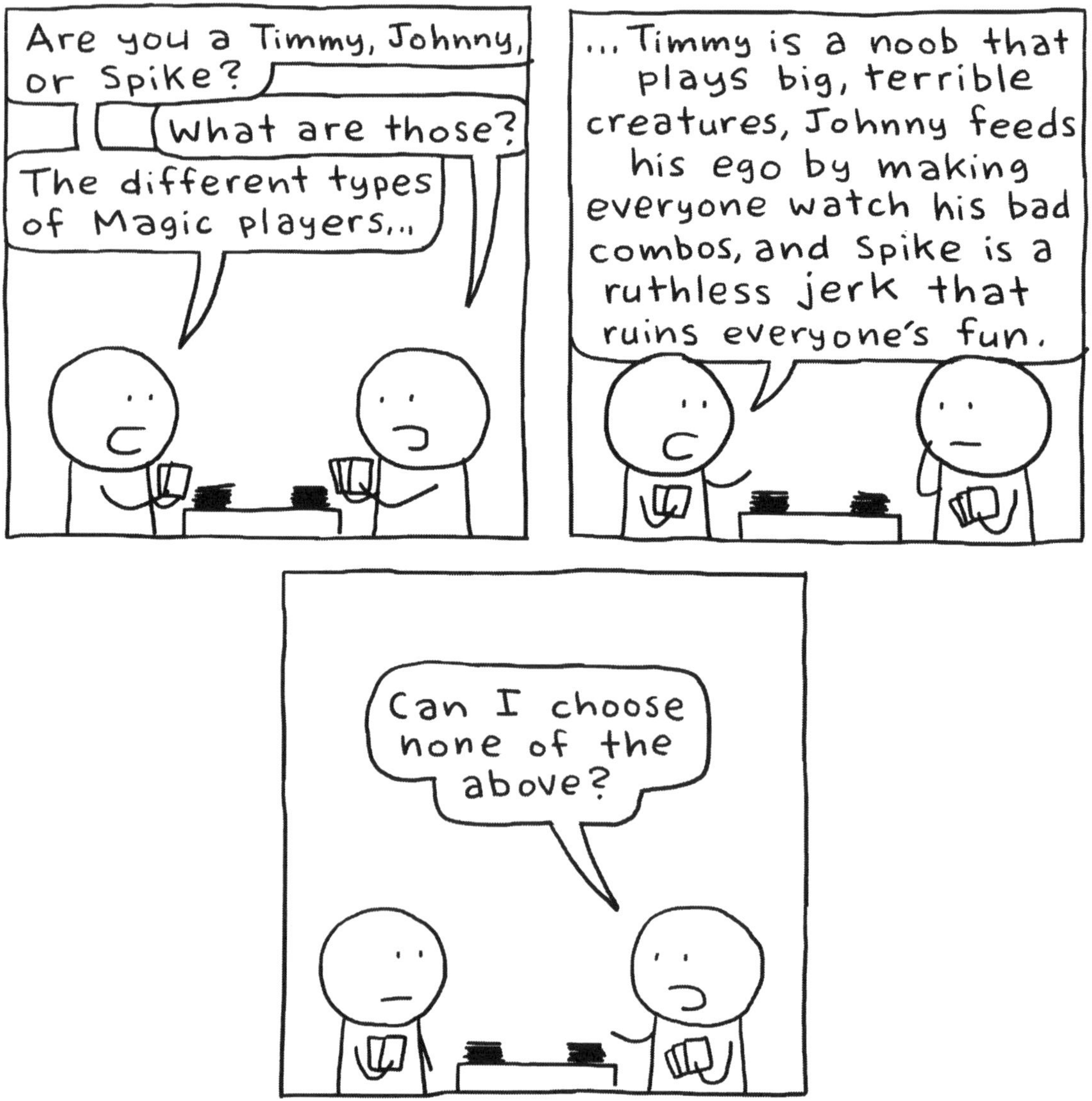
Are you a Timmy, Johnny, or Spike?
What are those?
The different types of Magic players...
...Timmy is a noob that plays big, terrible creatures, Johnny feeds his ego by making everyone watch his bad combos, and Spike is a ruthless jerk that ruins everyone's fun.
Can I choose none of the above?

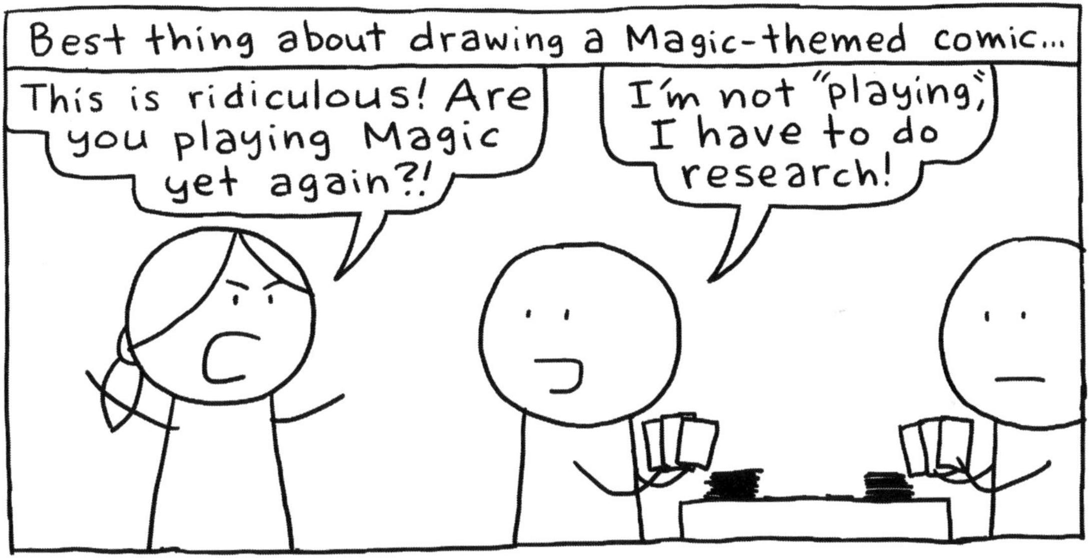

Best thing about drawing a Magic-themed comic...
This is ridiculous! Are you playing Magic yet again?!
I'm not "playing," I have to do research!

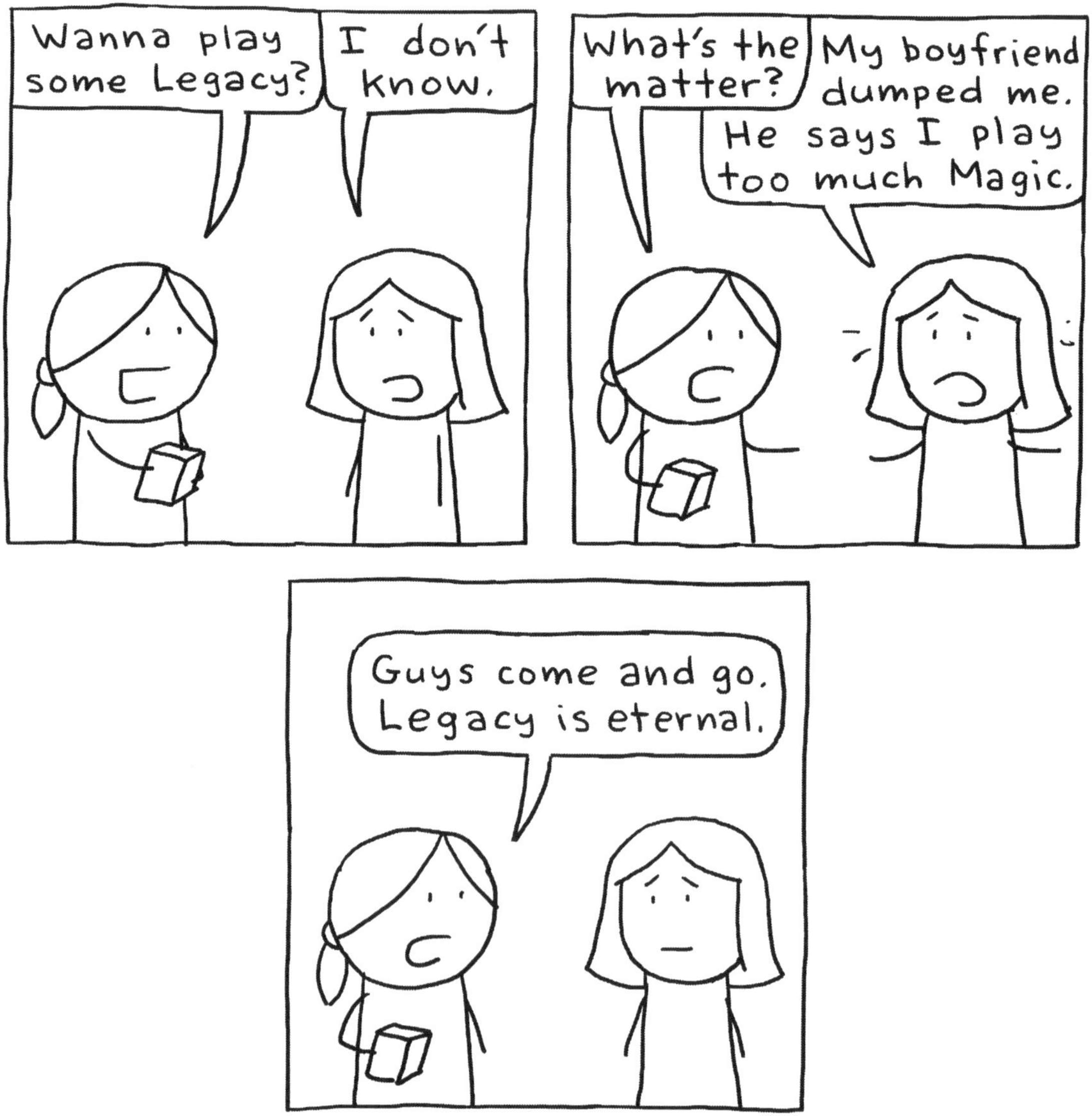
Wanna play some Legacy?
I don't know.
What's the matter?
My boyfriend dumped me. He says I play too much Magic.
Guys come and go. Legacy is eternal.

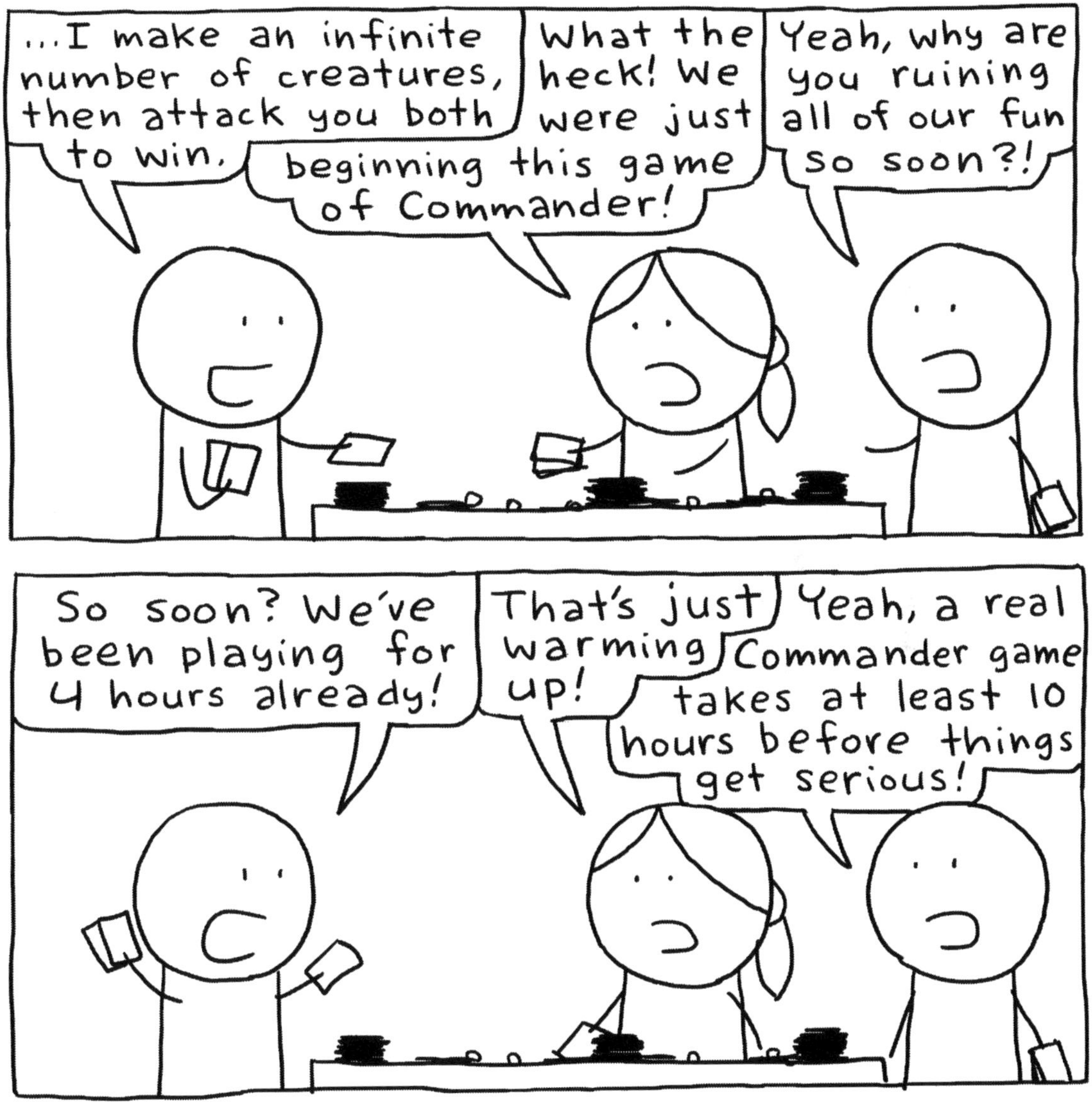
...I make an infinite number of creatures, then attack you both to win.
What the heck! We were just beginning this game of Commander!
Yeah, why are you ruining all of our fun so soon?!
So soon? We've been playing for 4 hours already!
That's just warming up!
Yeah, a real Commander game takes at least 10 hours before things get serious!

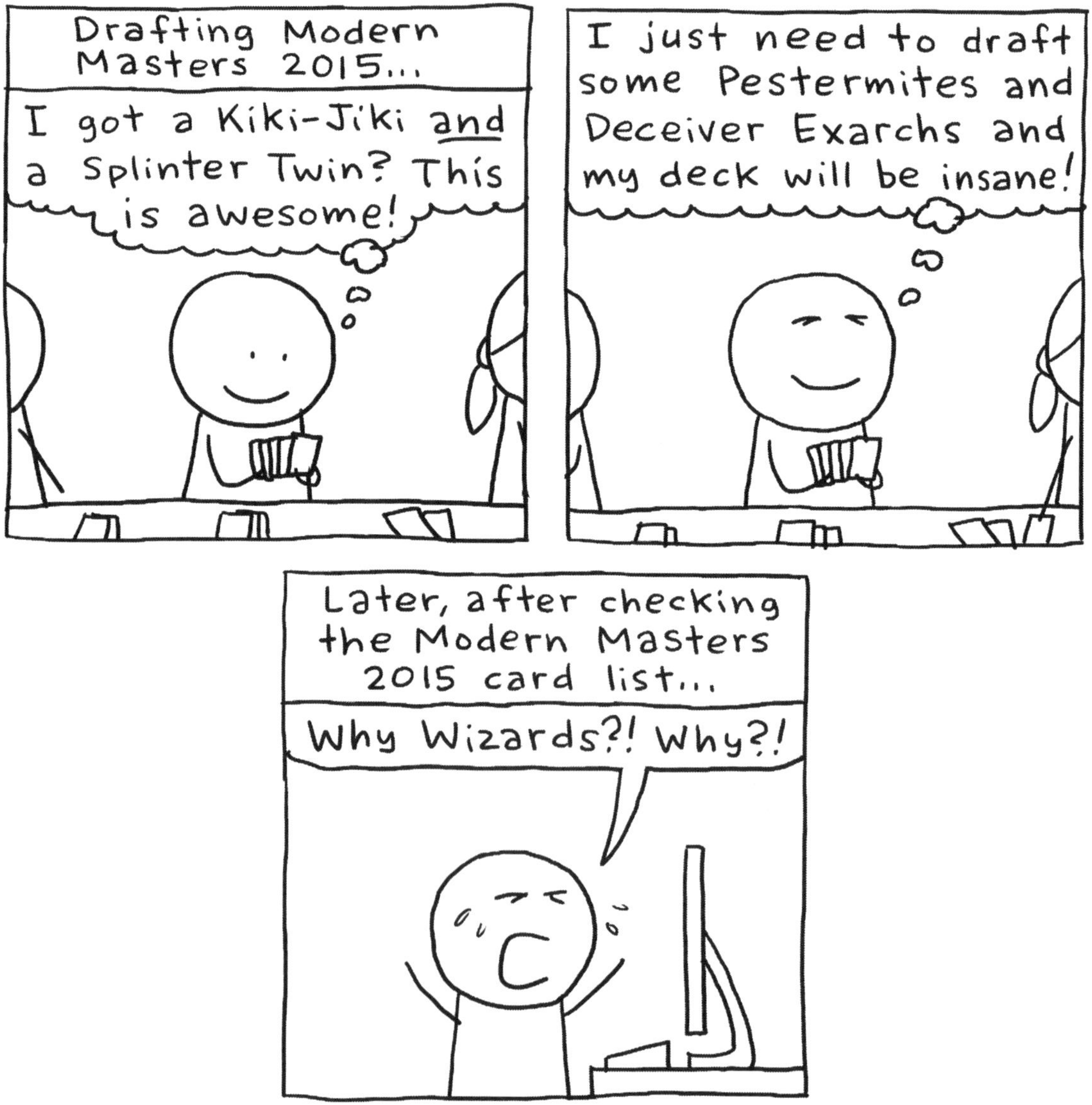
Drafting Modern Masters 2015...
I got a Kiki-Jiki and a Splinter Twin? This is awesome!
I just need to draft some Pestermites and Deceiver Exarchs and my deck will be insane!
Later, after checking the Modern Masters 2015 card list...
Why Wizards?! Why?!

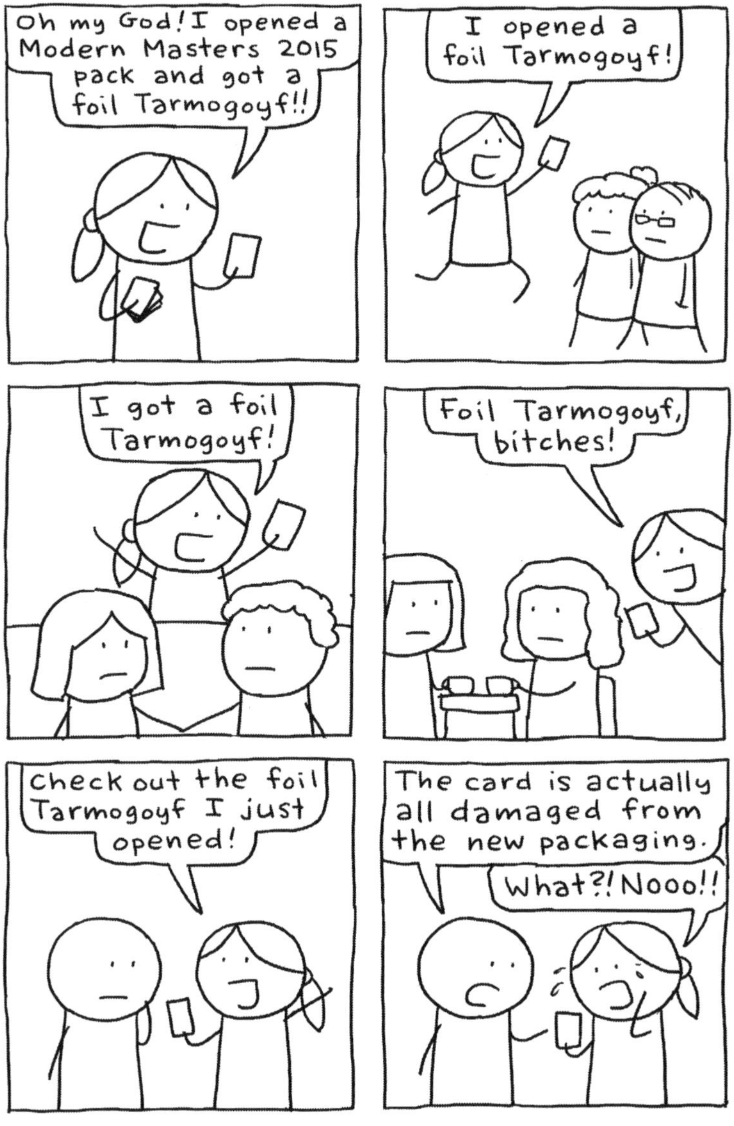
Oh my God! I opened a Modern Masters 2015 pack and got a foil Tarmogoyf!!
I opened a foil Tarmogoyf!
I got a foil Tarmogoyf!
Foil Tarmogoyf, bitches!
Check out the foil Tarmogoyf I just opened!
The card is actually all damaged from the new packaging.
What?! Nooo!!

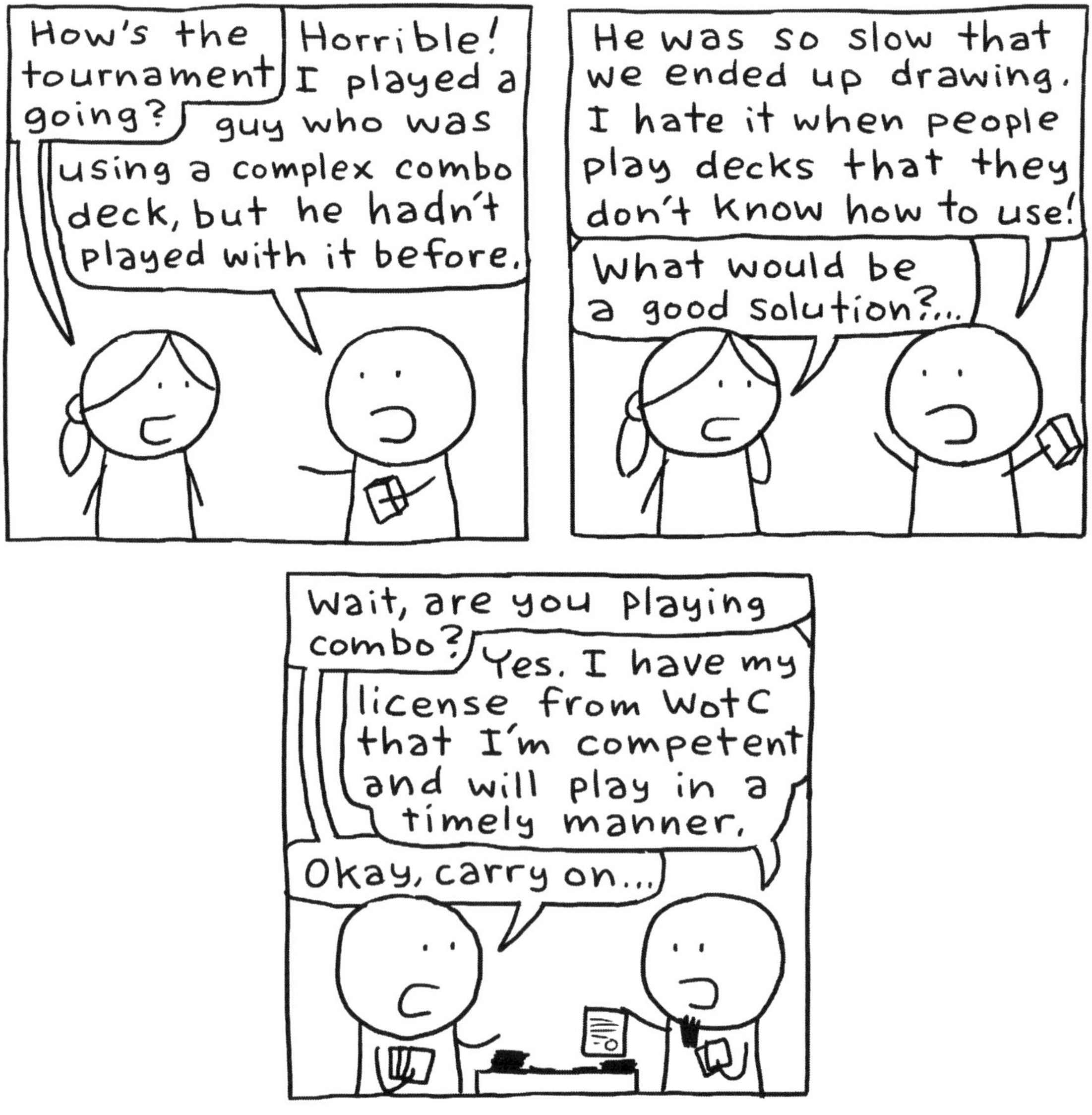
How's the tournament going?
Horrible! I played a guy who was using a complex combo deck, but he hadn't played with it before.
He was so slow that we ended up drawing. I hate it when people play decks that they don't know how to use!
What would be a good solution?...
Wait, are you playing combo?
Yes. I have my license from WotC that I'm competent and will play in a timely manner.
Okay, carry on...

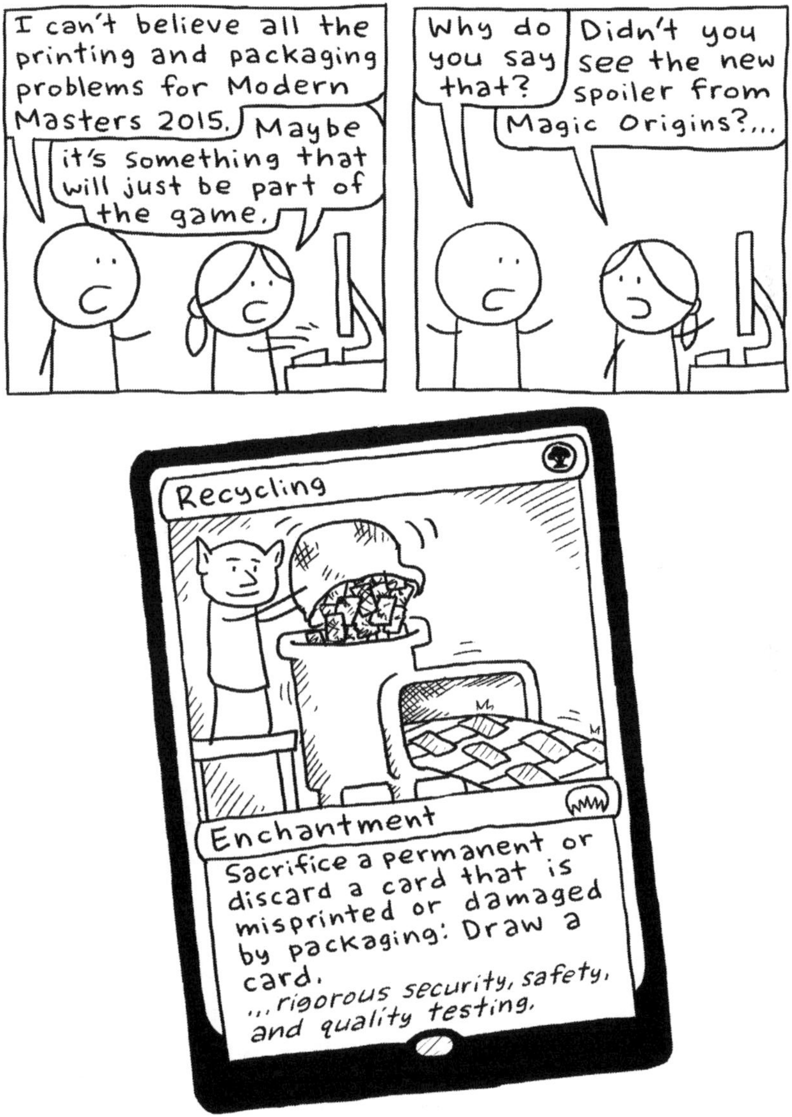
I can't believe all the printing and packaging problems for Modern Masters 2015.
Maybe it's something that will just be part of the game.
Why do you say that?
Didn't you see the new spoiler from Magic Origins?...
Recycling
Enchantment
Sacrifice a permanent or discard a card that is misprinted or damaged by packaging: Draw a card.
...rigorous security, safety, and quality testing.

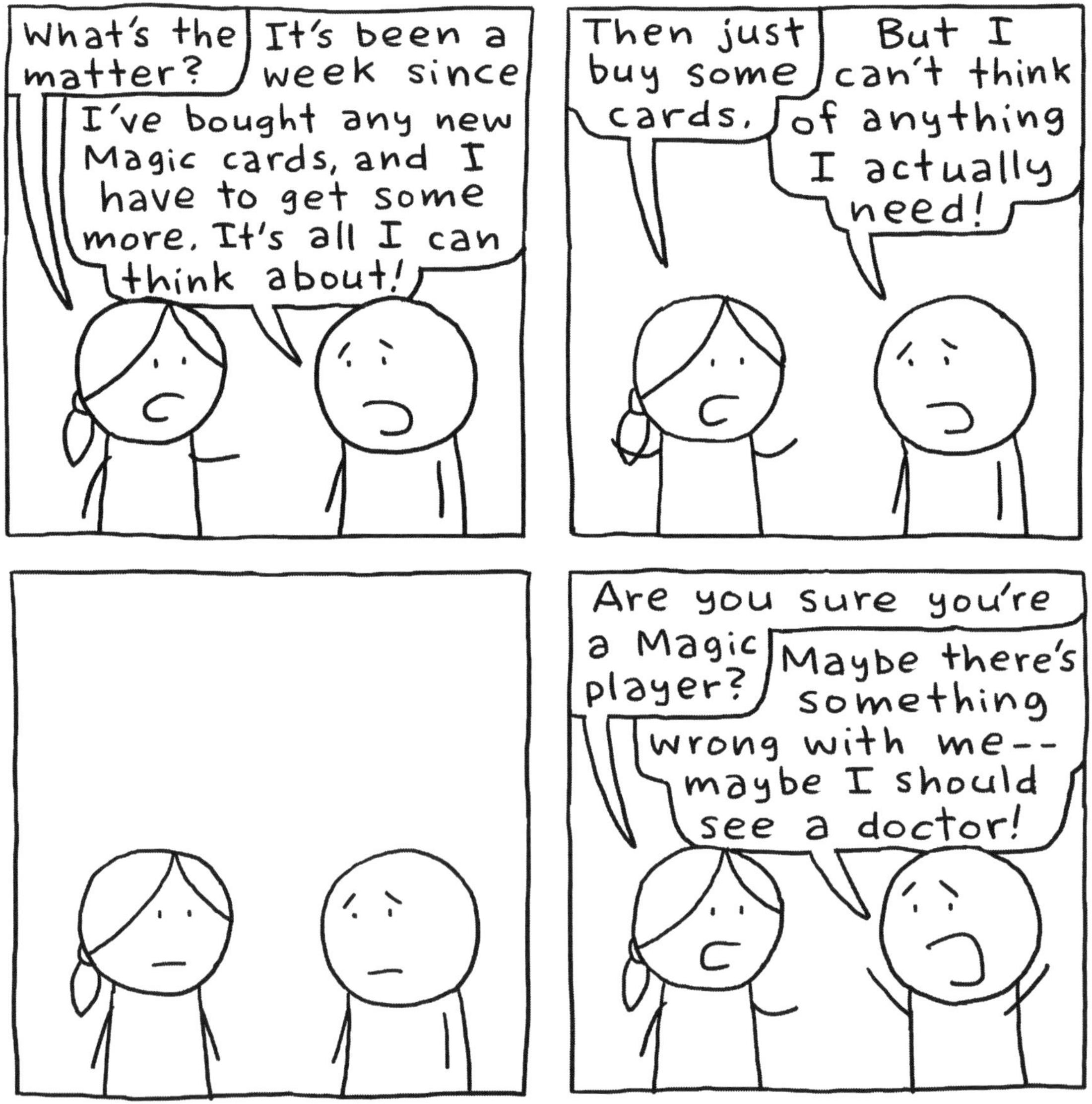
What's the matter?
It's been a week since I've bought any new Magic cards, and I have to get some more. It's all I can think about!
Then just buy some cards.
But I can't think of anything I actually need!
Are you sure you're a Magic player?
Maybe there's something wrong with me--maybe I should see a doctor!

Wow! How long have you been playing Magic?
Just about a week...
...Why? Isn't this normal?

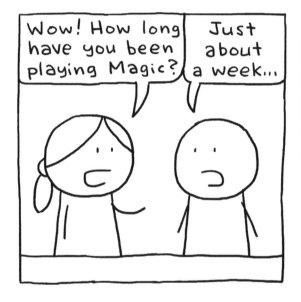

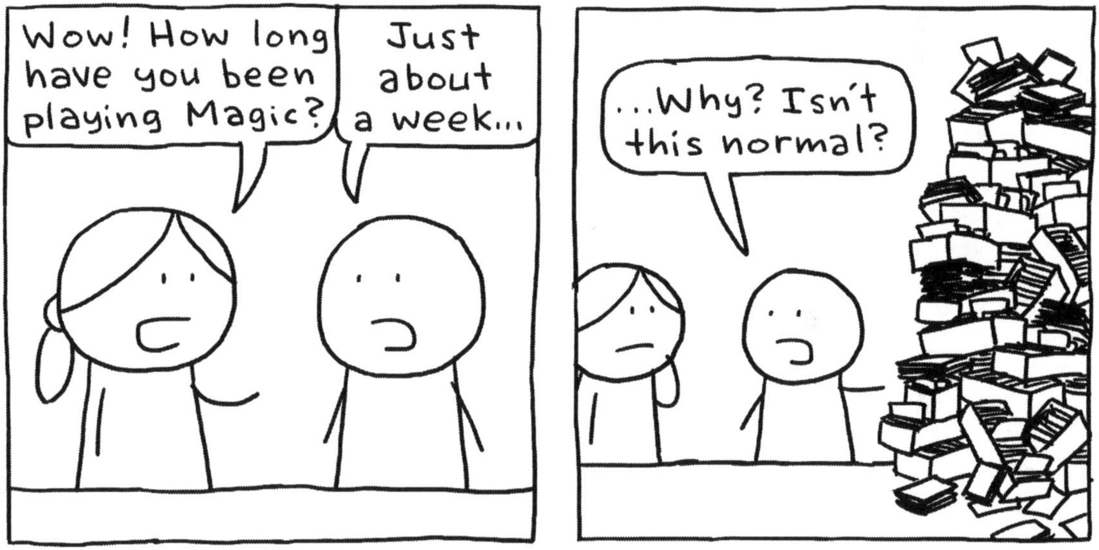

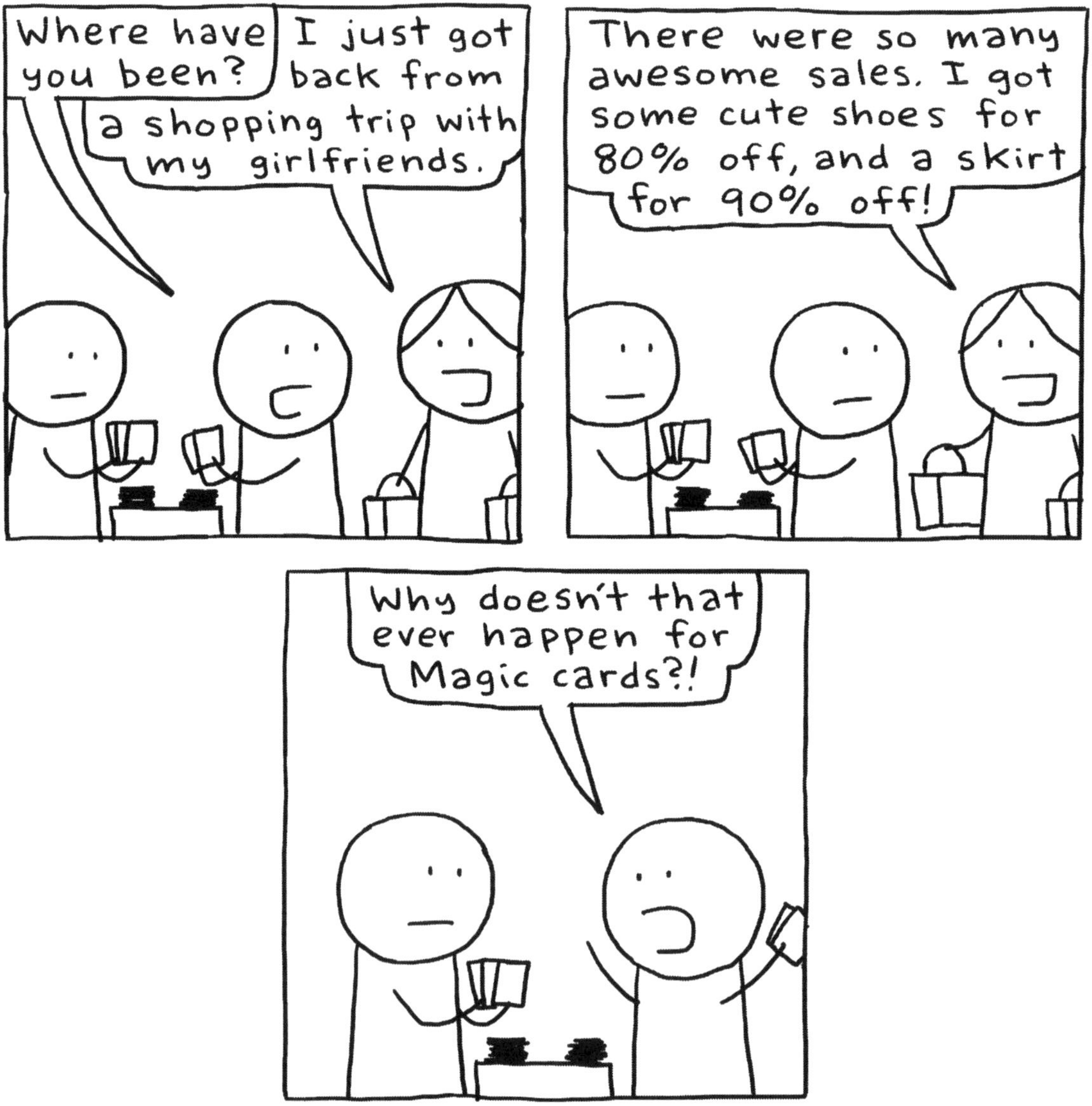
Where have you been?
I just got back from a shopping trip with my girlfriends.
There were so many awesome sales. I got some cute shoes for 80% off, and a skirt for 90% off!
Why doesn't that ever happen for Magic cards?!

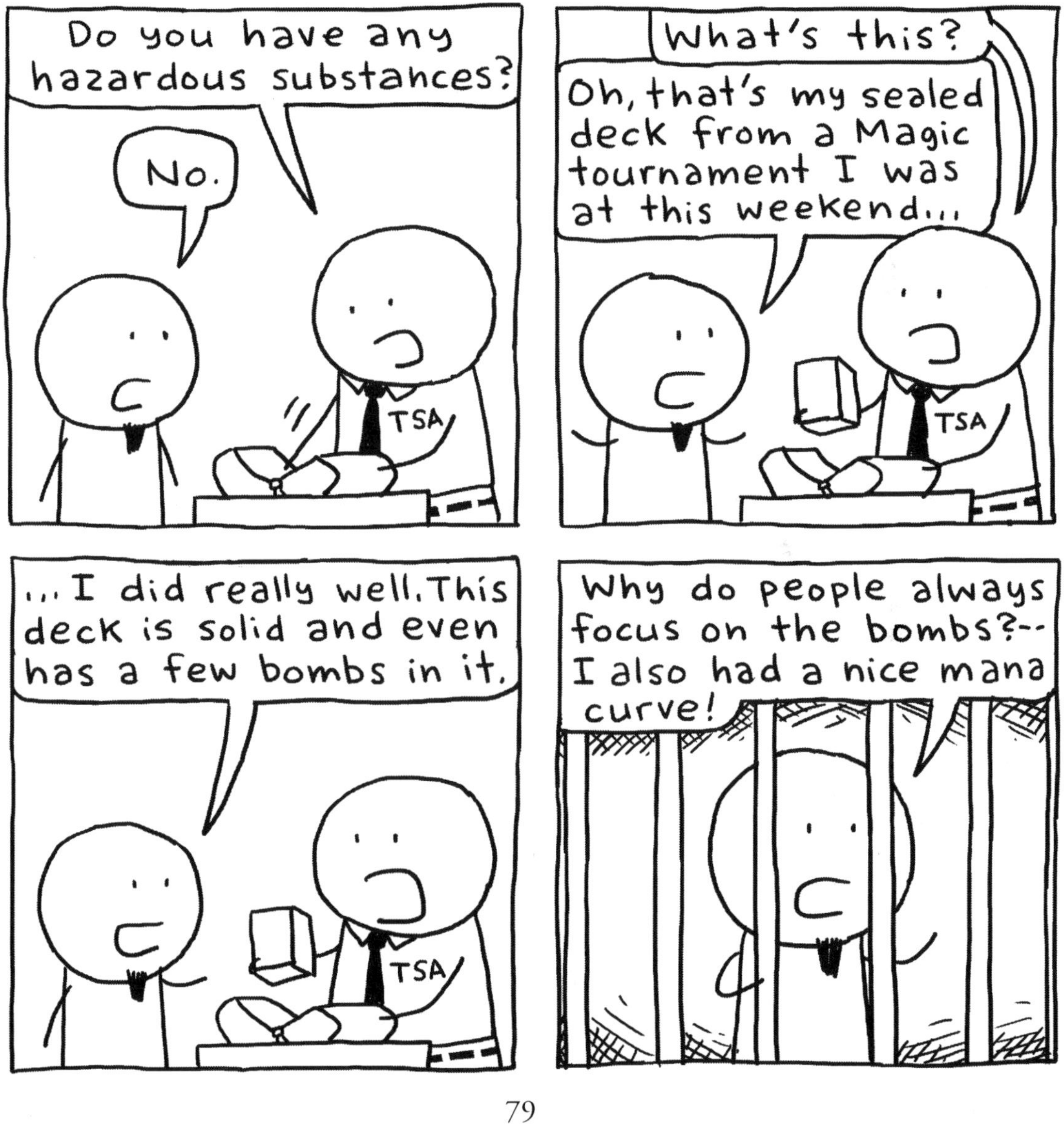
Do you have any hazardous substances?
No.
What's this?
Oh, that's my sealed deck from a Magic tournament I was at this weekend...
...I did really well. This deck is solid and even has a few bombs in it.
Why do people always focus on the bombs?-- I also had a nice mana curve!

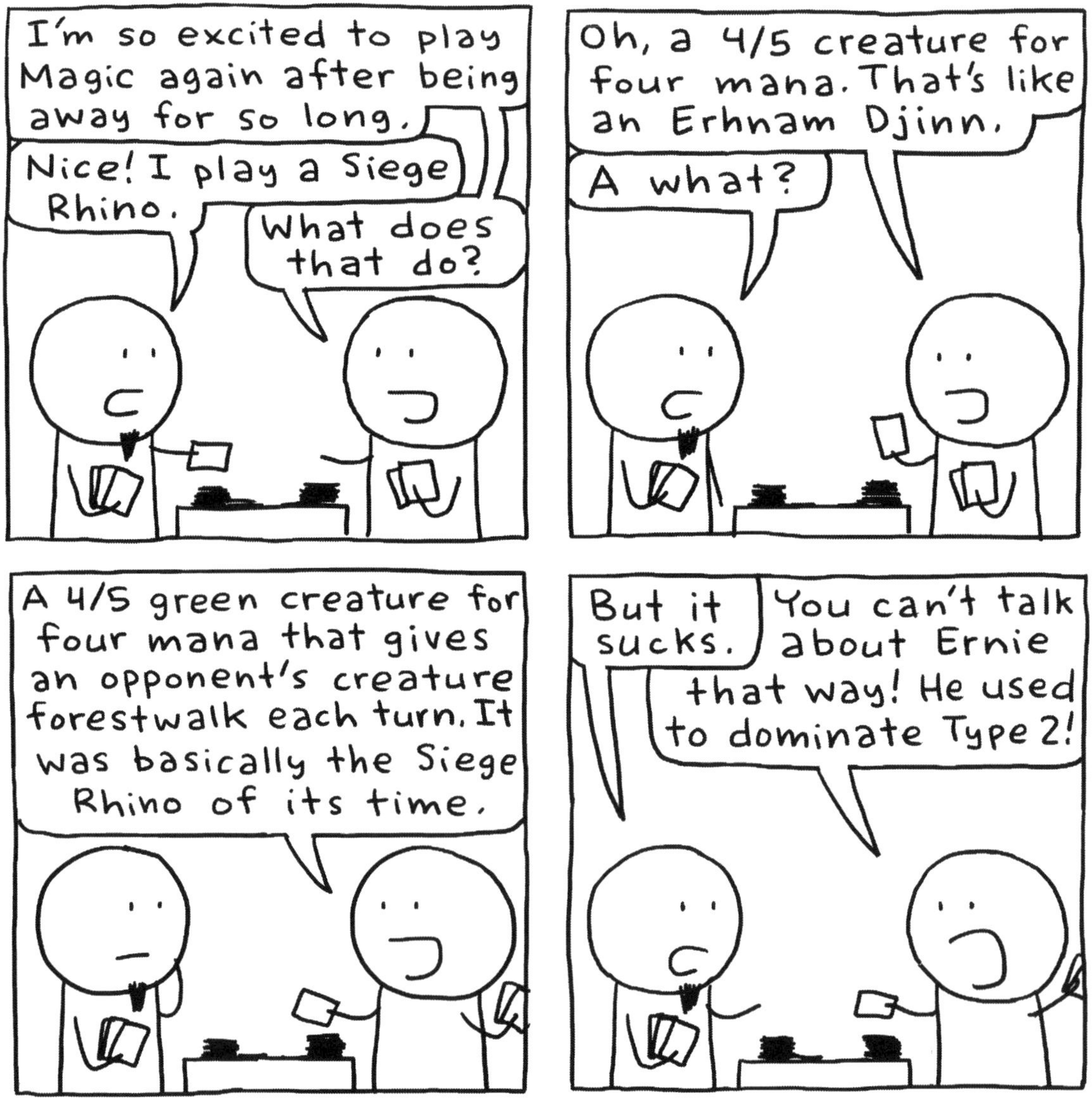
I'm so excited to play Magic again after being away for so long.
Nice! I play a Siege Rhino.
What does that do?
Oh, a 4/5 creature for four mana. That's like an Erhnam Djinn.
A what?
A 4/5 green creature for four mana that gives an opponent's creature forestwalk each turn. It was basically the Siege Rhino of its time.
But it sucks.
You can't talk about Ernie that way! He used to dominate Type 2!

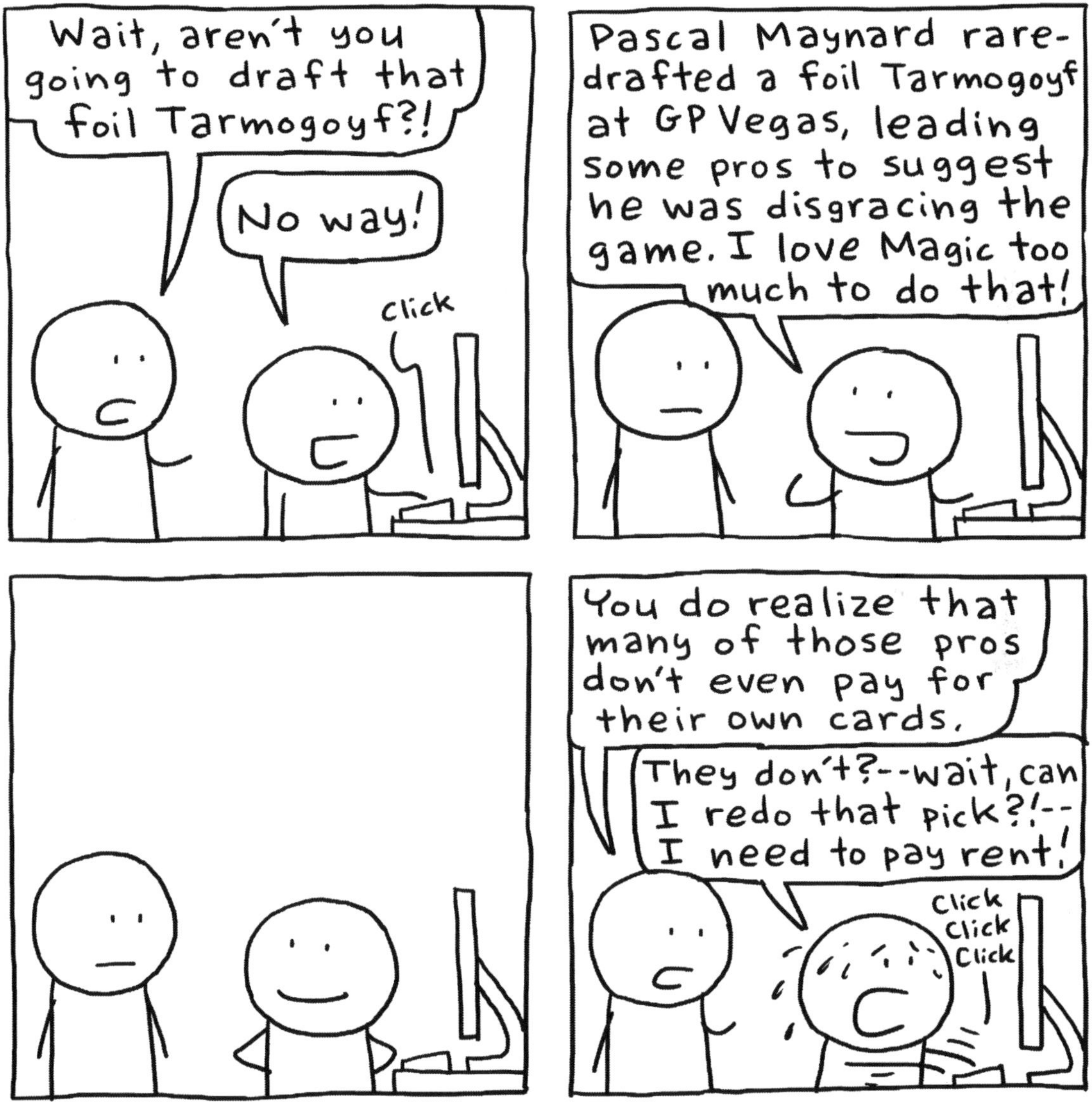
Wait, aren't you going to draft that foil Tarmogoyf?!
No way!
Click
Pascal Maynard rare-drafted a foil Tarmogoyf at GP Vegas, leading some pros to suggest he was disgracing the game. I love Magic too much to do that!
You do realize that many of those pros don't even pay for their own cards.
They don't?--wait, can I redo that pick?!--I need to pay rent!
Click
Click
Click

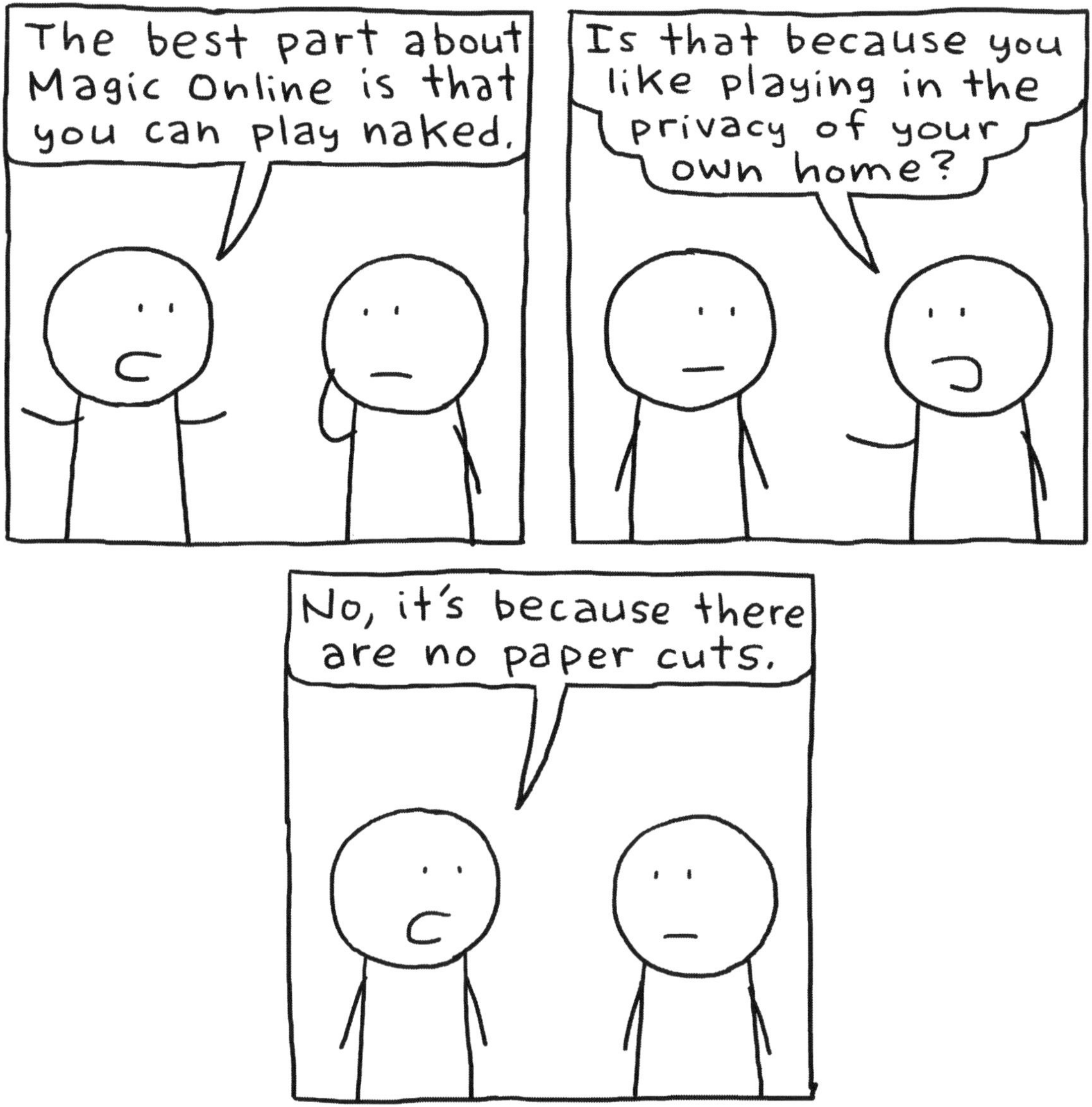
The best part about Magic Online is that you can play naked.
Is that because you like playing in the privacy of your own home?
No, it's because there are no paper cuts.

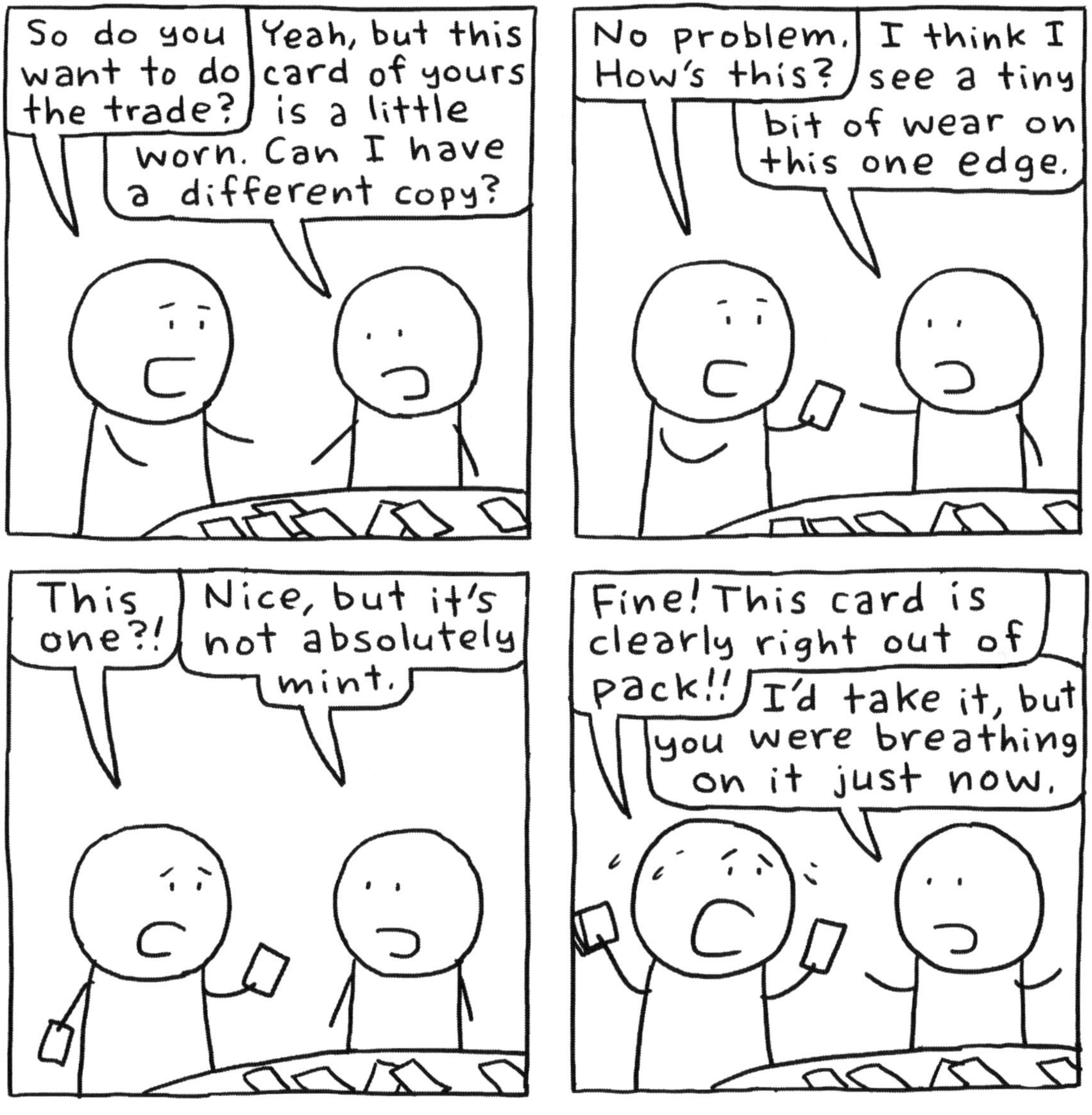
So do you want to do the trade?
Yeah, but this card of yours is a little worn. Can I have a different copy?
No problem. How's this?
I think I see a tiny bit of wear on this one edge.
This one?!
Nice, but it's not absolutely mint.
Fine! This card is clearly right out of pack!!
I'd take it, but you were breathing on it just now.

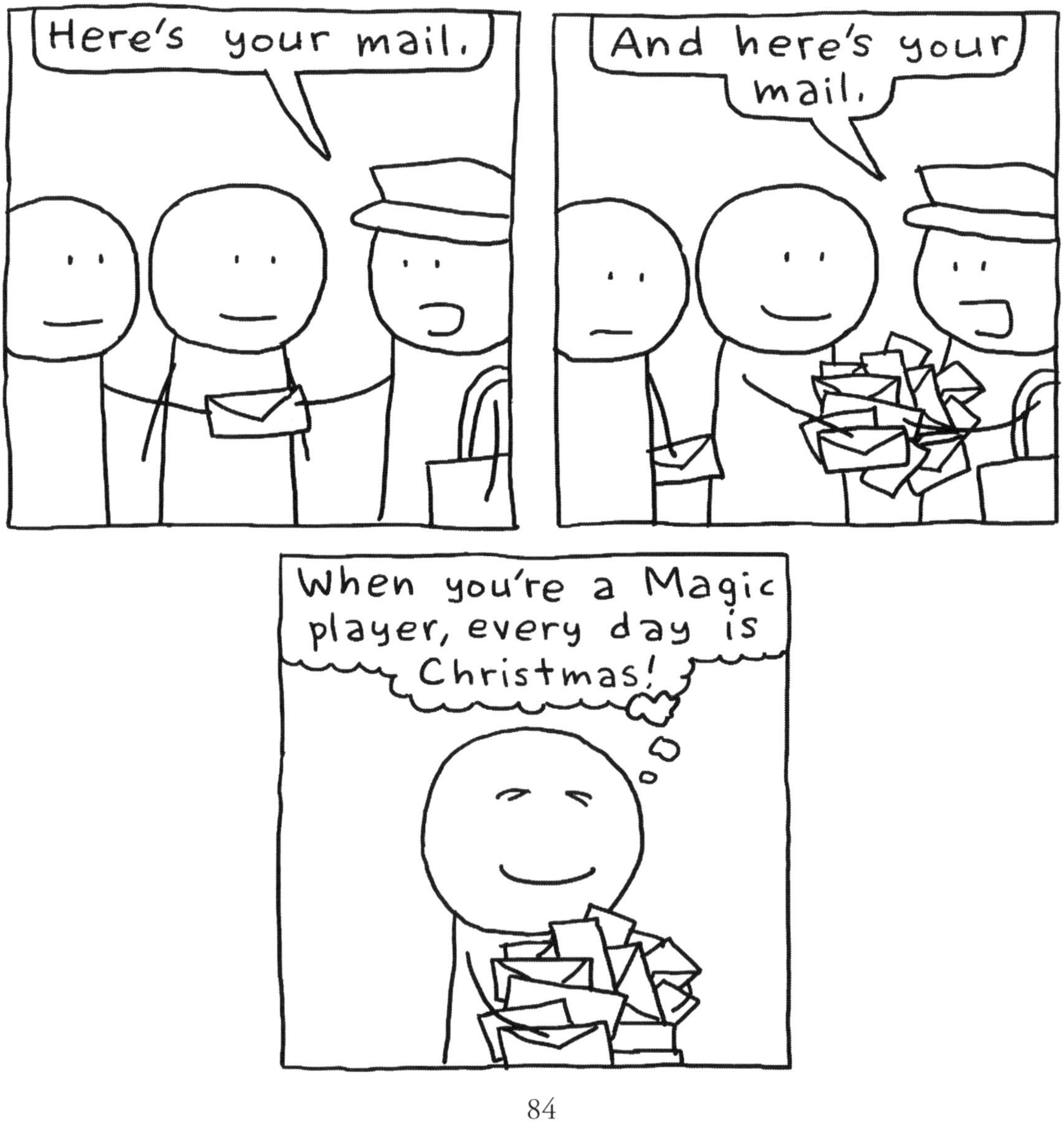
Here's your mail.
And here's your mail.
When you're a Magic player, every day is Christmas!

I'm sorry. He passed away due to some strange complications after the surgery.
What happened?
Earlier...
Okay, time to sew him up.
Let us finish this game of Magic first.
Has anyone seen my Mountain?

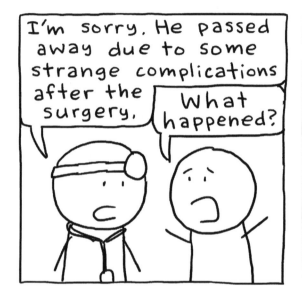

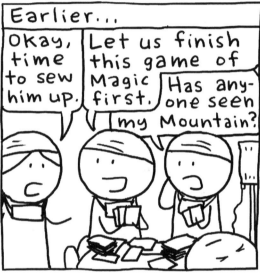

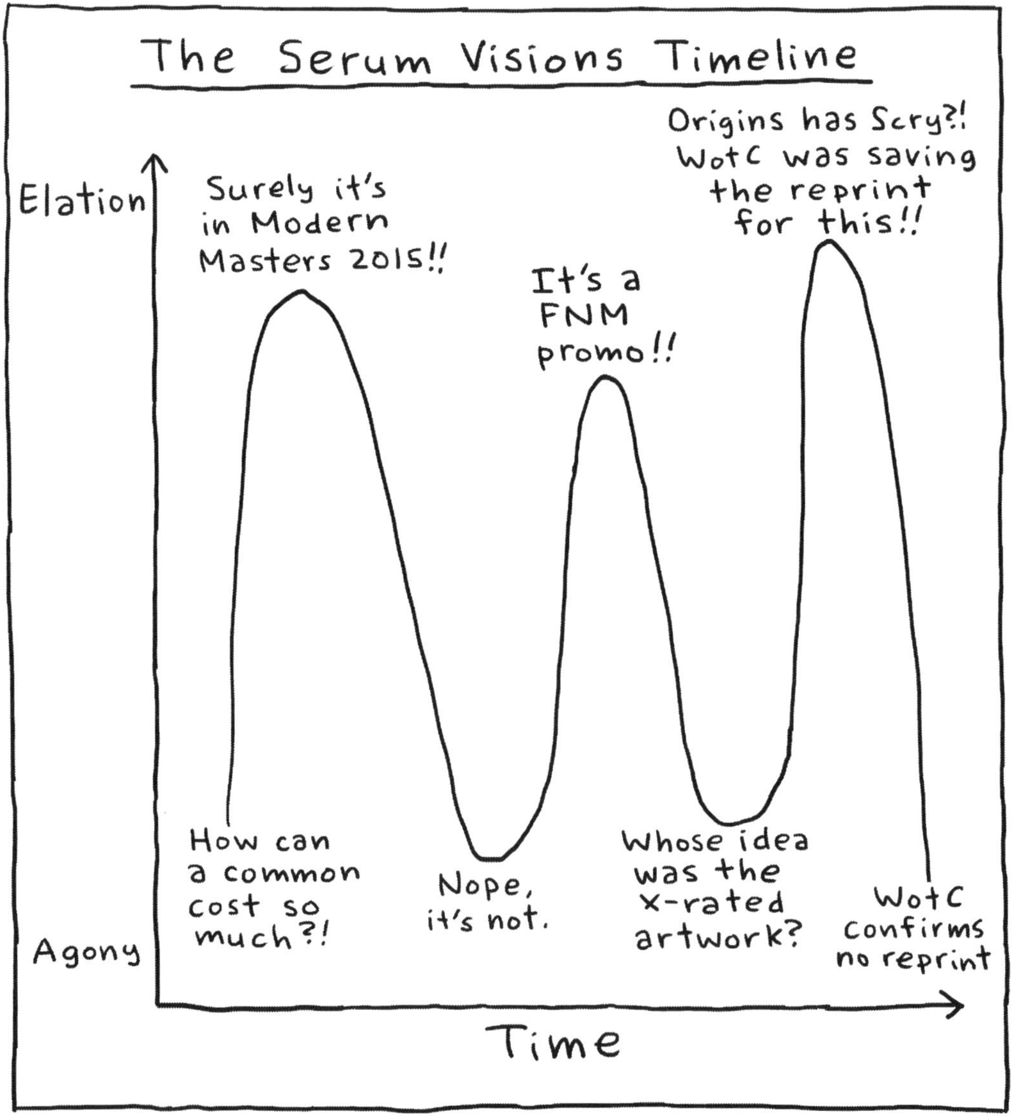
The Serum Visions Timeline
Elation
Agony
Time
Surely it's in Modern Masters 2015!!
It's a FNM promo!!
Origins has Scry?! WotC was saving the reprint for this!!
How can a common cost so much?!
Nope, it's not.
Whose idea was the x-rated artwork?
WotC confirms no reprint

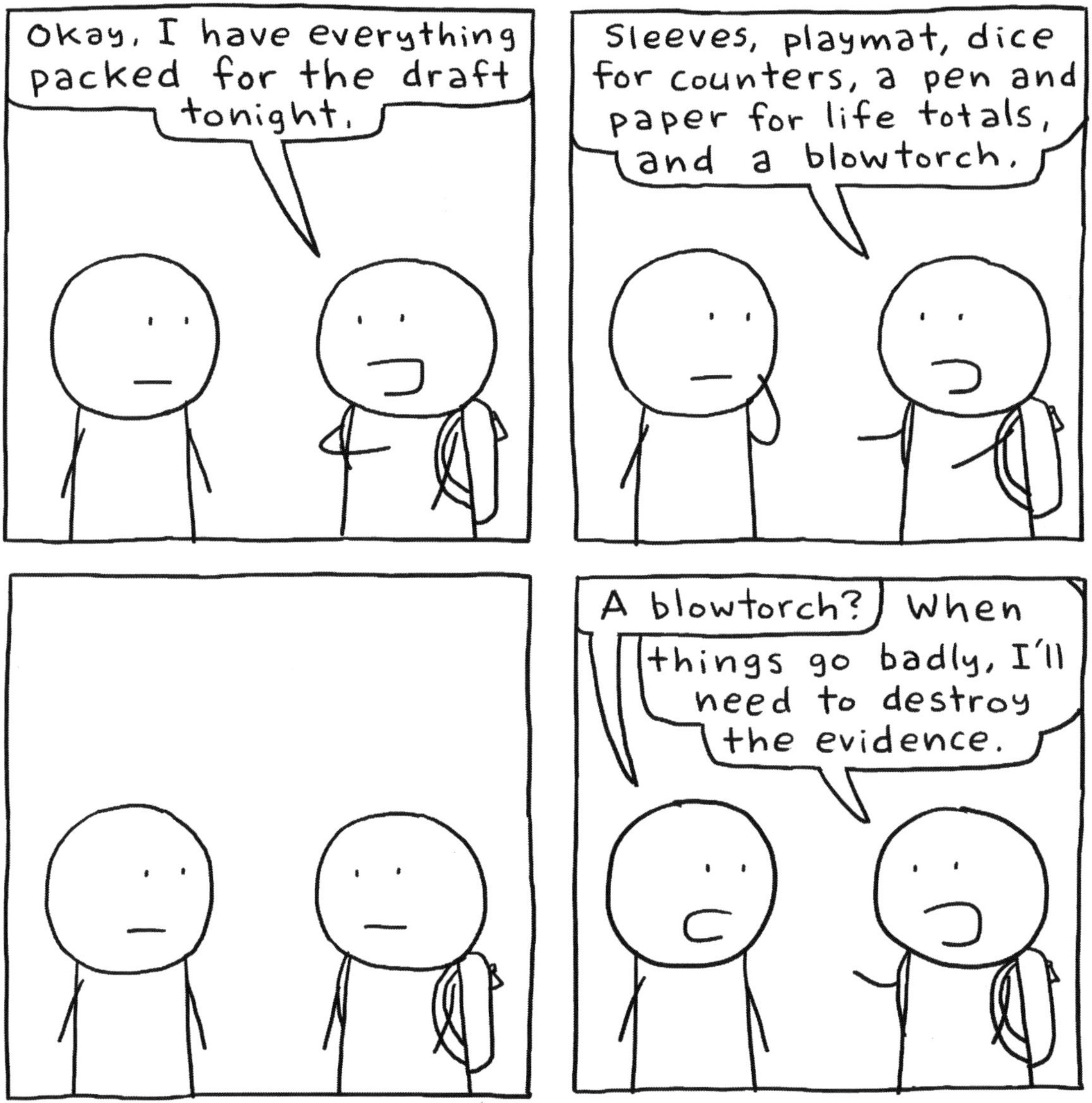
Okay, I have everything packed for the draft tonight.
Sleeves, playmat, dice for counters, a pen and paper for life totals, and a blowtorch.
A blowtorch?
When things go badly, I'll need to destroy the evidence.

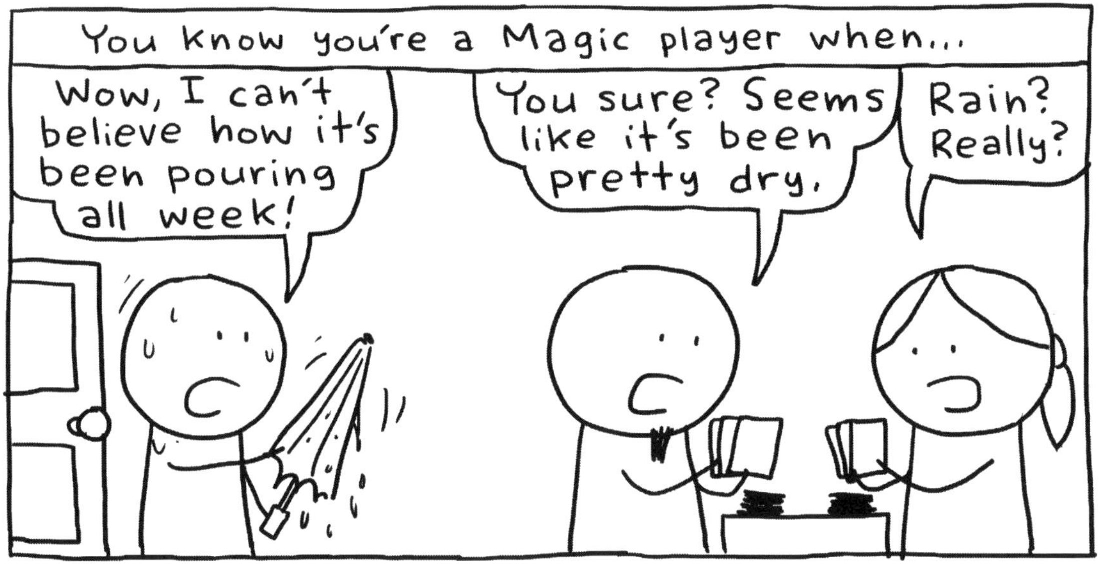
You know you're a Magic player when...
Wow, I can't believe how it's been pouring all week!
You sure? Seems like it's been pretty dry.
Rain? Really?

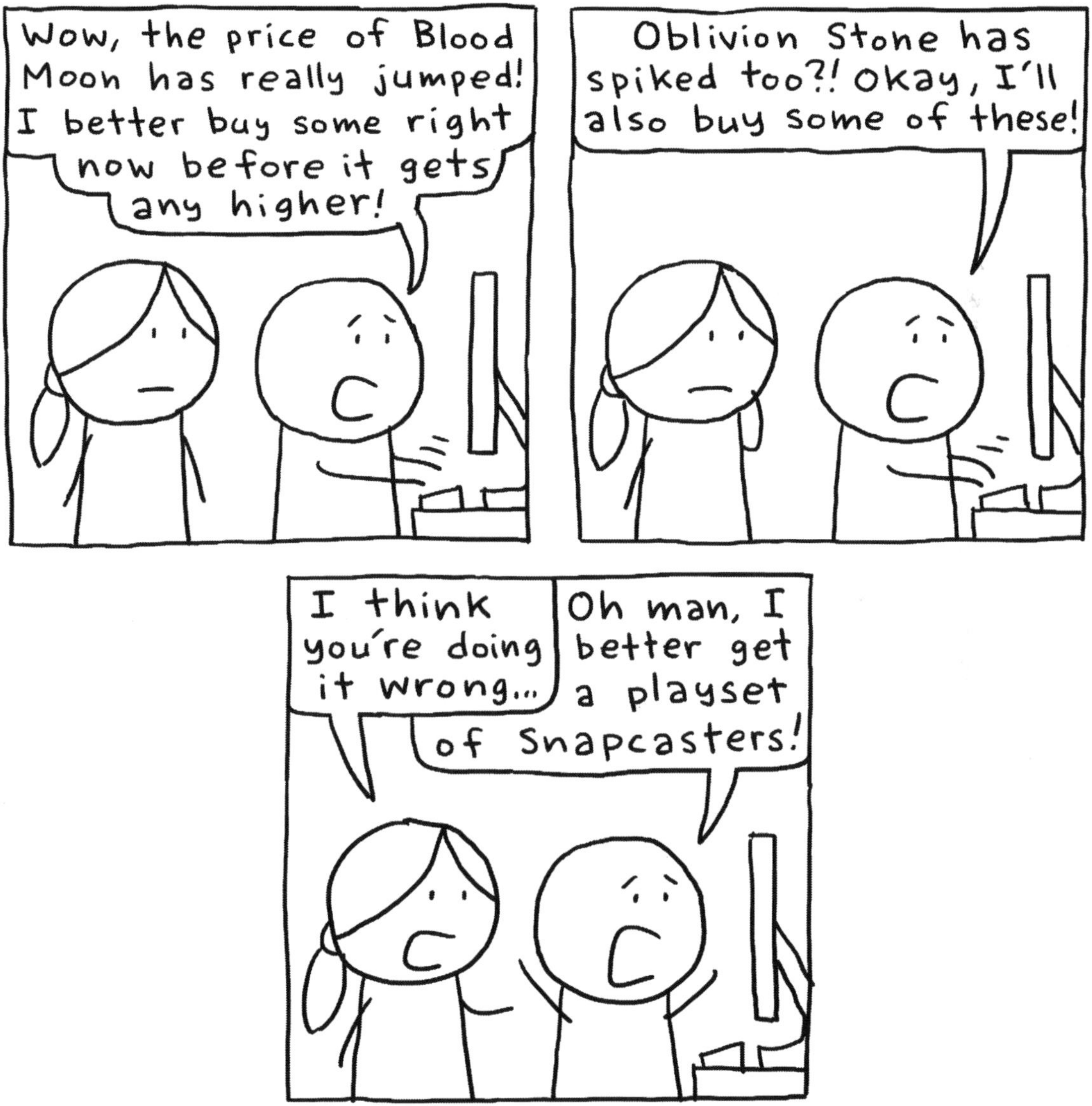
Wow, the price of Blood Moon has really jumped! I better buy some right now before it gets any higher!
Oblivion Stone has spiked too?! Okay, I'll also buy some of these!
I think you're doing it wrong...
Oh man, I better get a playset of Snapcasters!

Back in January...
Banning Birthing Pod is a tragedy! All my cards are worthless! I'm quitting Magic forever!
Now...
Enjoying your Abzan Collected Company deck?
I get the point -- stop asking me that!

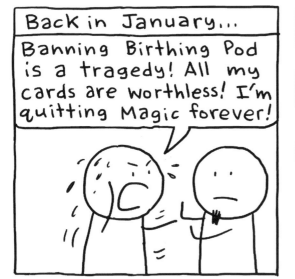

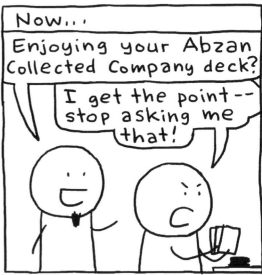

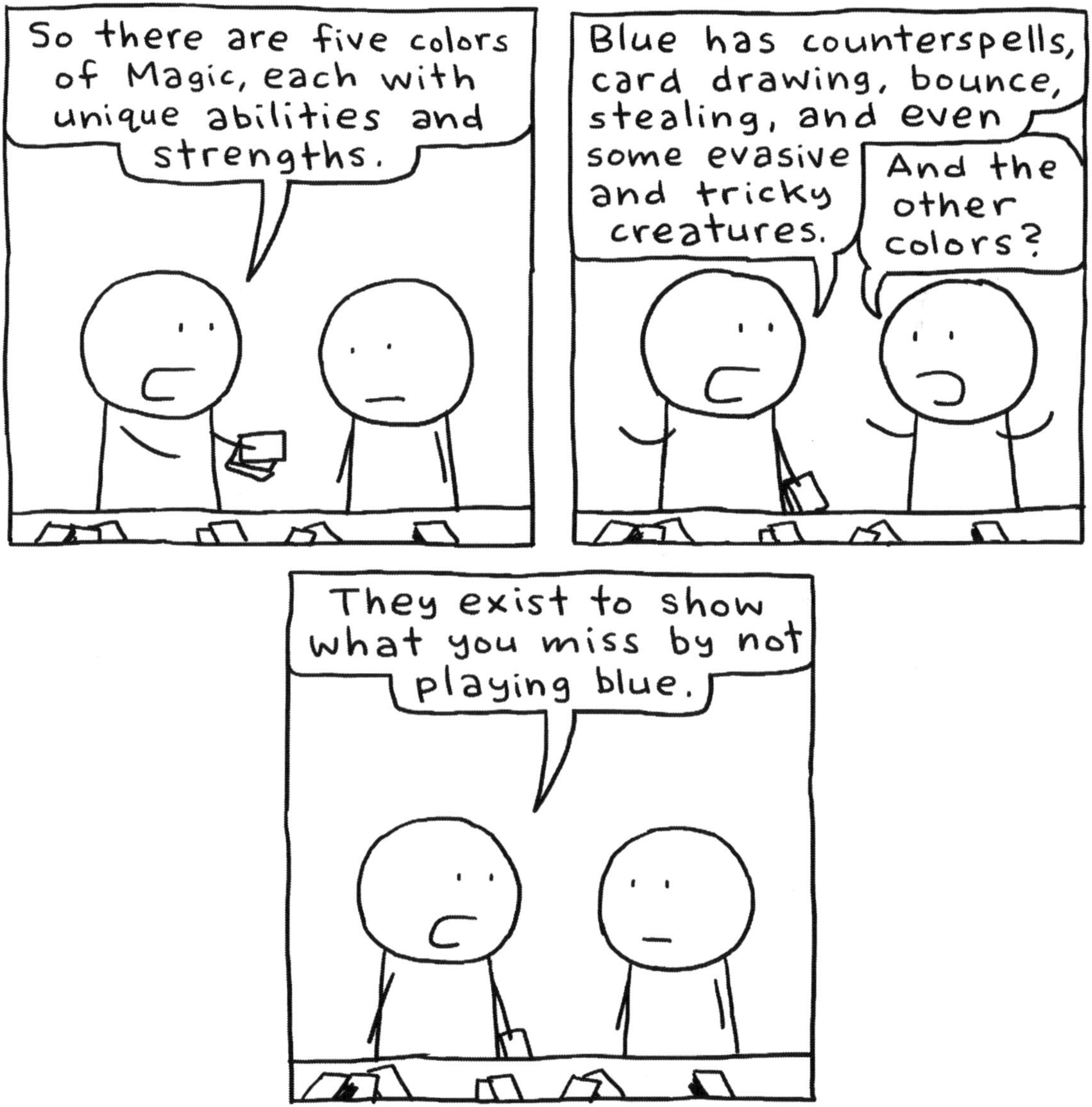
So there are five colors of Magic, each with unique abilities and strengths.
Blue has counterspells, card drawing, bounce, stealing, and even some evasive and tricky creatures.
And the other colors?
They exist to show what you miss by not playing blue.

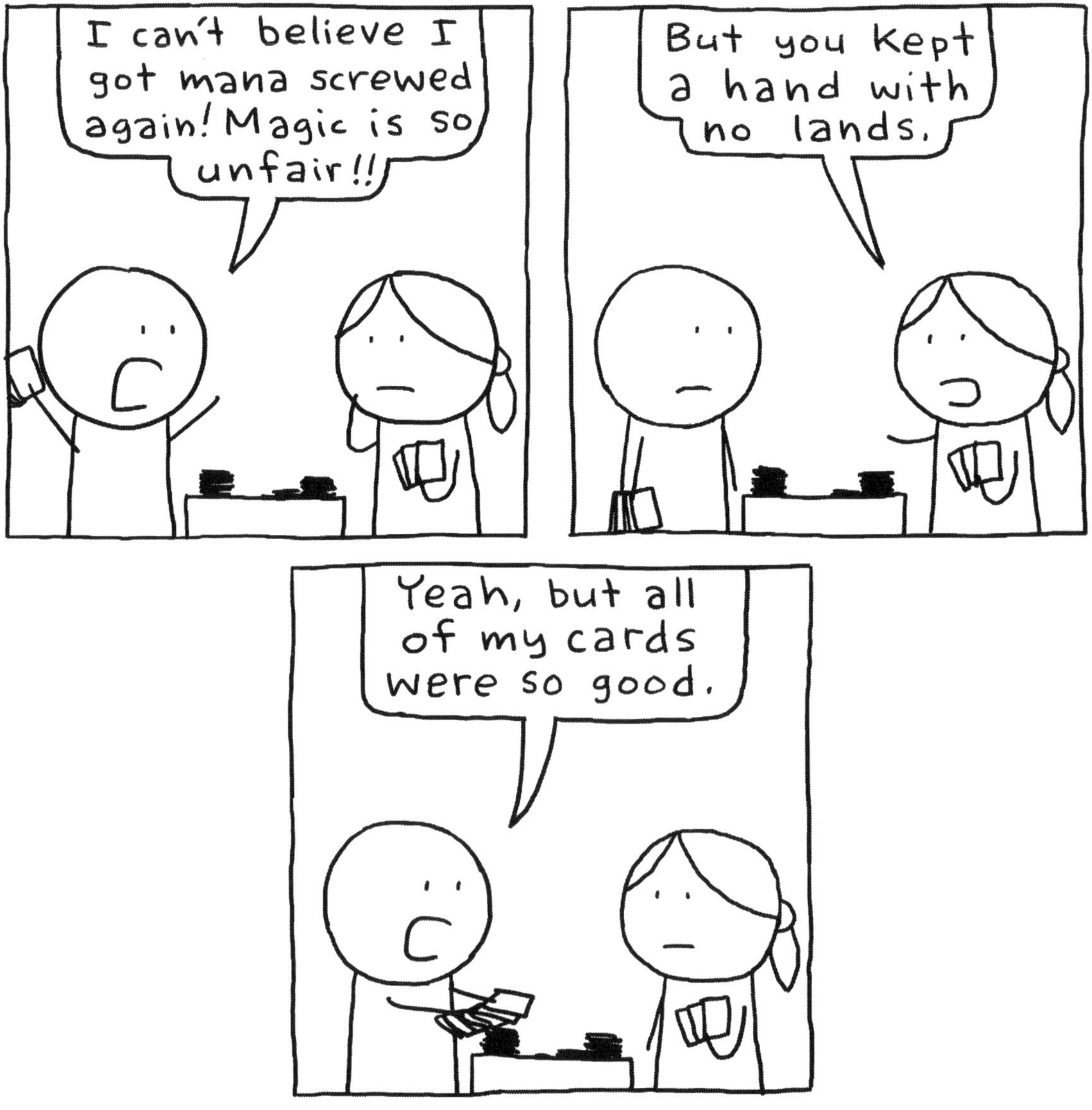
I can't believe I got mana screwed again! Magic is so unfair!!
But you kept a hand with no lands.
Yeah, but all of my cards were so good.

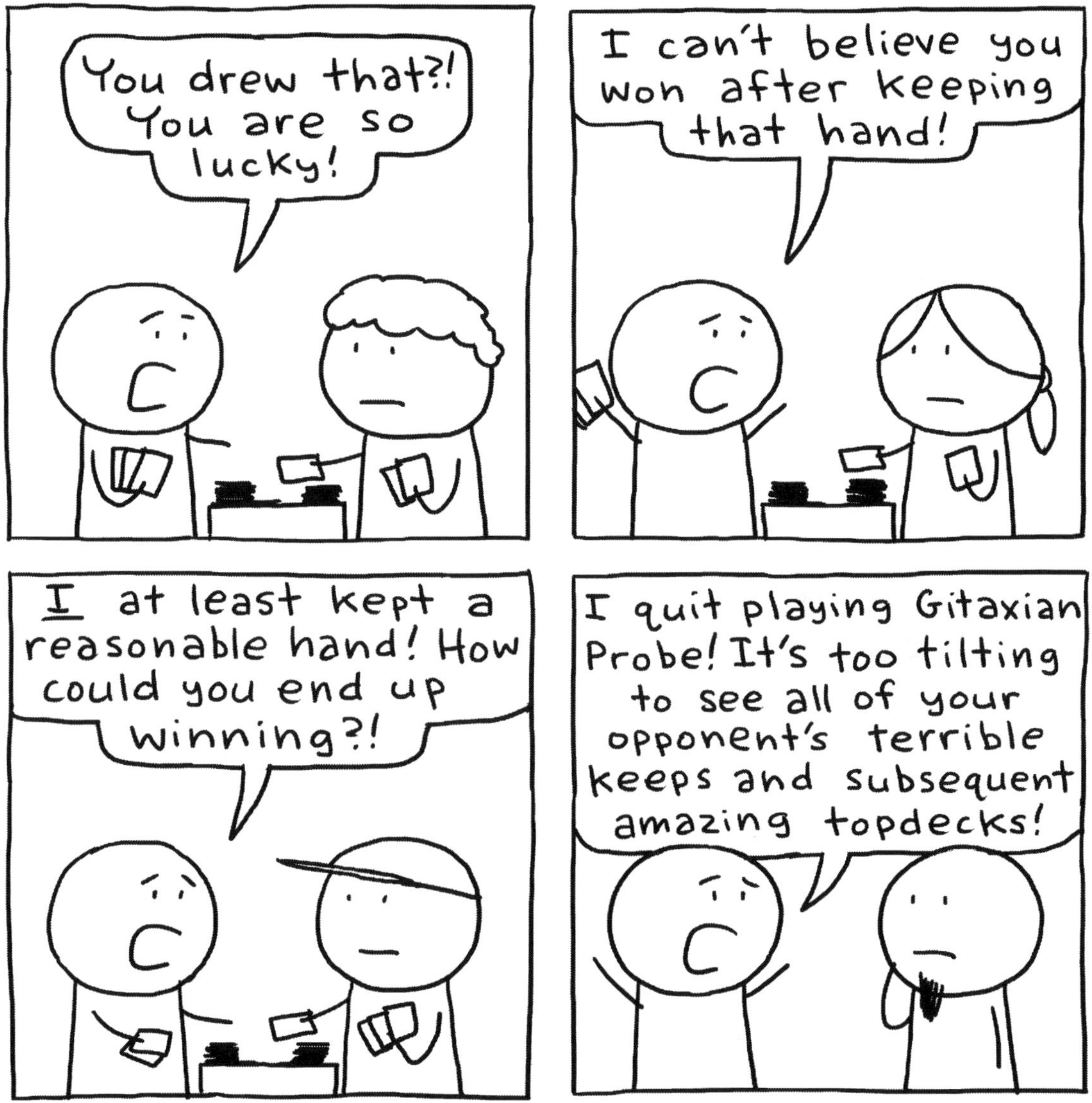
You drew that?! You are so lucky!
I can't believe you won after keeping that hand!
I at least kept a reasonable hand! How could you end up winning?!
I quit playing Gitaxian Probe! It's too tilting to see all of your opponent's terrible keeps and subsequent amazing topdecks!

Being a new Magic player in the past...
This huge creature is awesome!
Sorry newb, Actually, it's terrible.
Being a new Magic player now...
This huge creature is awesome!
Yup.

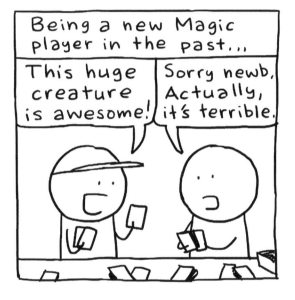

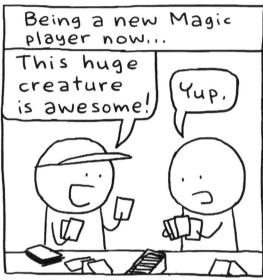

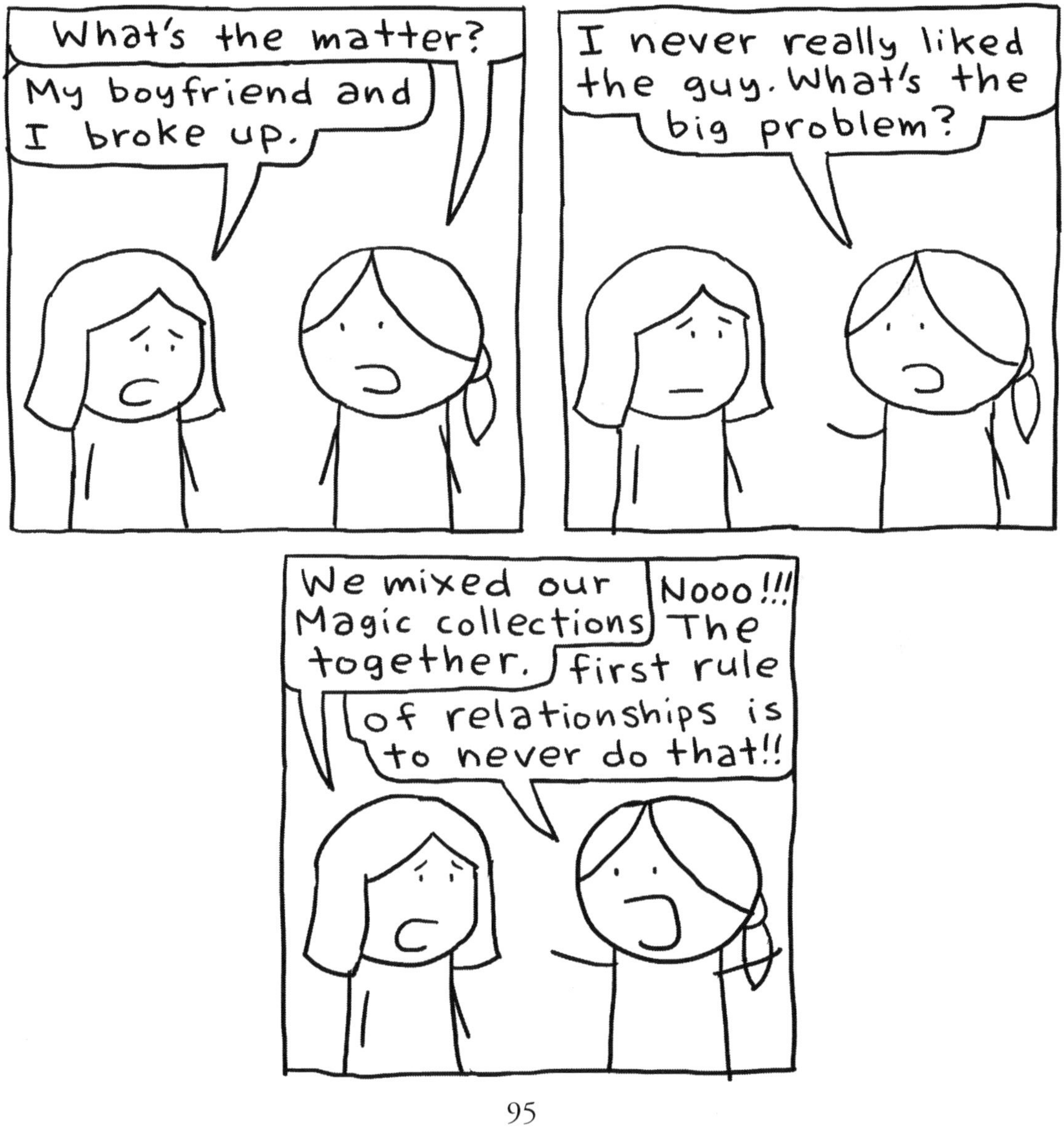
What's the matter?
My boyfriend and I broke up.
I never really liked the guy. What's the big problem?
We mixed our Magic collections together.
Nooo!!! The first rule of relationships is to never do that!!

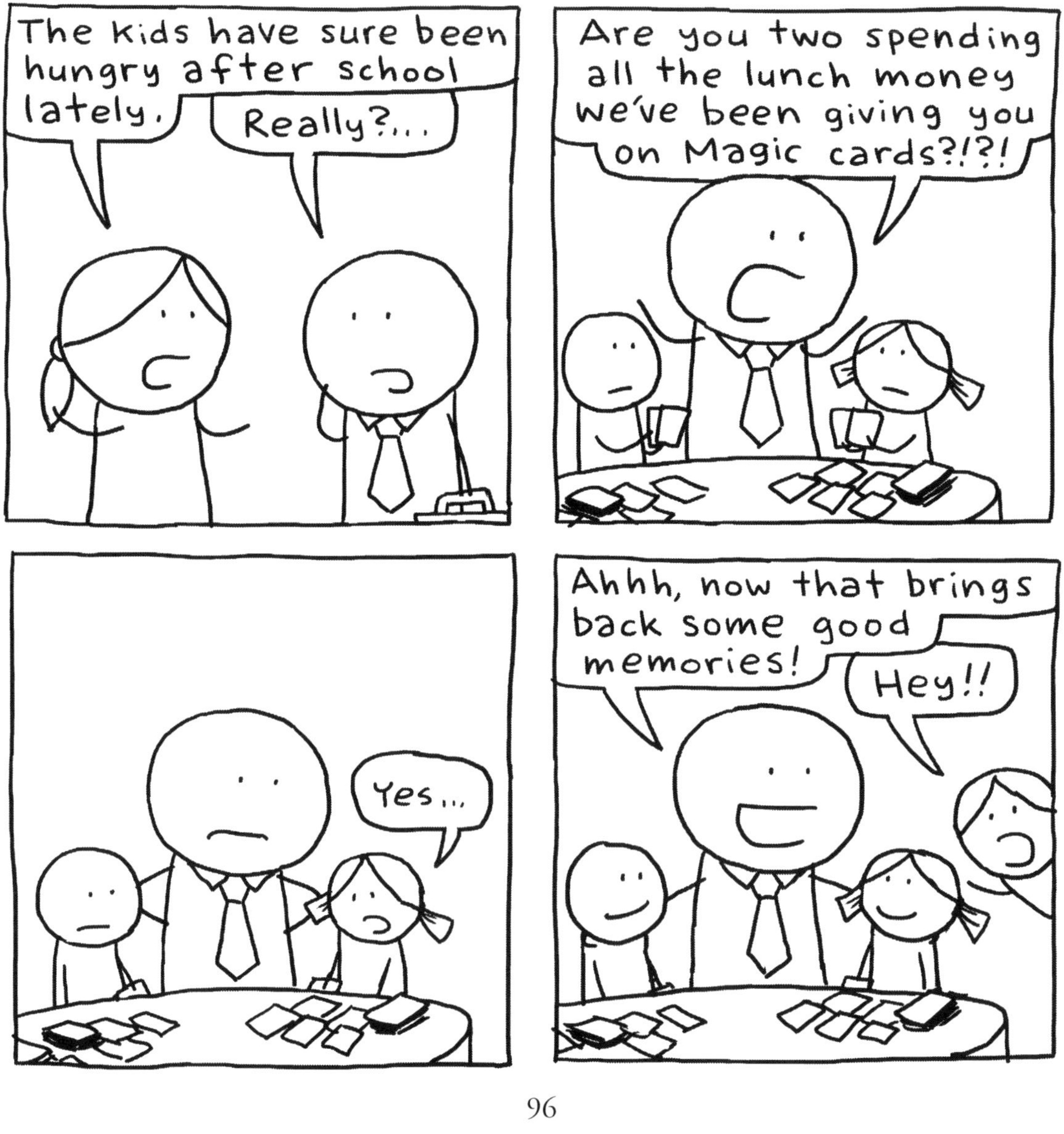
The kids have sure been hungry after school lately.
Really?...
Are you two spending all the lunch money we've been giving you on Magic cards?!?!
Yes...
Ahhh, now that brings back some good memories!
Hey!!

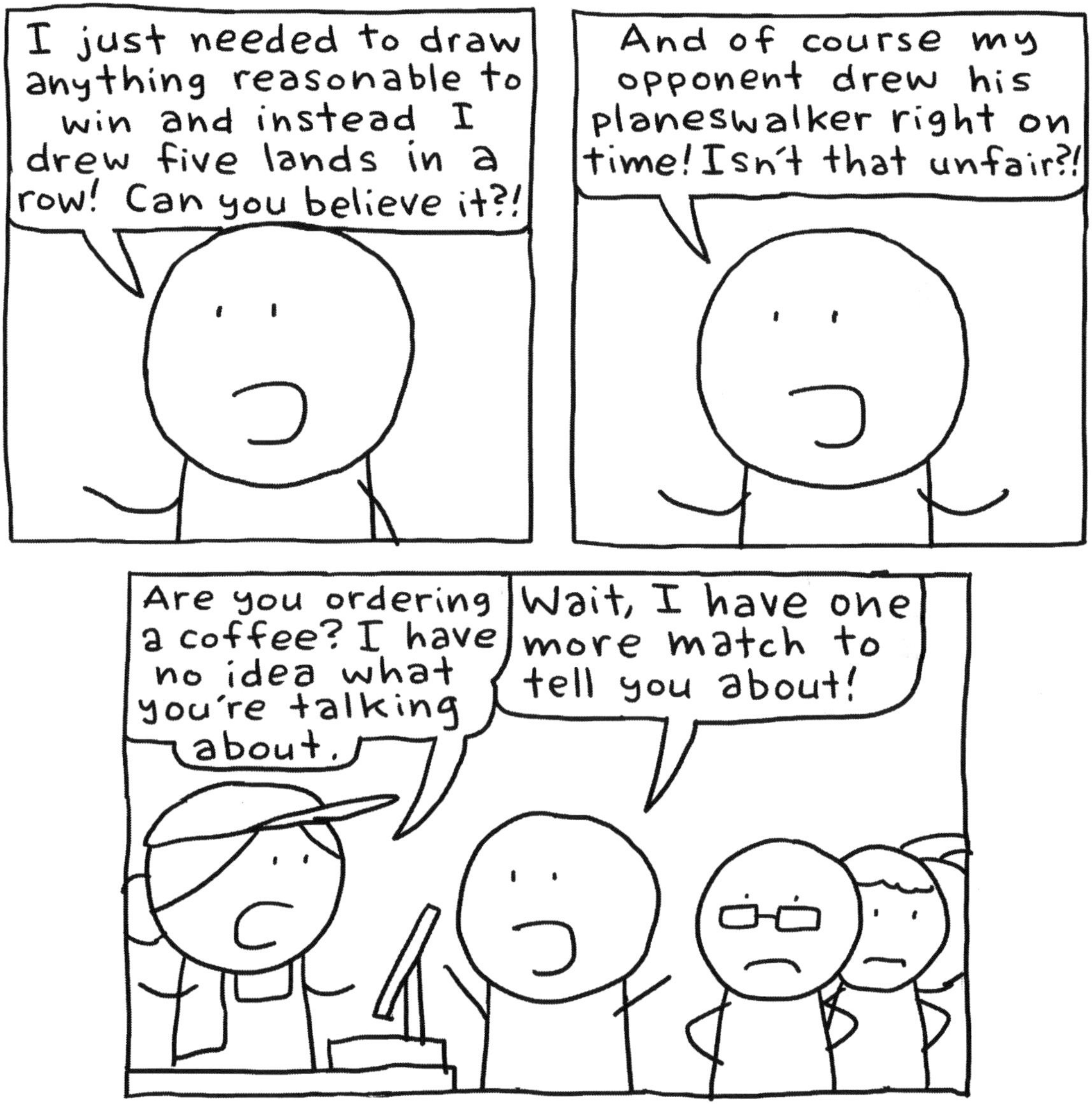
I just needed to draw anything reasonable to win and instead I drew five lands in a row! Can you believe it?!
And of course my opponent drew his planeswalker right on time! Isn't that unfair?!
Are you ordering a coffee? I have no idea what you're talking about.
Wait, I have one more match to tell you about!

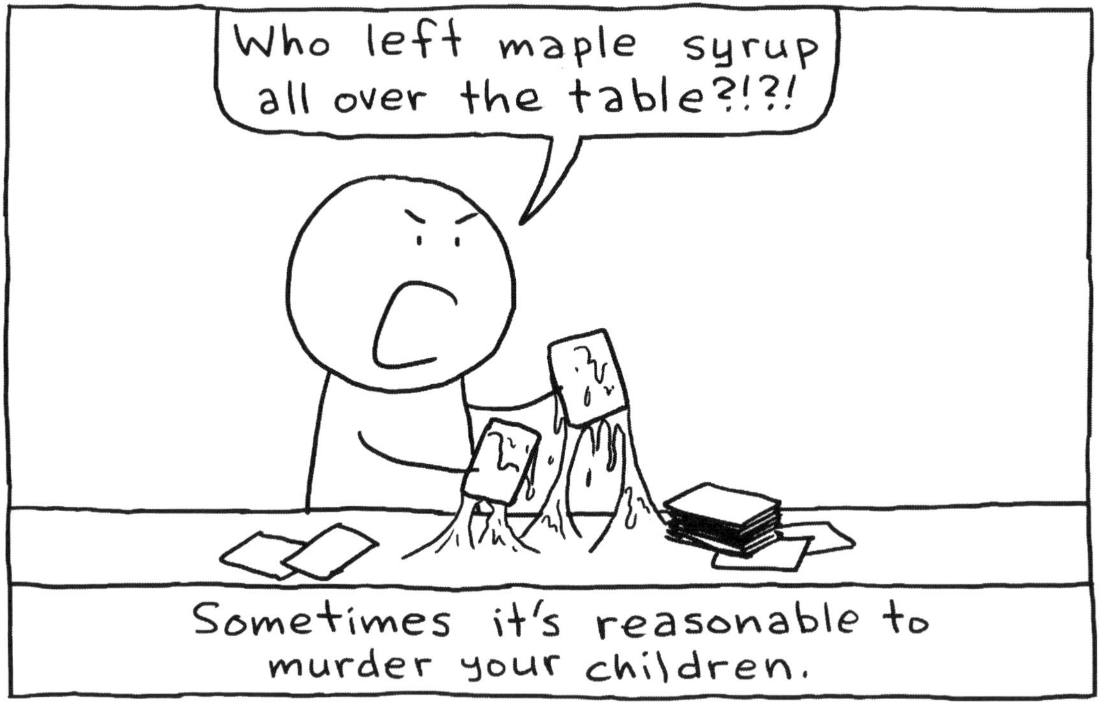
Who left maple syrup all over the table?!?!
Sometimes it's reasonable to murder your children.

What your basic lands say about you...

Alpha/Beta – You are old as #6%*!

Full art Unhinged/Zendikar – You're trying to make your deck special and unique by using the same lands as everyone else

5th Edition – You're a terrible person

Guru – You're a terrible person (although maybe I'm just insanely jealous)

Summer Magic – You have way, way too much money

APAC/Euro – Okay, these are actually pretty cool

Normal, regular lands – What?! You spend your time actually honing your play skills rather than agonizing over what basic lands you play?!?!

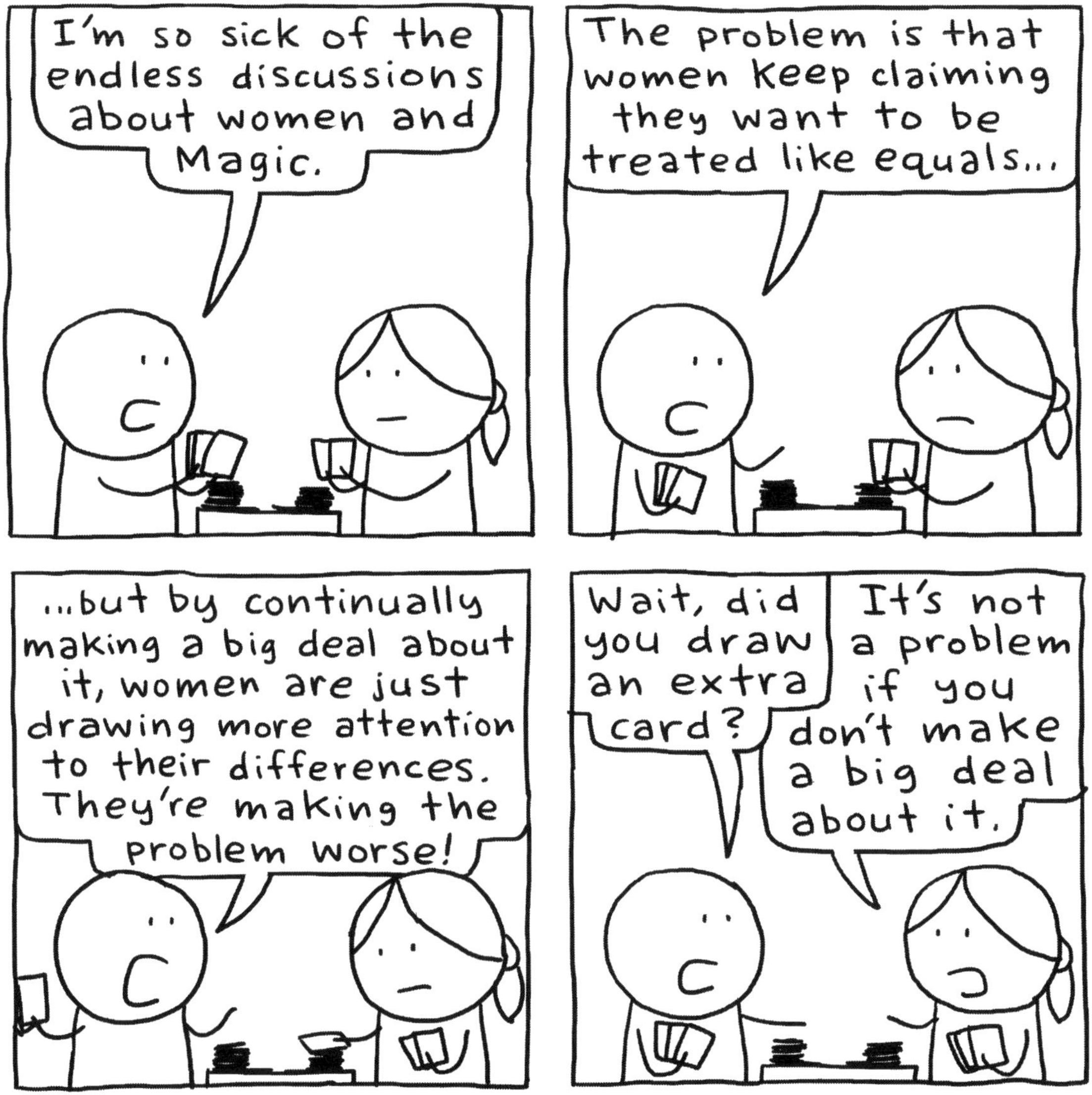
I'm so sick of the endless discussions about women and Magic.
The problem is that women keep claiming they want to be treated like equals...
...but by continually making a big deal about it, women are just drawing more attention to their differences. They're making the problem worse!
Wait, did you draw an extra card?
It's not a problem if you don't make a big deal about it.

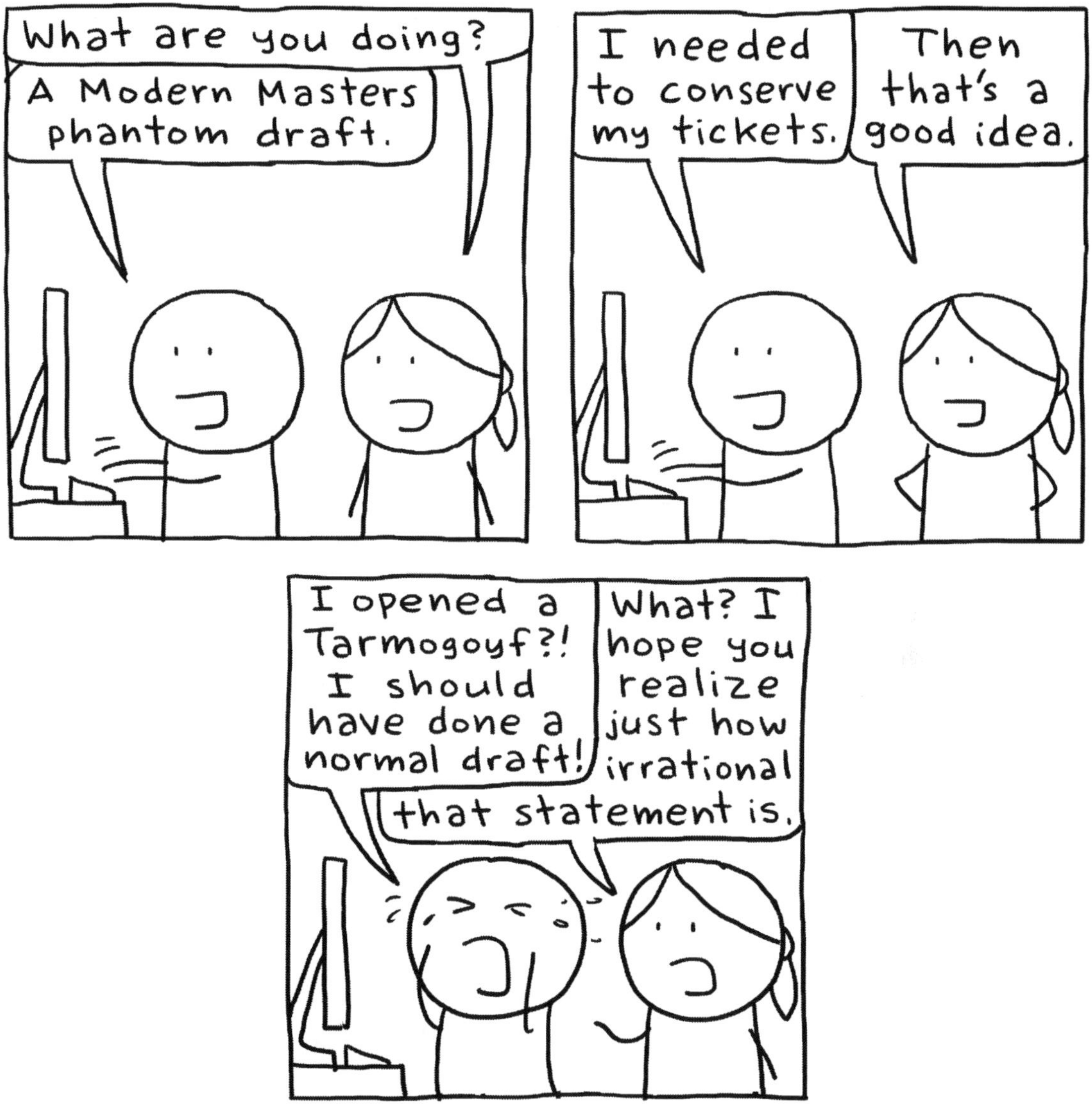
What are you doing?
A Modern Masters phantom draft.
I needed to conserve my tickets.
Then that's a good idea.
I opened a Tarmogoyf?! I should have done a normal draft!
What? I hope you realize just how irrational that statement is.

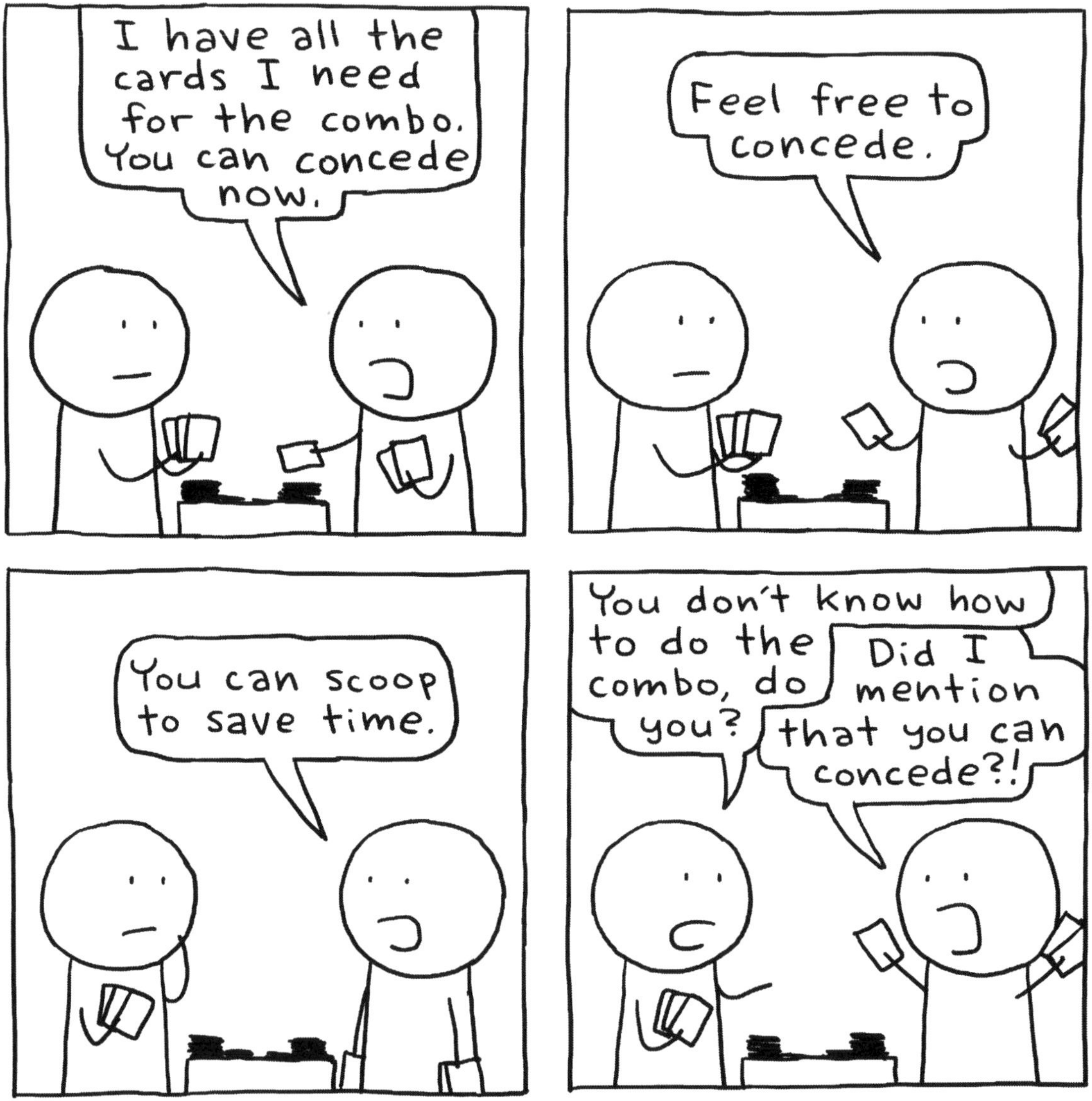
I have all the cards I need for the combo. You can concede now.
Feel free to concede.
You can scoop to save time.
You don't know how to do the combo, do you?
Did I mention that you can concede?!

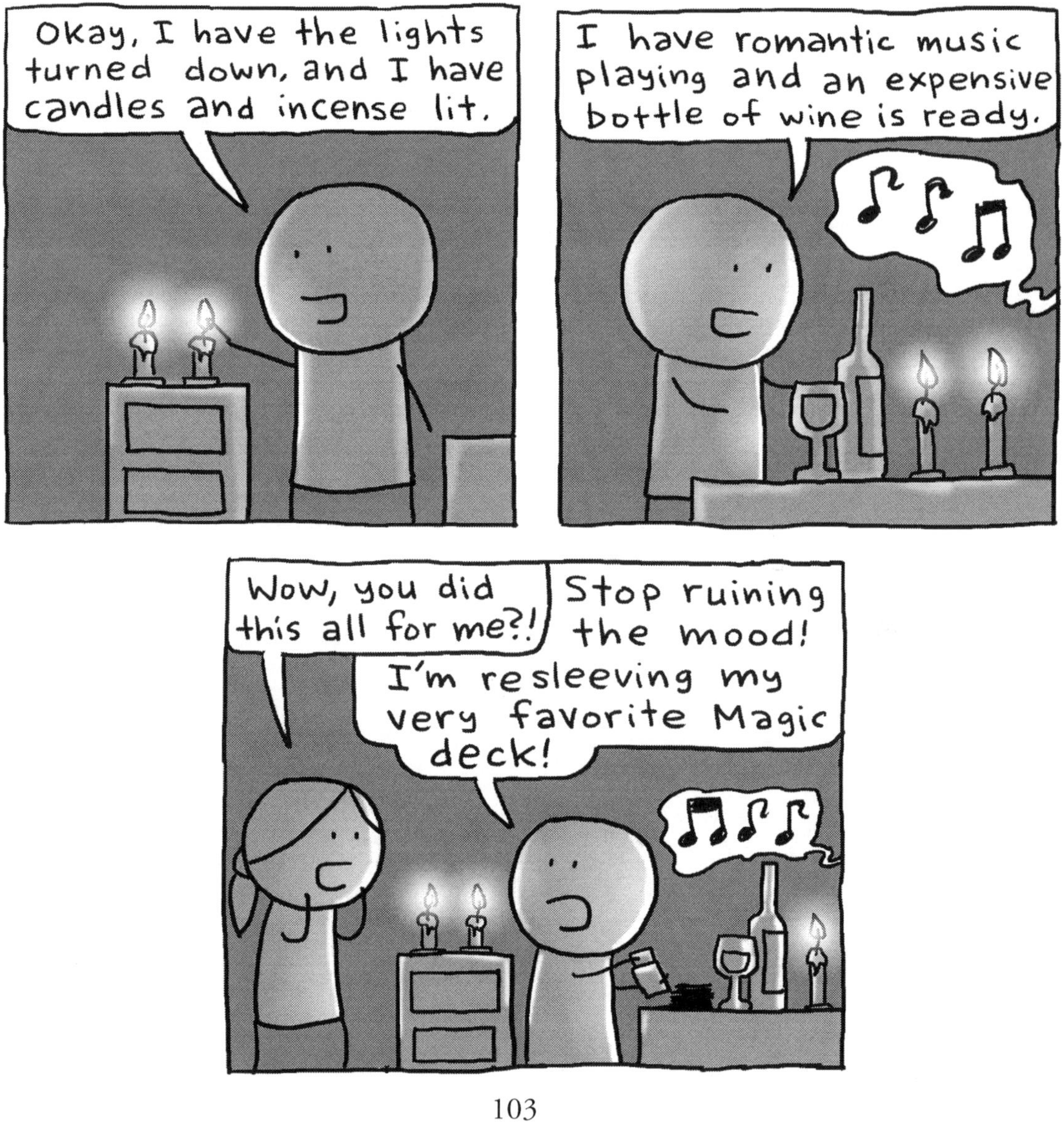
Okay, I have the lights turned down, and I have candles and incense lit.
I have romantic music playing and an expensive bottle of wine is ready.
Wow, you did this all for me?!
Stop ruining the mood!
I'm resleeving my very favorite Magic deck!

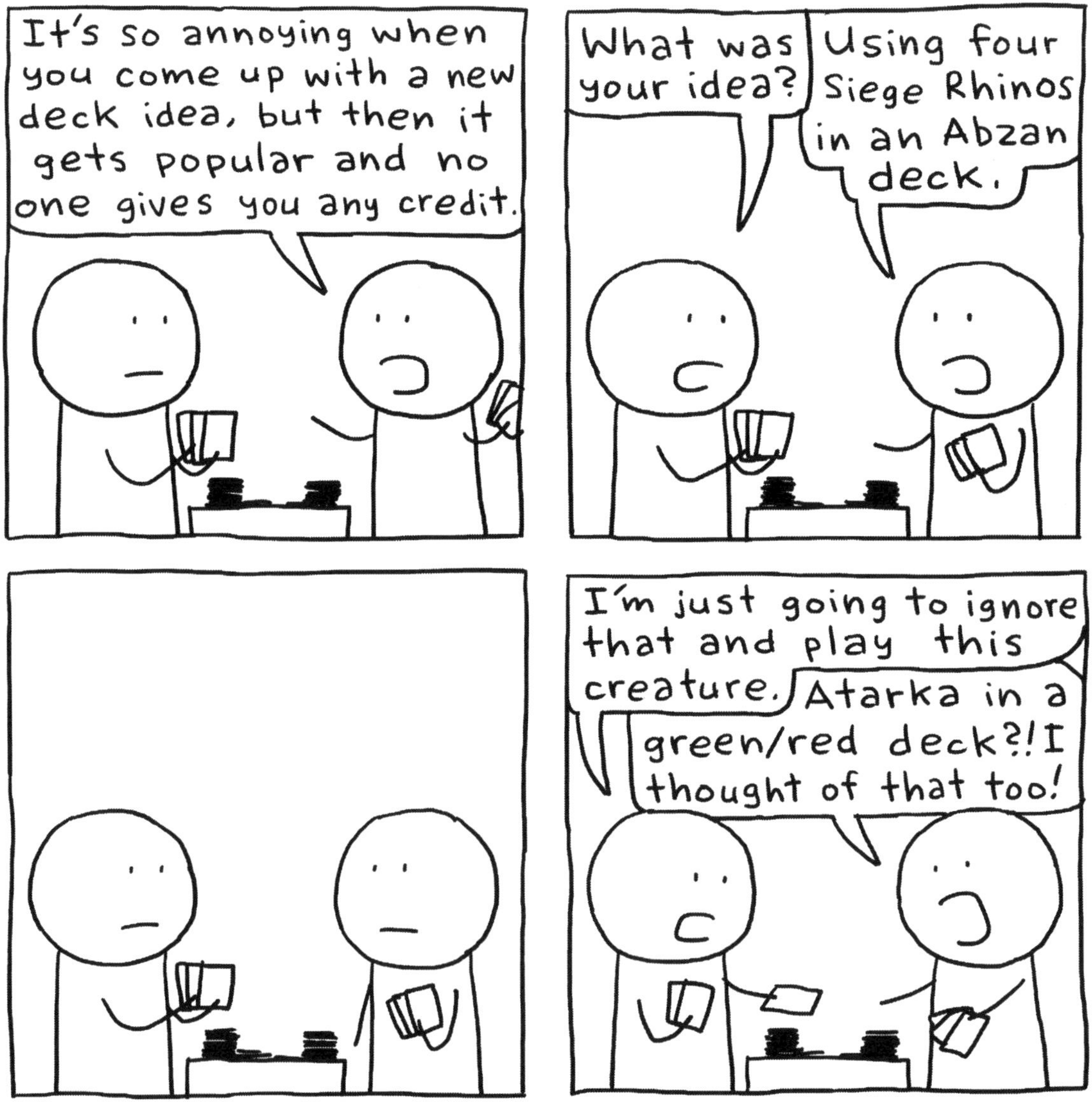
It's so annoying when you come up with a new deck idea, but then it gets popular and no one gives you any credit.
What was your idea?
Using four Siege Rhinos in an Abzan deck.
I'm just going to ignore that and play this creature.
Atarka in a green/red deck?! I thought of that too!

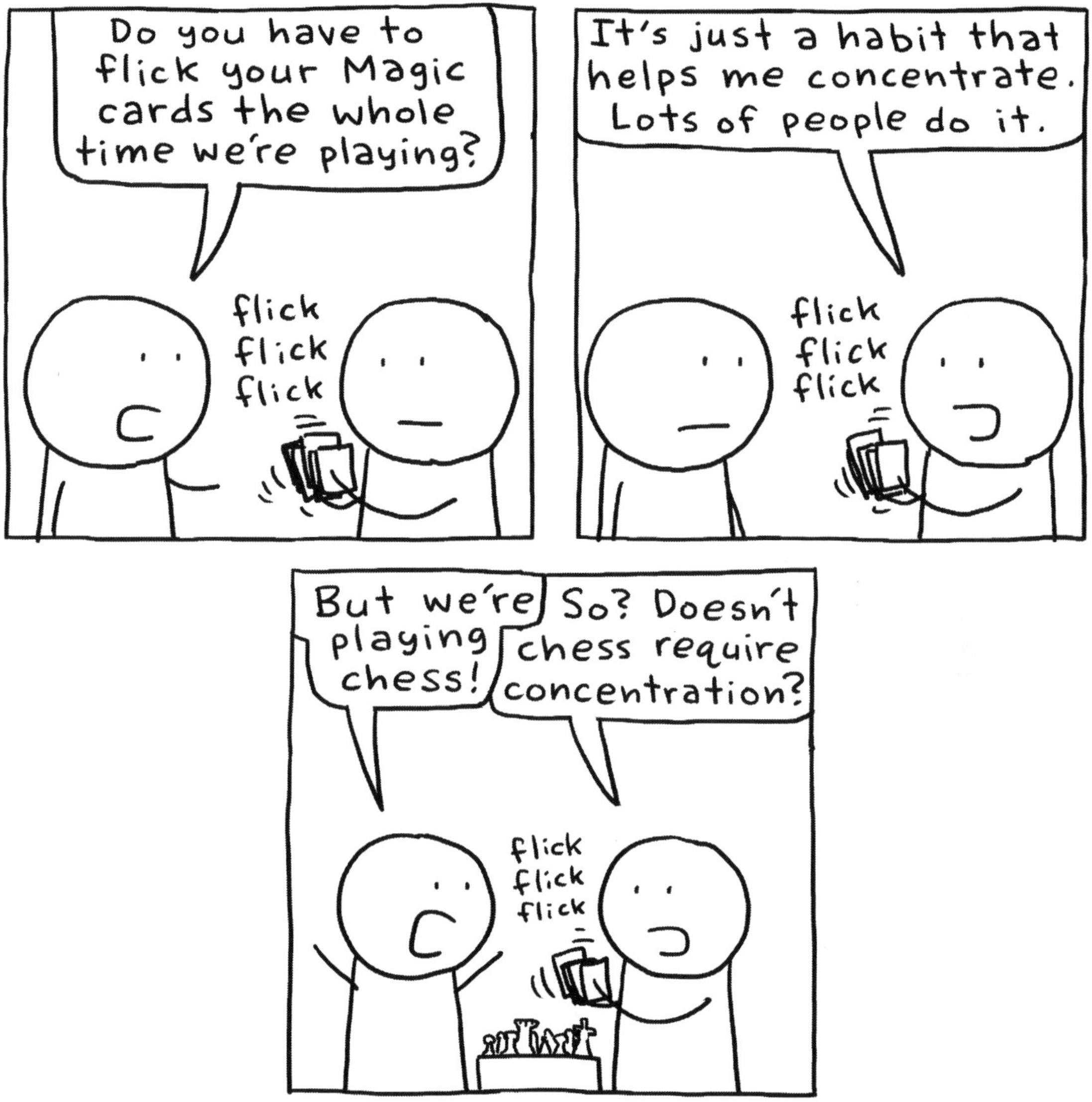
Do you have to flick your Magic cards the whole time we're playing?
flick flick flick
It's just a habit that helps me concentrate. Lots of people do it.
flick flick flick
But we're playing chess!
So? Doesn't chess require concentration?
flick flick flick

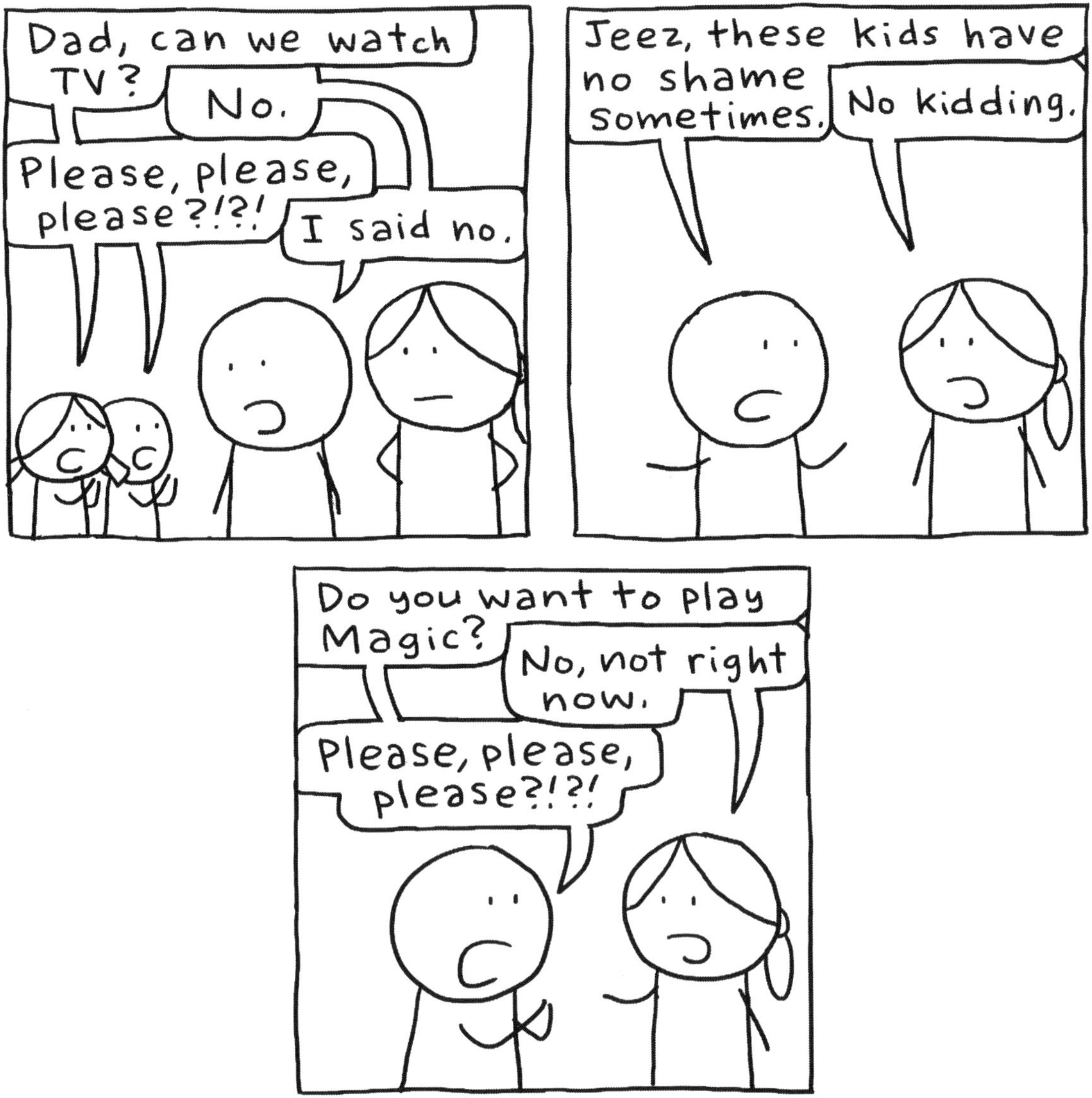
Dad, can we watch TV?
No.
Please, please, please?!?!
I said no.
Jeez, these kids have no shame sometimes.
No kidding.
Do you want to play Magic?
No, not right now.
Please, please, please?!?!

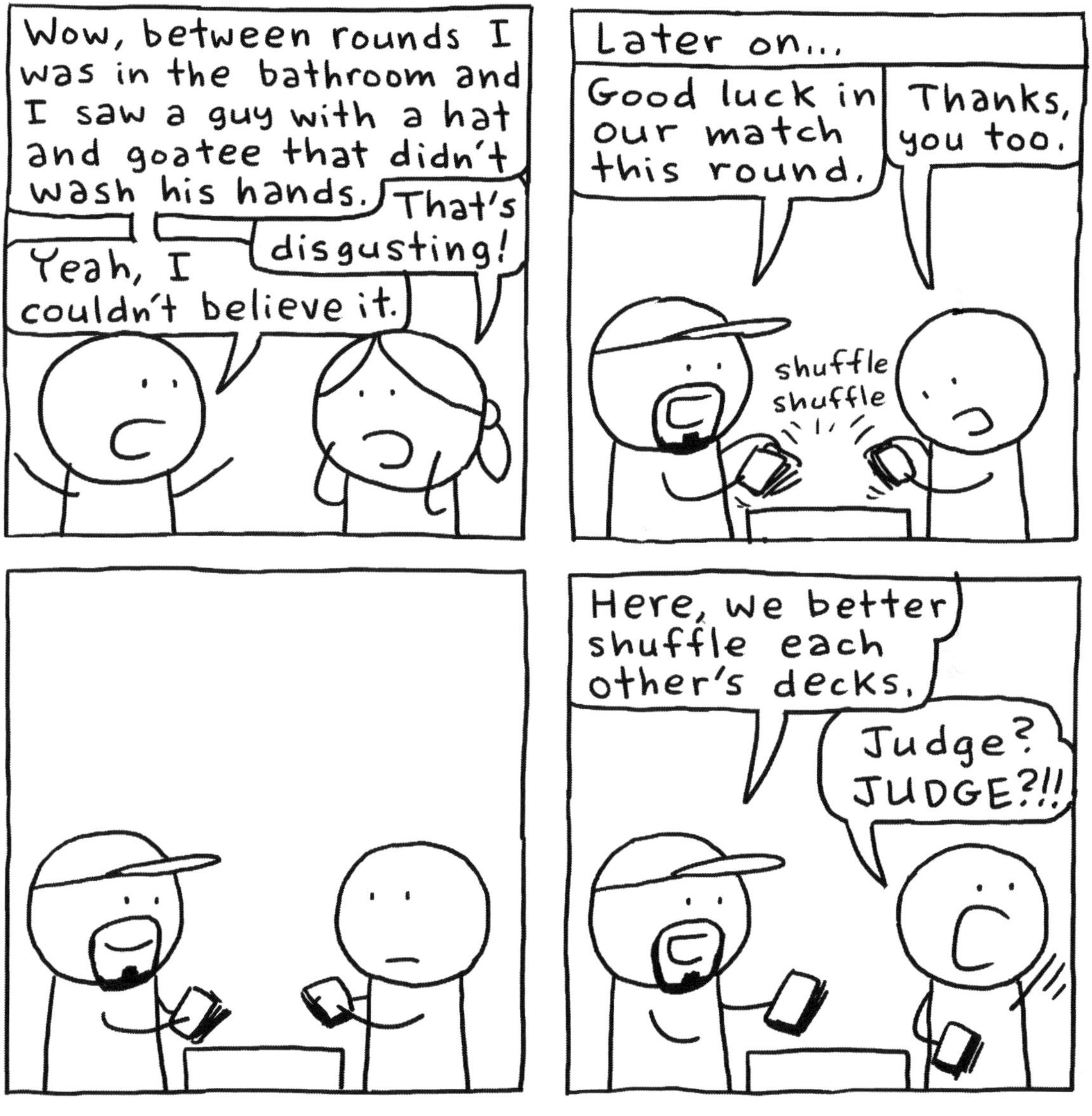
Wow, between rounds I was in the bathroom and I saw a guy with a hat and goatee that didn't wash his hands.
Yeah, I couldn't believe it.
That's disgusting!
Later on...
Good luck in our match this round.
Thanks, you too.
shuffle shuffle
Here, we better shuffle each other's decks.
Judge? JUDGE?!!

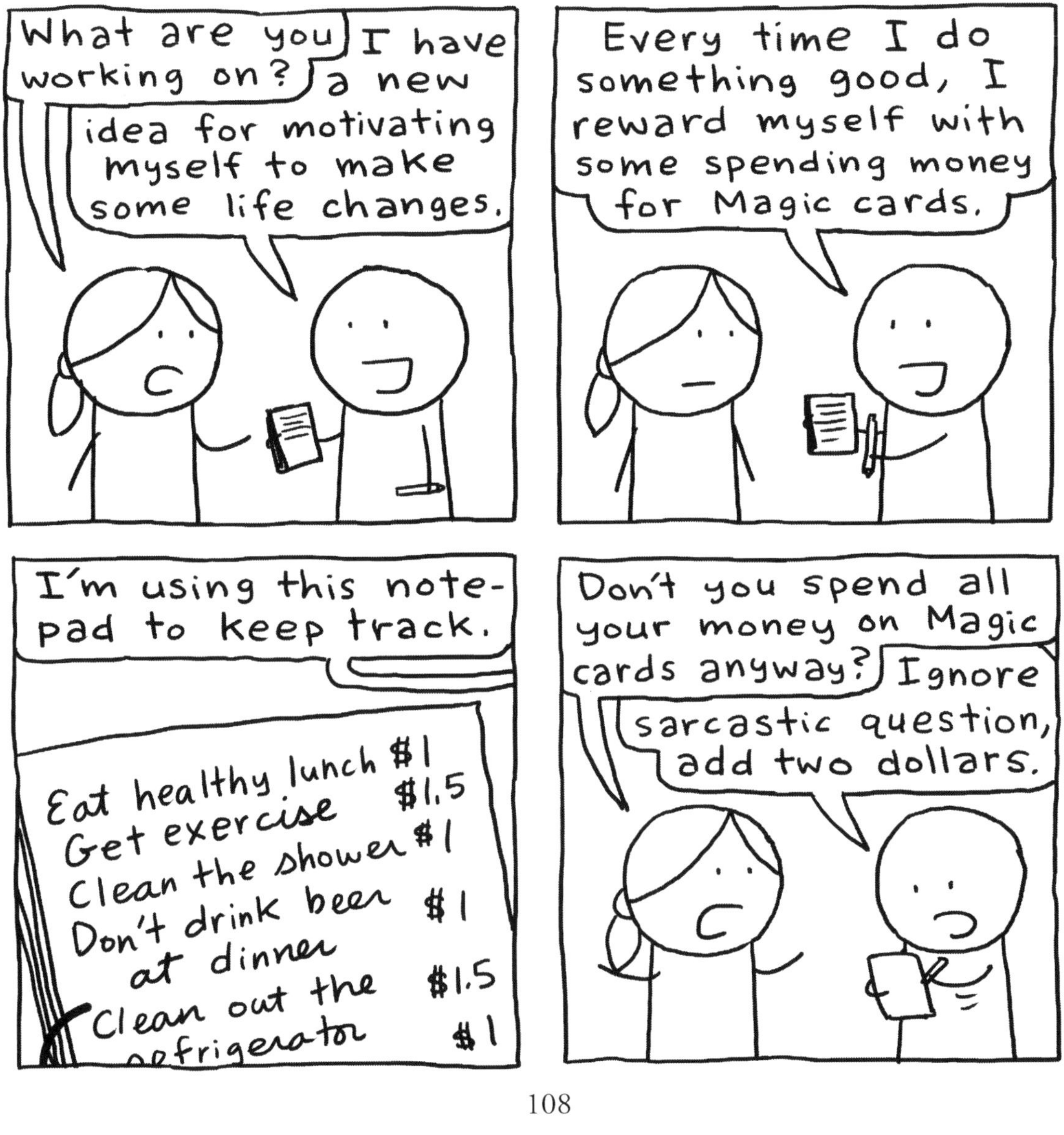
What are you working on?
I have a new idea for motivating myself to make some life changes.
Every time I do something good, I reward myself with some spending money for Magic cards.
I'm using this note-pad to keep track.
Eat healthy lunch $1
Get exercise $1.5
Clean the shower $1
Don't drink beer at dinner $1
Clean out the refrigerator $1.5
$1
Don't you spend all your money on Magic cards anyway?
Ignore sarcastic question, add two dollars.

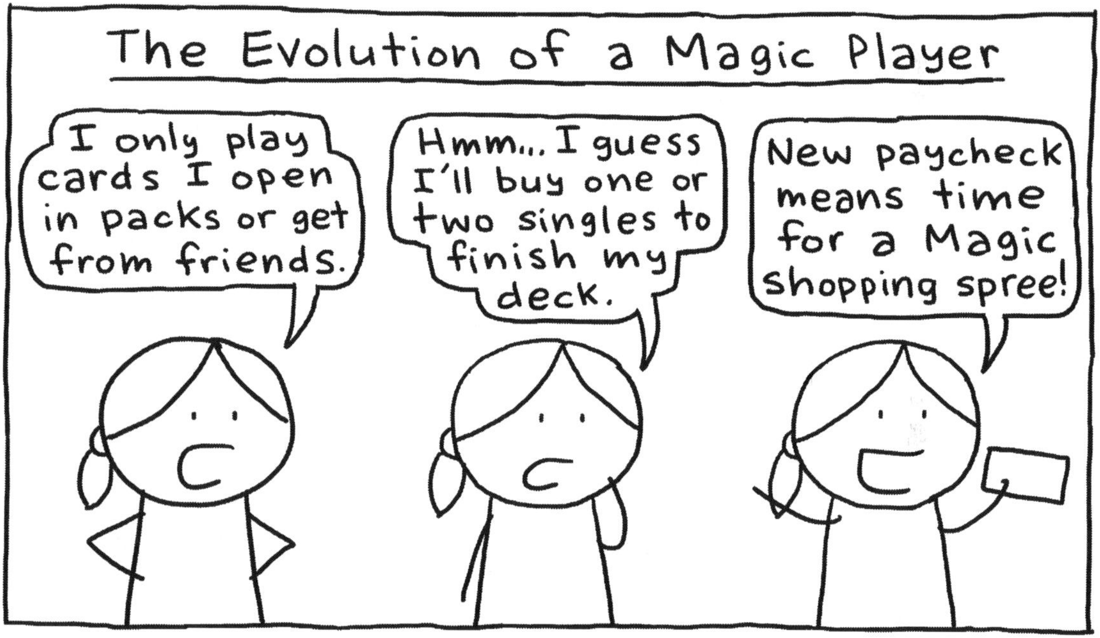
The Evolution of a Magic Player
I only play cards I open in packs or get from friends.
Hmm... I guess I'll buy one or two singles to finish my deck.
New paycheck means time for a Magic shopping spree!

I'm completely broke! How am I going to get the money I need for Magic cards?...
Do you want to pay me for sex?
Nope.

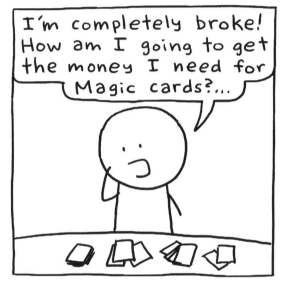

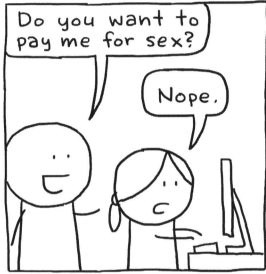

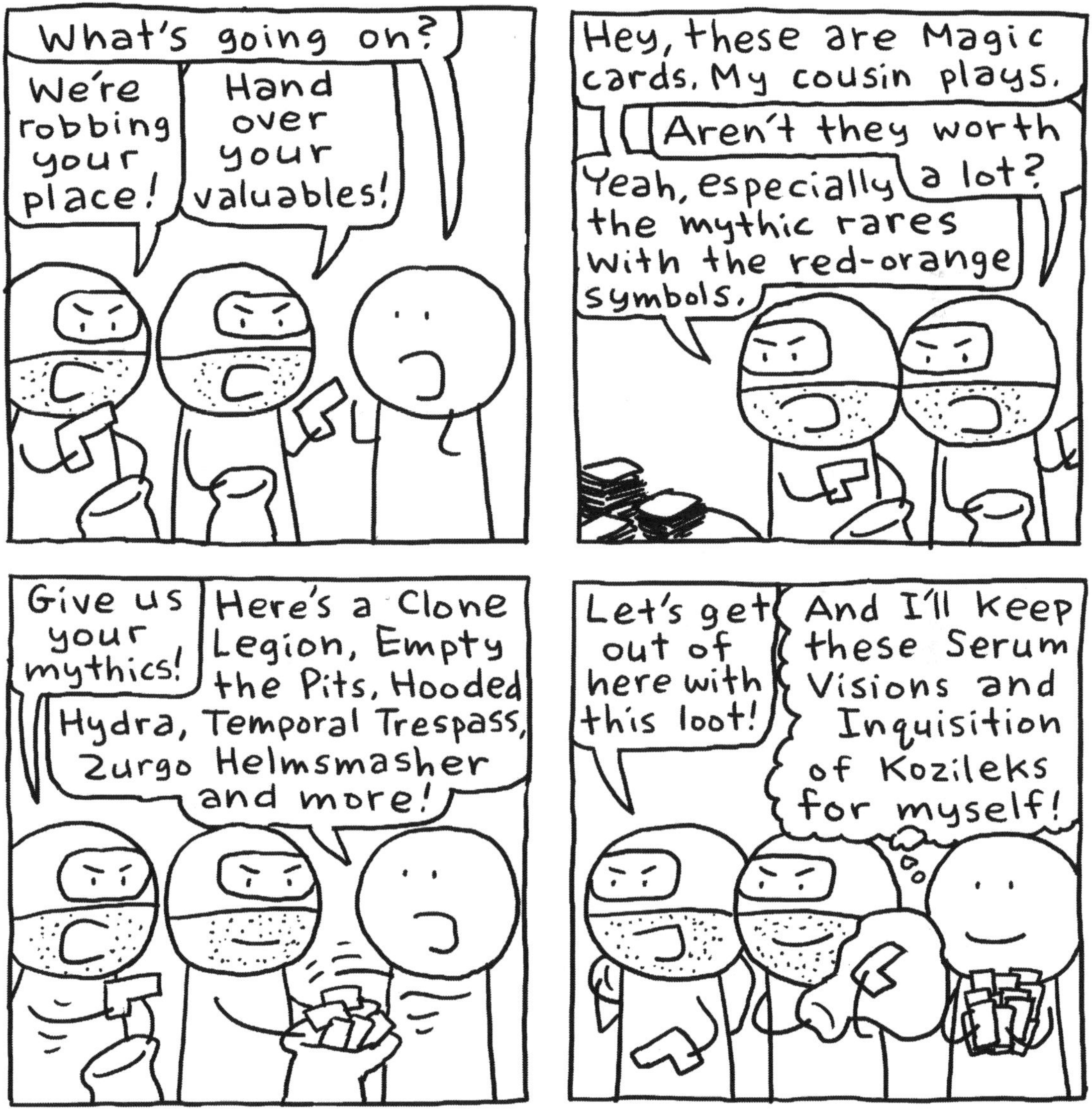
What's going on?
We're robbing your place!
Hand over your valuables!
Hey, these are Magic cards. My cousin plays.
Aren't they worth a lot?
Yeah, especially the mythic rares with the red-orange symbols.
Give us your mythics!
Here's a Clone Legion, Empty the Pits, Hooded Hydra, Temporal Trespass, Zurgo Helmsmasher and more!
Let's get out of here with this loot!
And I'll keep these Serum Visions and Inquisition of Kozileks for myself!

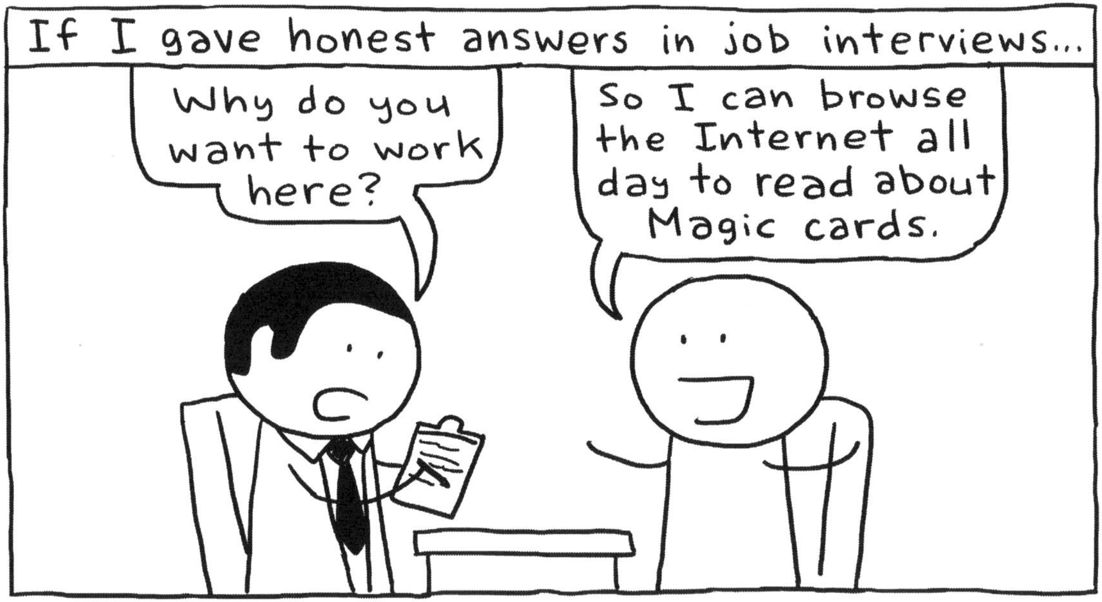
If I gave honest answers in job interviews...
Why do you want to work here?
So I can browse the Internet all day to read about Magic cards.

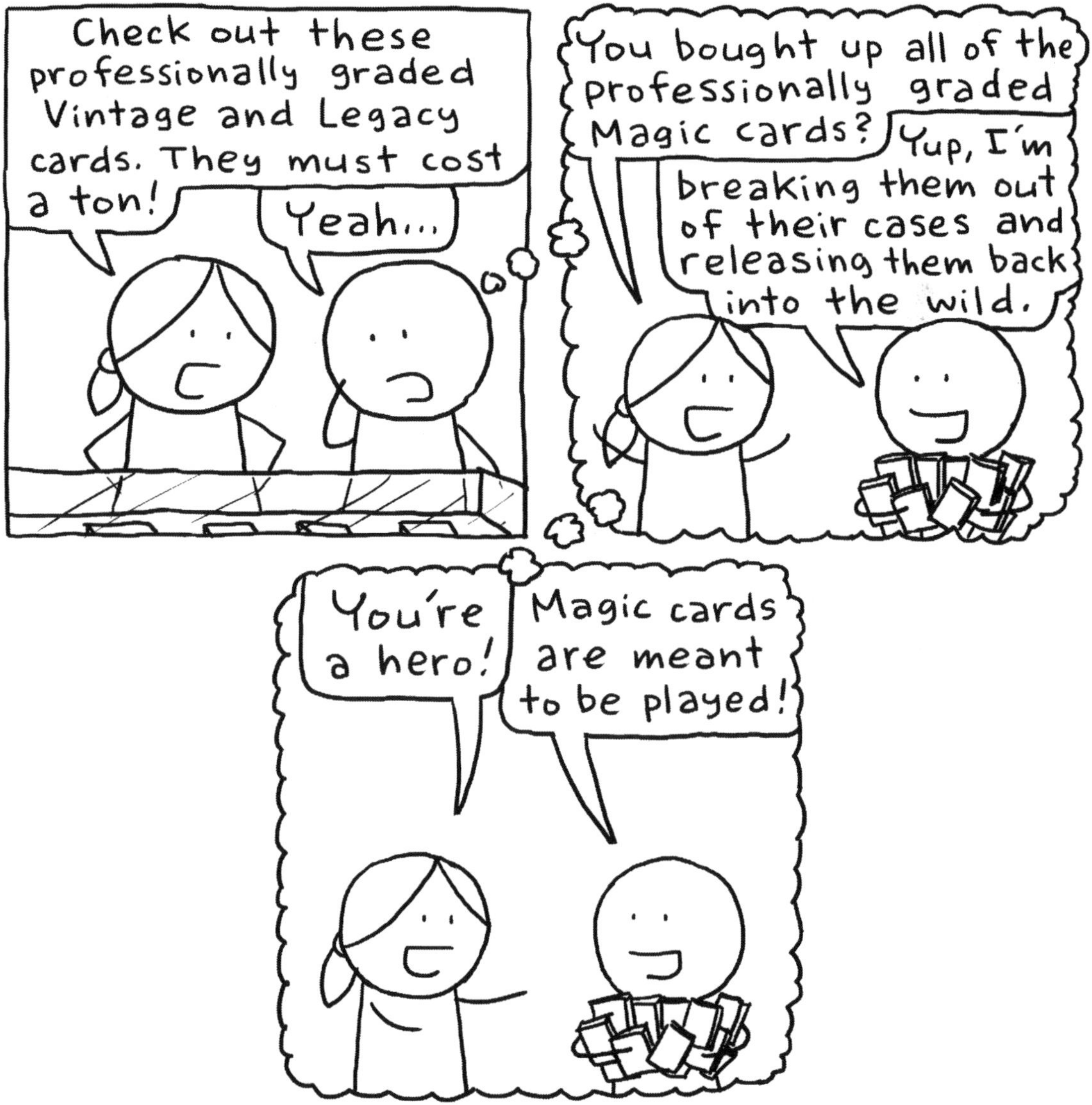
Check out these professionally graded Vintage and Legacy cards. They must cost a ton!
Yeah...
You bought up all of the professionally graded Magic cards?
Yup, I'm breaking them out of their cases and releasing them back into the wild.
You're a hero!
Magic cards are meant to be played!

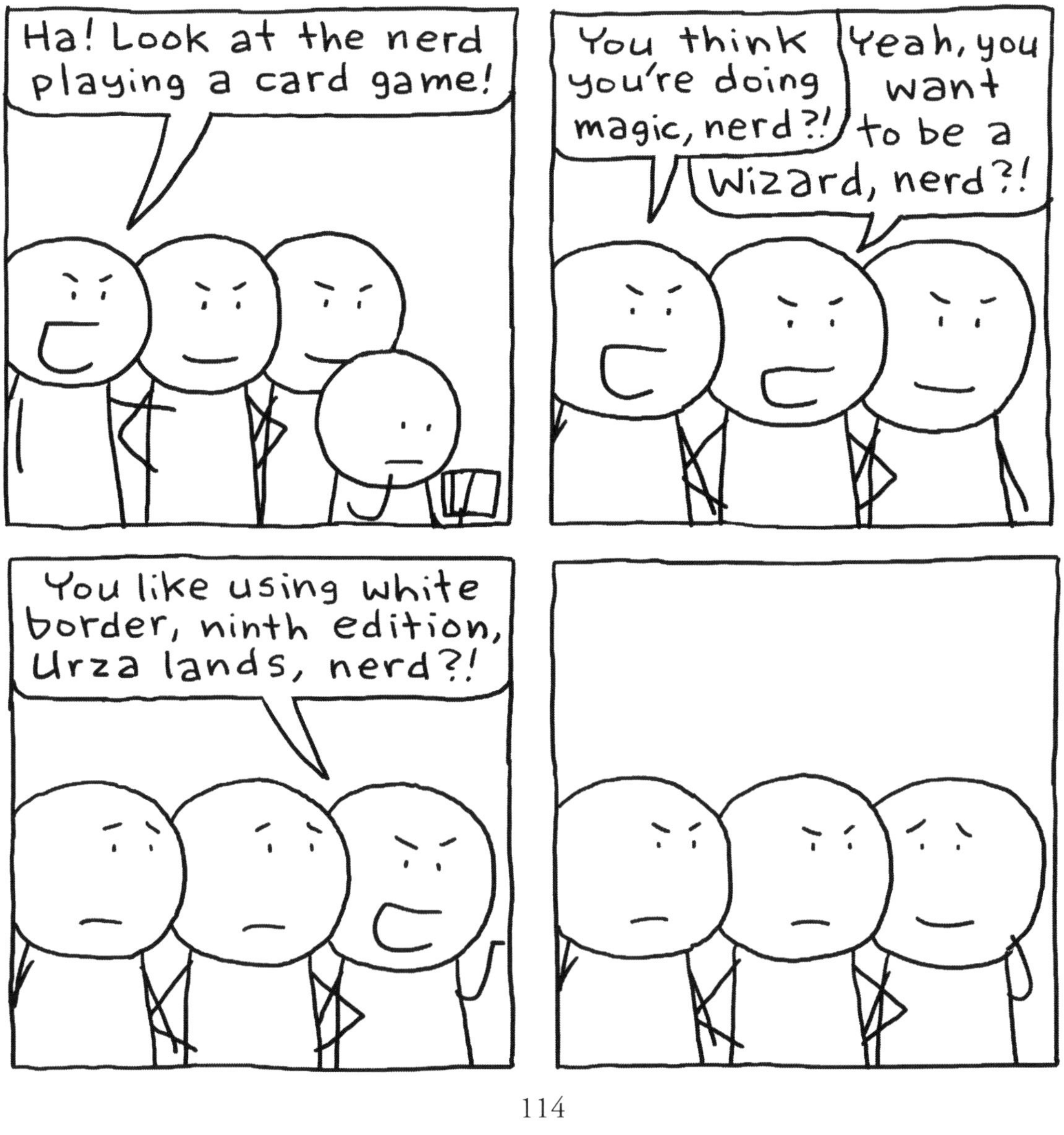
Ha! Look at the nerd playing a card game!
You think you're doing magic, nerd?!
Yeah, you want to be a Wizard, nerd?!
You like using white border, ninth edition, Urza lands, nerd?!

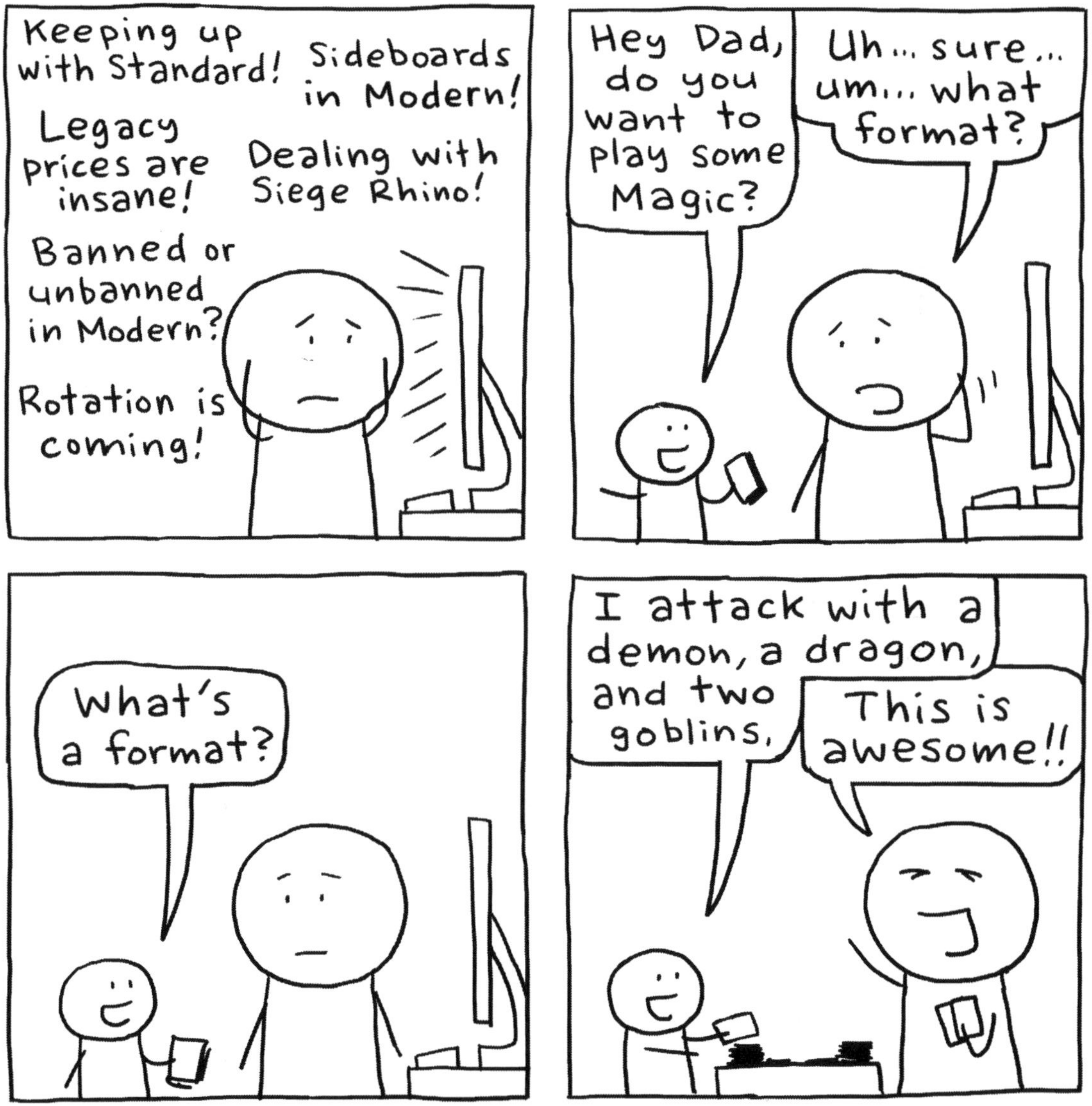

Keeping up with Standard!
Sideboards in Modern!
Legacy prices are insane!
Dealing with Siege Rhino!
Banned or unbanned in Modern?
Rotation is coming!
Hey Dad, do you want to play some Magic?
Uh... sure... um... what format?
What's a format?
I attack with a demon, a dragon, and two goblins,
This is awesome!!

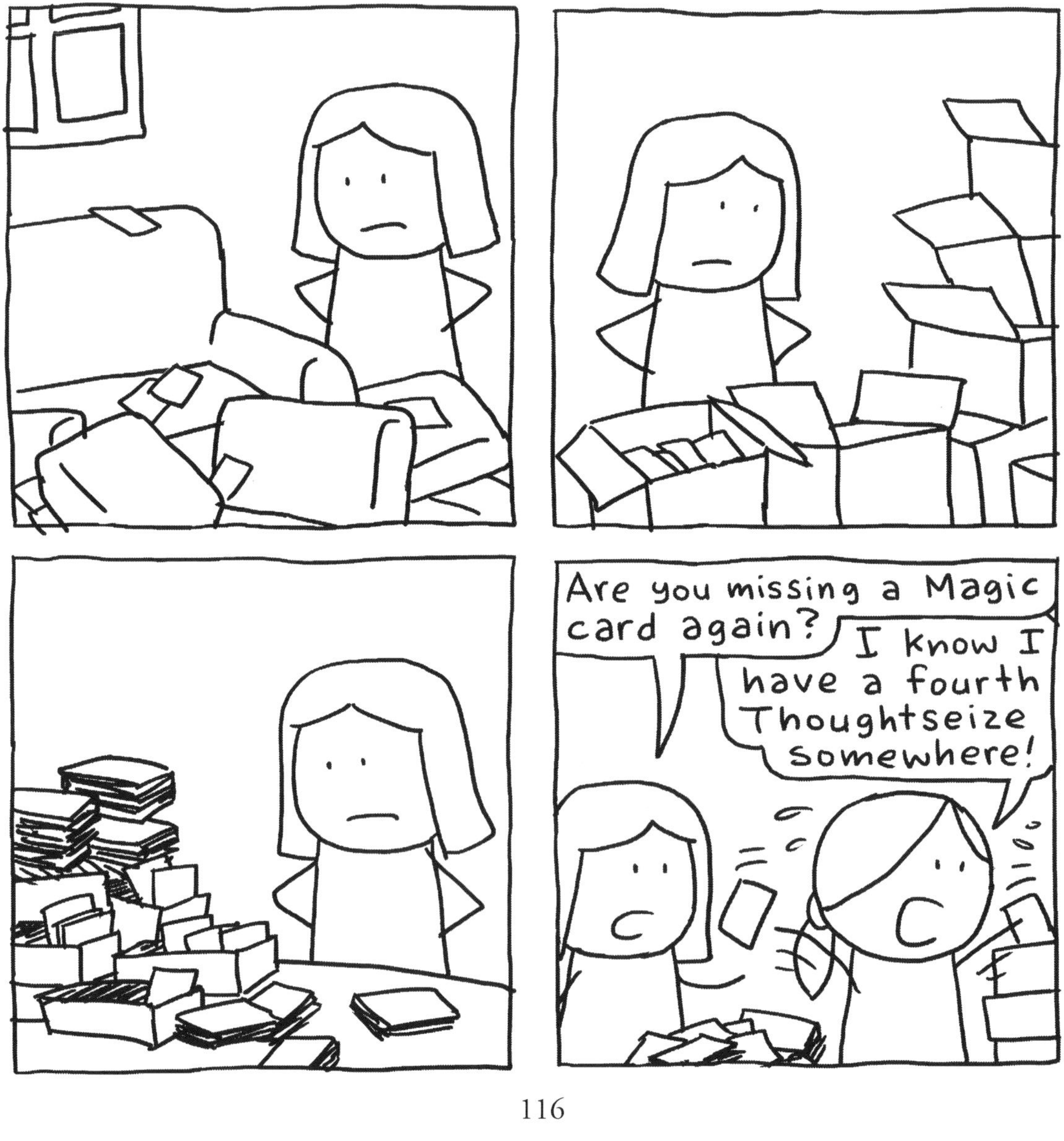
Are you missing a Magic card again?
I know I have a fourth Thoughtseize somewhere!

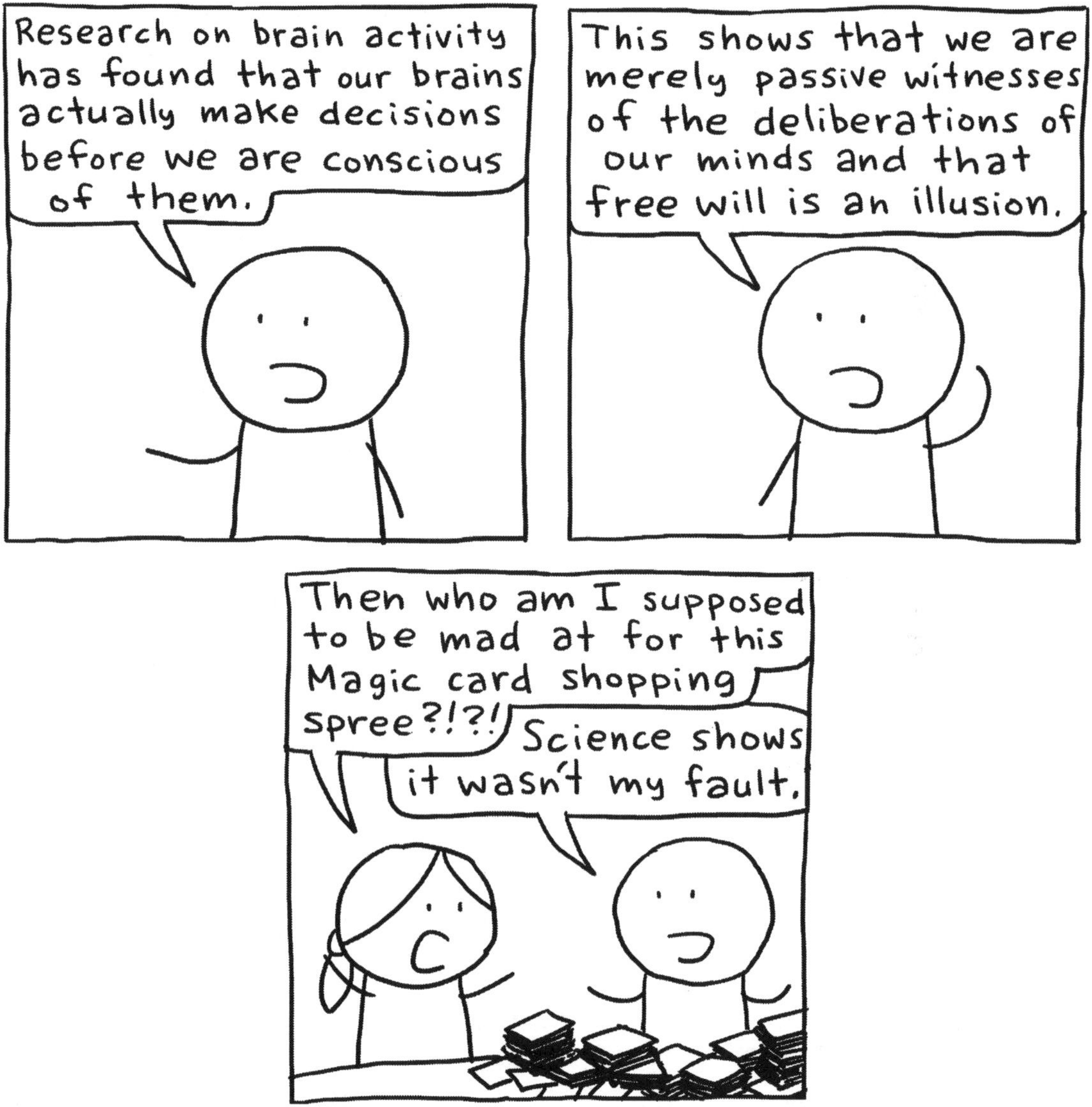
Research on brain activity has found that our brains actually make decisions before we are conscious of them.
This shows that we are merely passive witnesses of the deliberations of our minds and that free will is an illusion.
Then who am I supposed to be mad at for this Magic card shopping spree?!?!
Science shows it wasn't my fault.

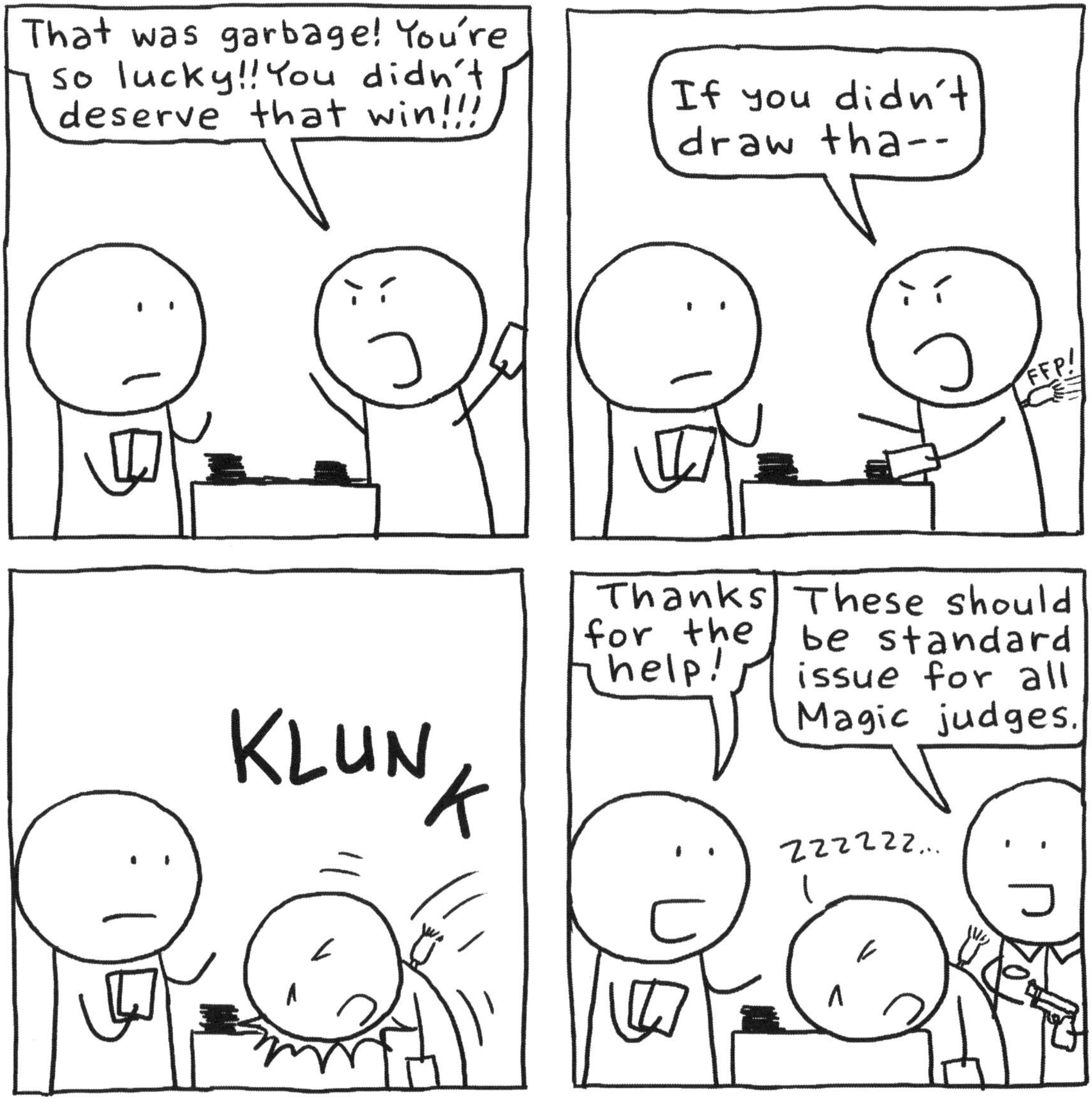
That was garbage! You're so lucky!! You didn't deserve that win!!!
If you didn't draw tha--
FFP!
KLUNK
Thanks for the help!
These should be standard issue for all Magic judges.
ZZZZZZ...

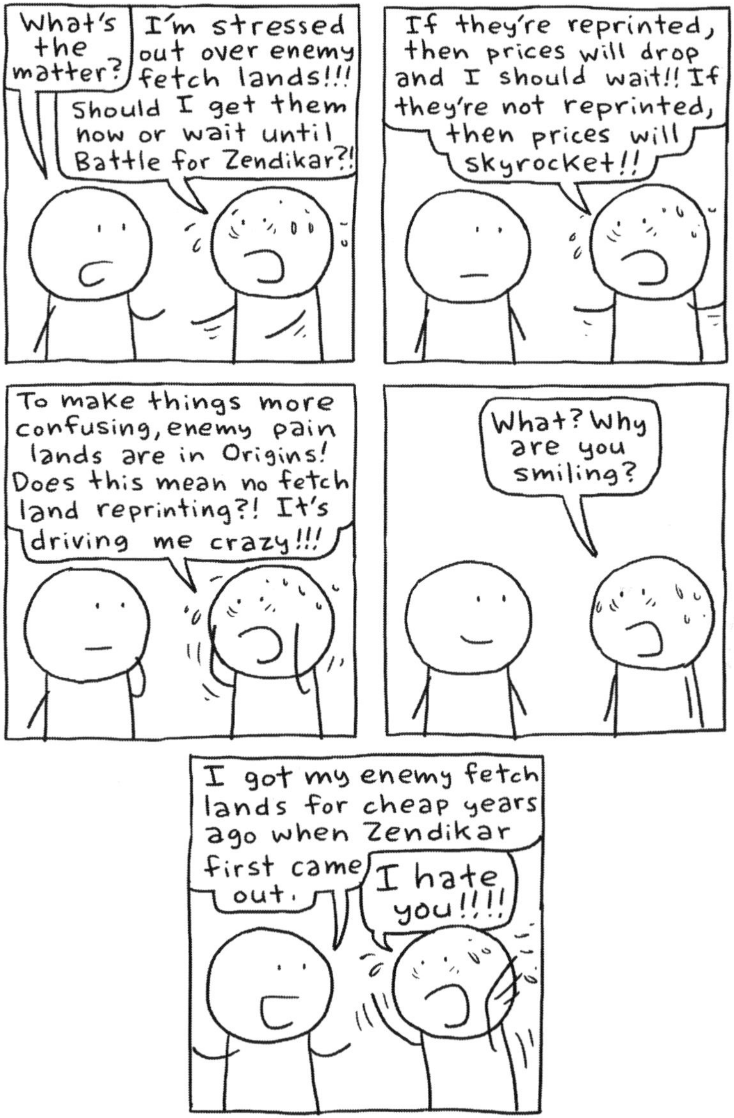
What's the matter?
I'm stressed out over enemy fetch lands!!! Should I get them now or wait until Battle for Zendikar?!
If they're reprinted, then prices will drop and I should wait!! If they're not reprinted, then prices will skyrocket!!
To make things more confusing, enemy pain lands are in Origins! Does this mean no fetch land reprinting?! It's driving me crazy!!!
What? Why are you smiling?
I got my enemy fetch lands for cheap years ago when Zendikar first came out.
I hate you!!!!

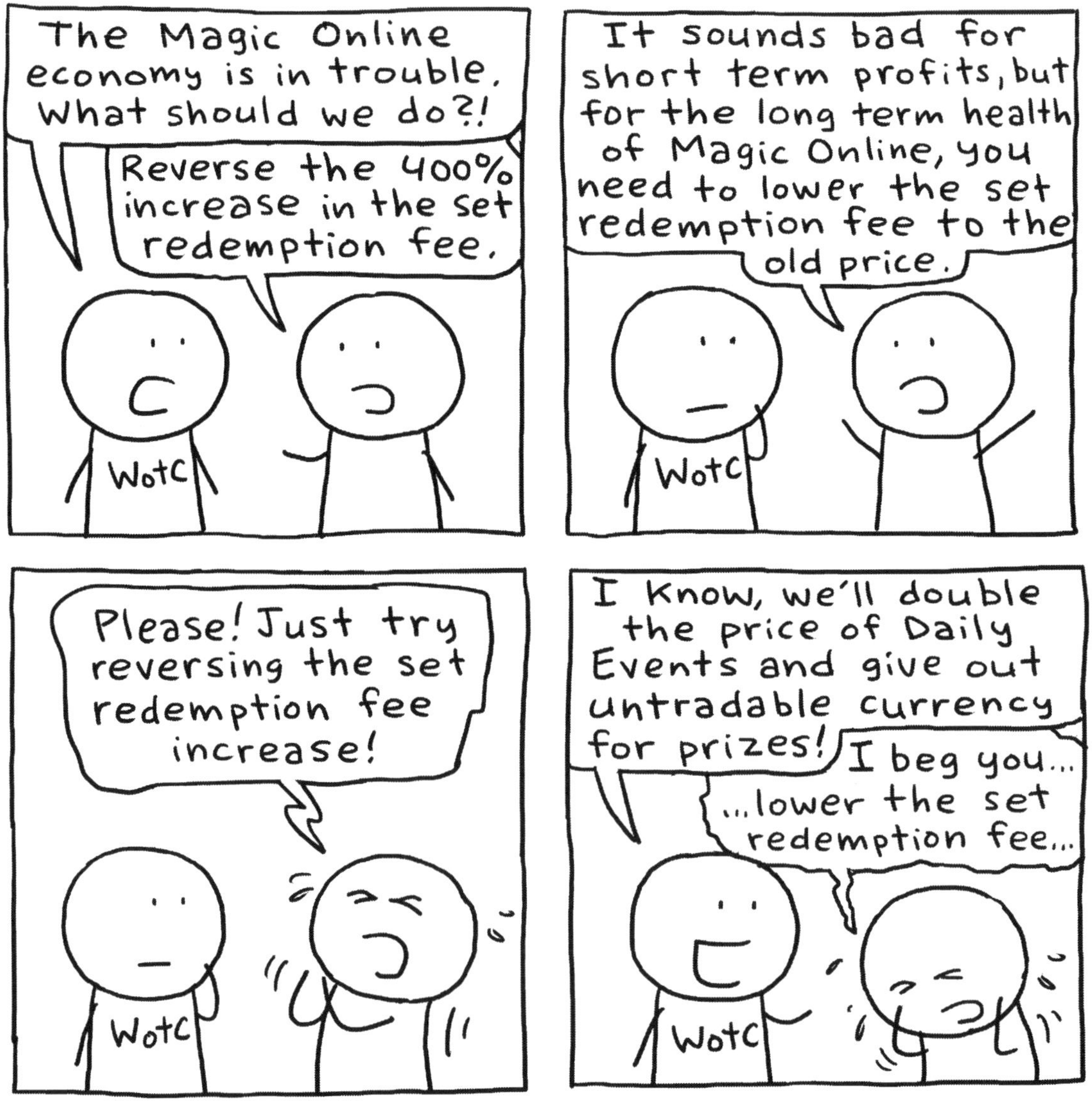
The Magic Online economy is in trouble. What should we do?!
Reverse the 400% increase in the set redemption fee.
It sounds bad for short term profits, but for the long term health of Magic Online, you need to lower the set redemption fee to the old price.
Please! Just try reversing the set redemption fee increase!
I know, we'll double the price of Daily Events and give out untradable currency for prizes!
I beg you... ...lower the set redemption fee...
WotC

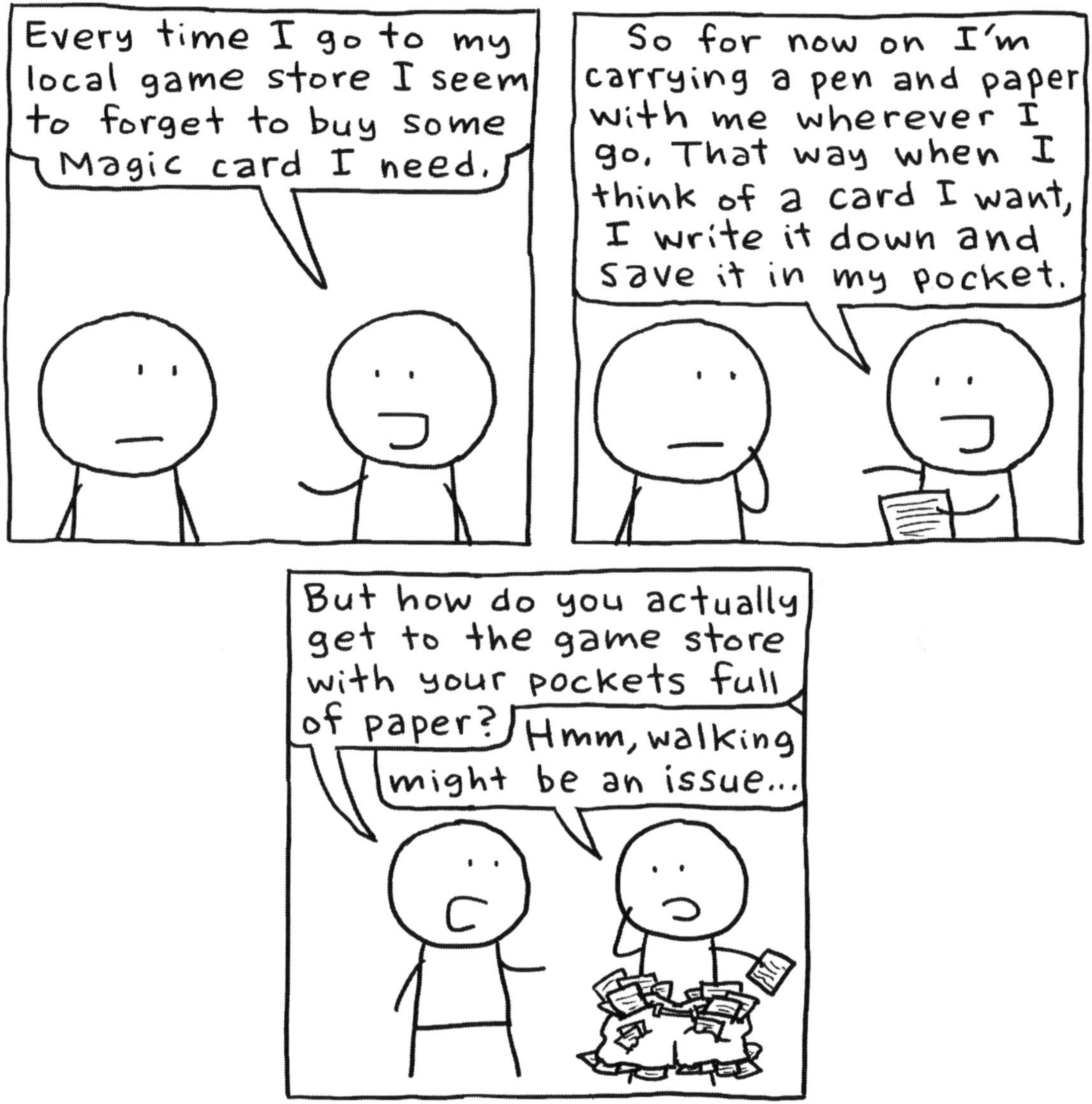
Every time I go to my local game store I seem to forget to buy some Magic card I need.
So for now on I'm carrying a pen and paper with me wherever I go. That way when I think of a card I want, I write it down and save it in my pocket.
But how do you actually get to the game store with your pockets full of paper?
Hmm, walking might be an issue...

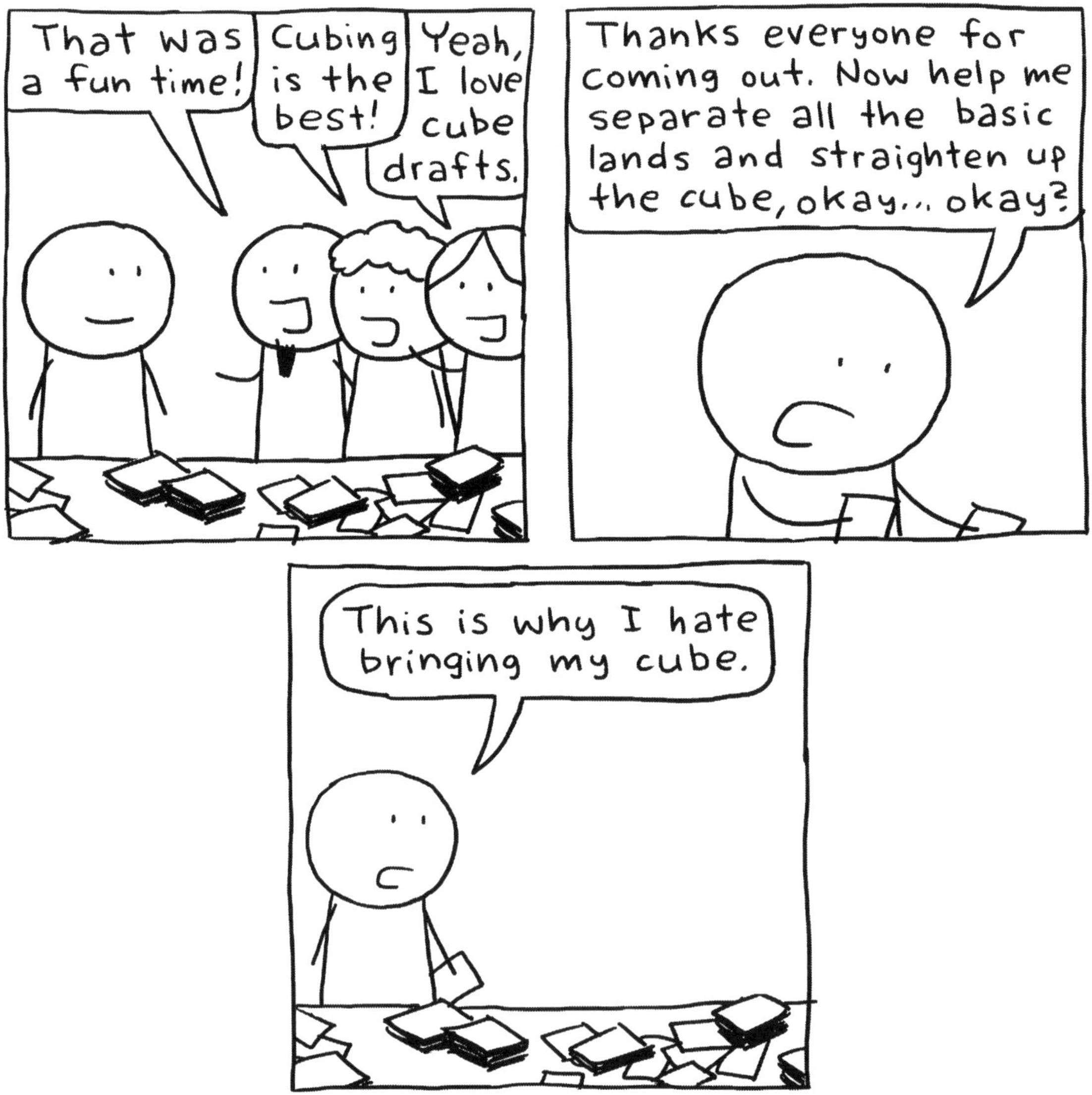

That was a fun time!
Cubing is the best!
Yeah, I love cube drafts.
Thanks everyone for coming out. Now help me separate all the basic lands and straighten up the cube, okay... okay?
This is why I hate bringing my cube.

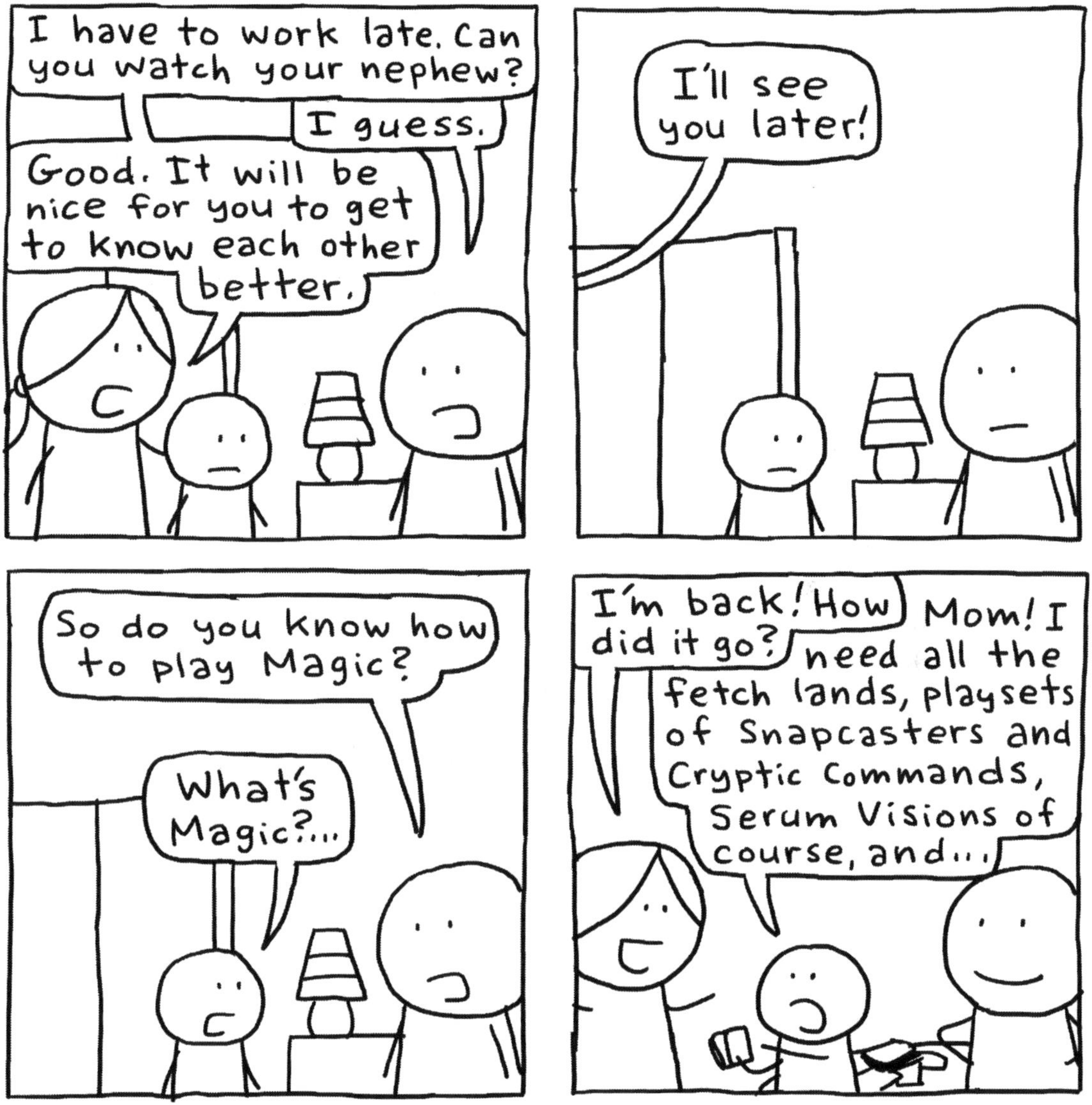
I have to work late. Can you watch your nephew?
I guess.
Good. It will be nice for you to get to know each other better.
I'll see you later!
So do you know how to play Magic?
What's Magic?...
I'm back! How did it go?
Mom! I need all the fetch lands, playsets of Snapcasters and Cryptic Commands, Serum Visions of course, and...

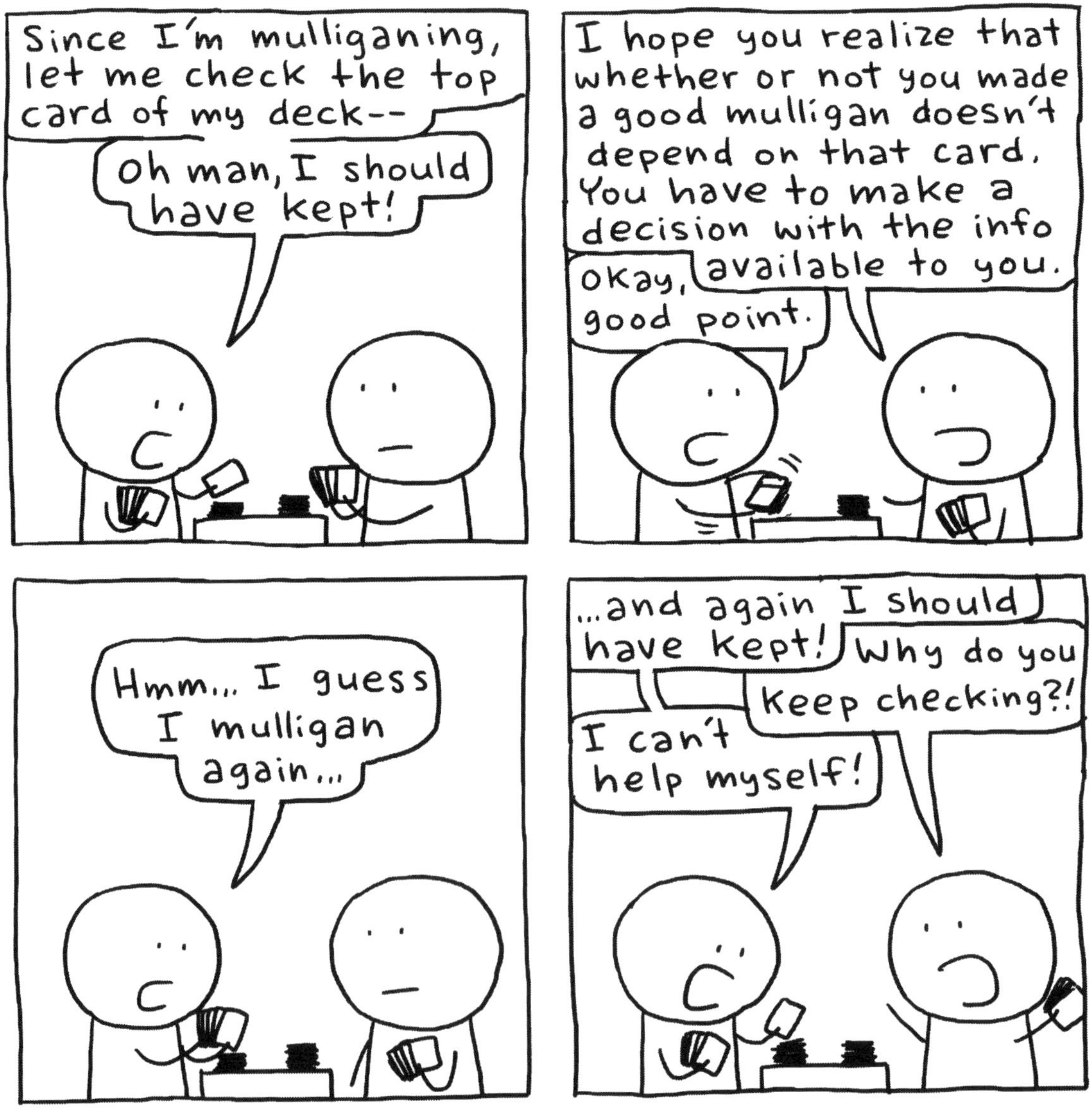
Since I'm mulliganing, let me check the top card of my deck--
Oh man, I should have kept!
I hope you realize that whether or not you made a good mulligan doesn't depend on that card. You have to make a decision with the info available to you.
Okay, good point.
Hmm... I guess I mulligan again...
...and again I should have kept!
Why do you keep checking?!
I can't help myself!

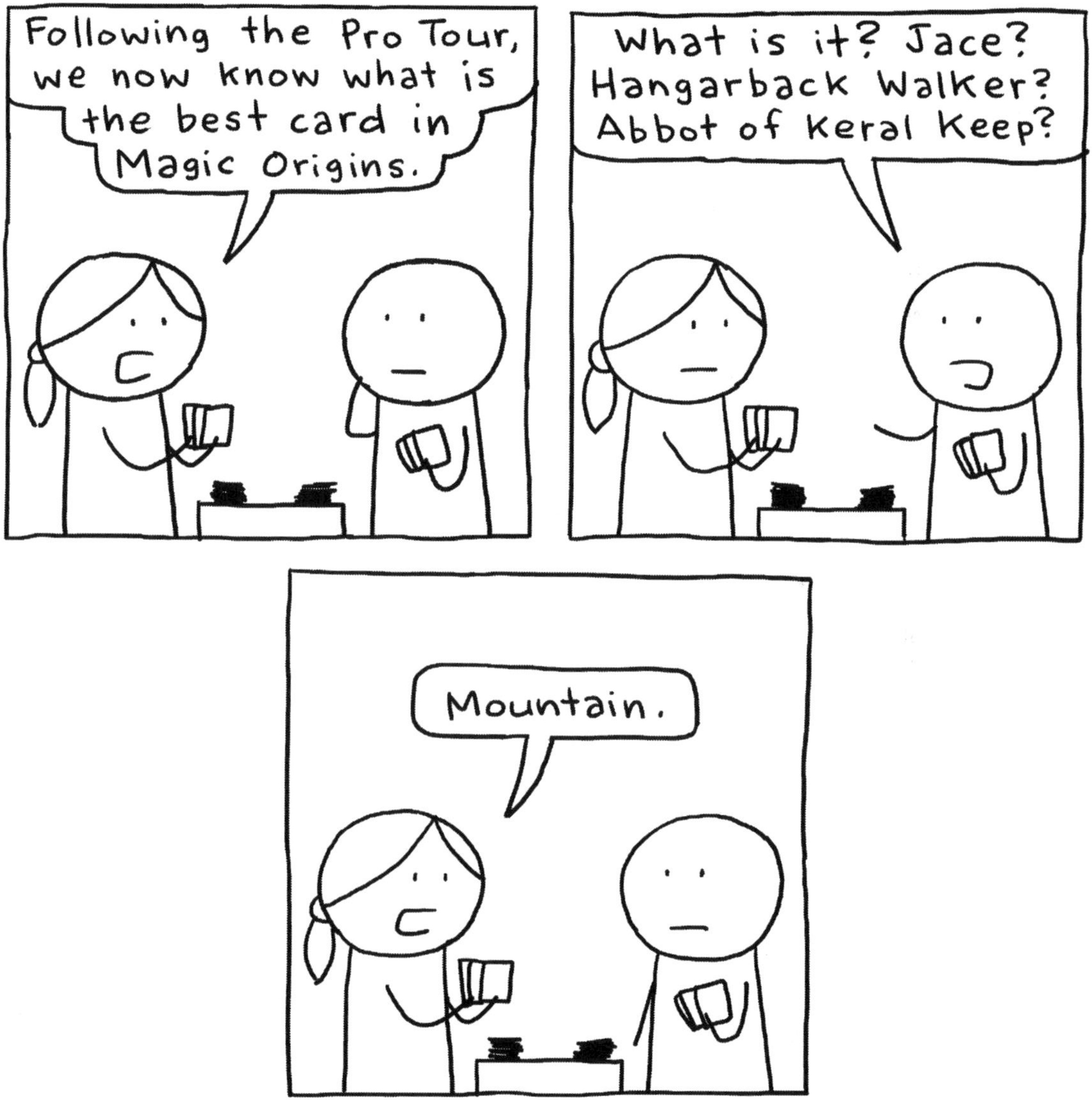
Following the Pro Tour, we now know what is the best card in Magic Origins.
What is it? Jace? Hangarback Walker? Abbot of Keral Keep?
Mountain.

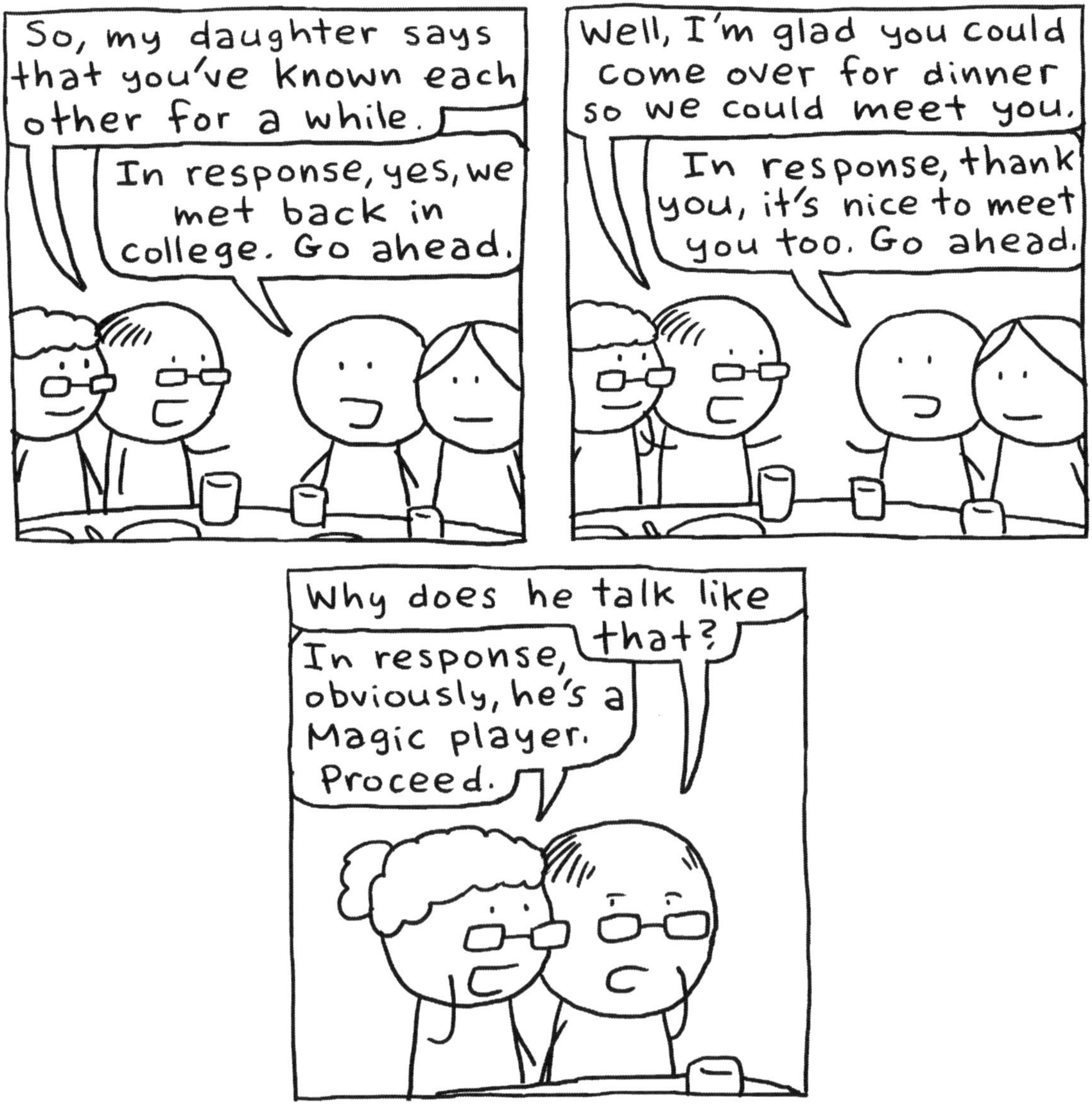
So, my daughter says that you've known each other for a while.
In response, yes, we met back in college. Go ahead.
Well, I'm glad you could come over for dinner so we could meet you.
In response, thank you, it's nice to meet you too. Go ahead.
Why does he talk like that?
In response, obviously, he's a Magic player. Proceed.

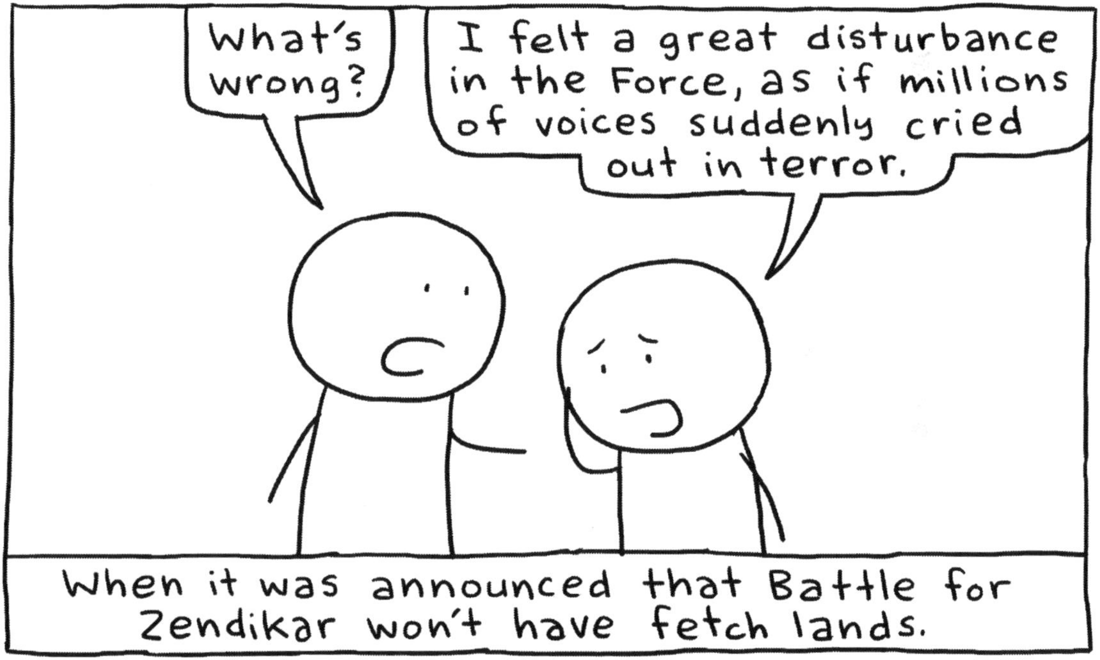
What's wrong?
I felt a great disturbance in the Force, as if millions of voices suddenly cried out in terror.
When it was announced that Battle for Zendikar won't have fetch lands.

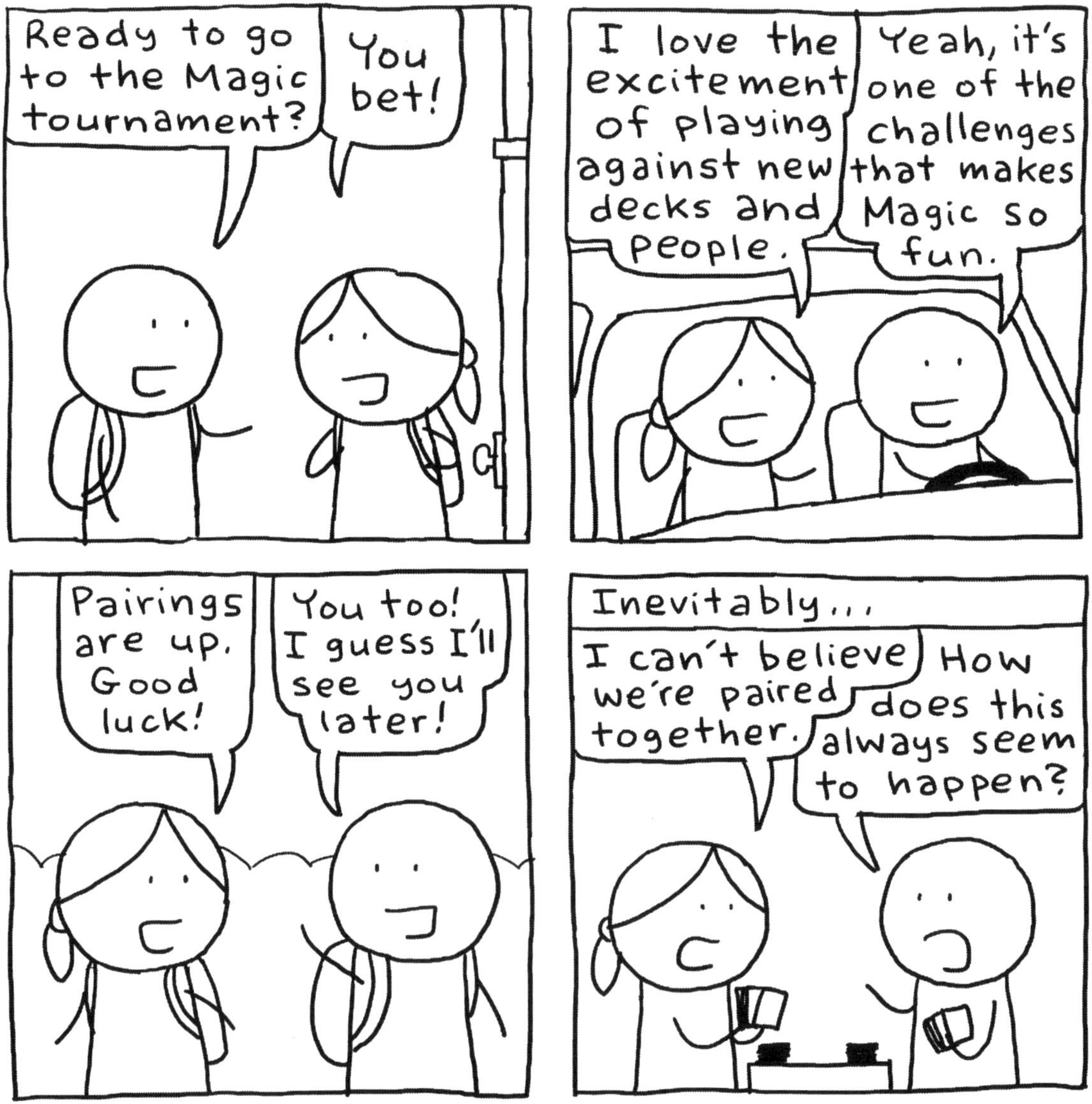
Ready to go to the Magic tournament?
You bet!
I love the excitement of playing against new decks and people.
Yeah, it's one of the challenges that makes Magic so fun.
Pairings are up. Good luck!
You too! I guess I'll see you later!
Inevitably...
I can't believe we're paired together.
How does this always seem to happen?

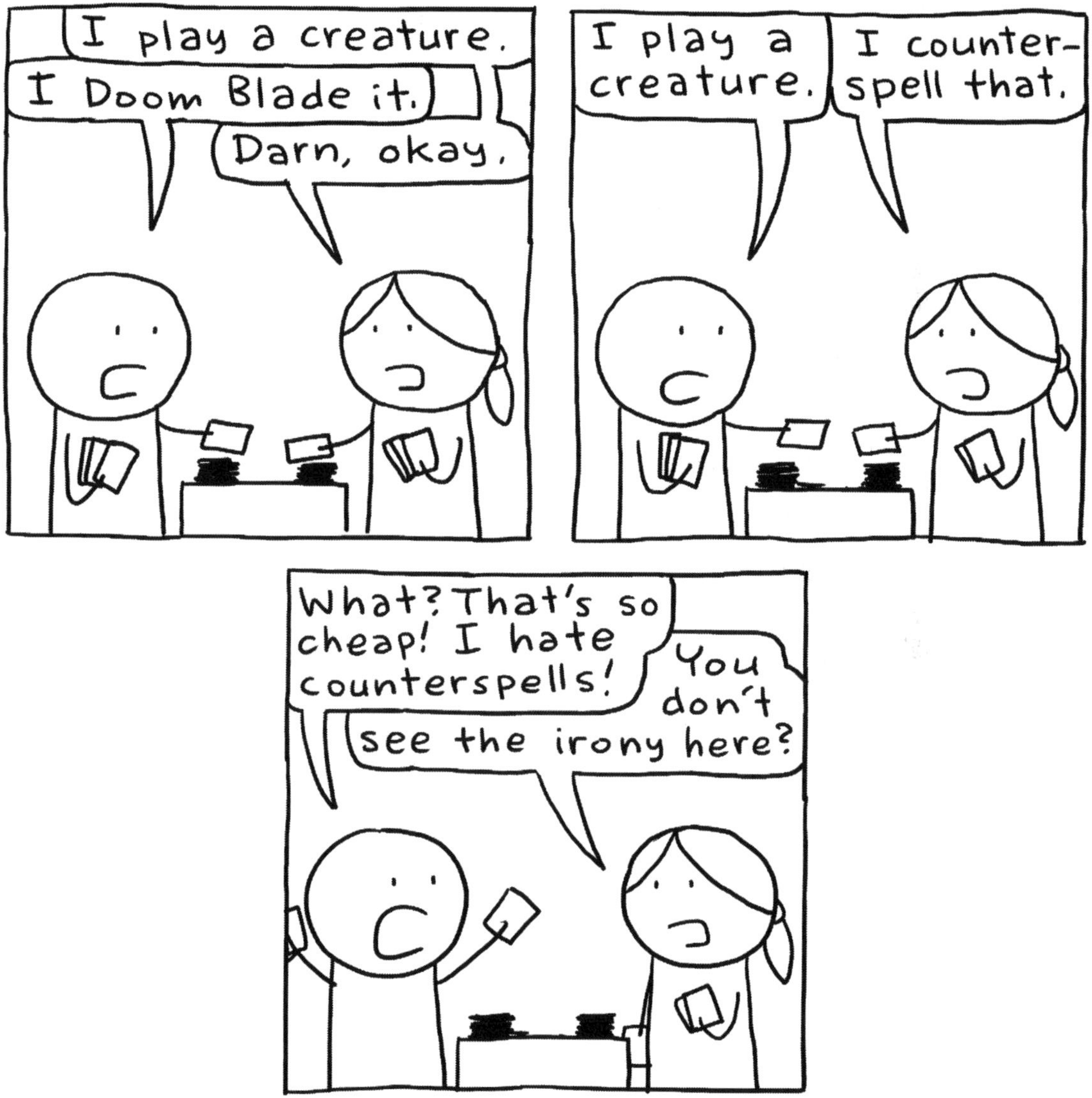
I play a creature.
I Doom Blade it.
Darn, okay.
I play a creature.
I counter-spell that.
What? That's so cheap! I hate counterspells!
You don't see the irony here?

Bonus Comics

The following pages feature comics that have never appeared on the Cardboard Crack website. I hope you enjoy the chance to see them here for the first time!

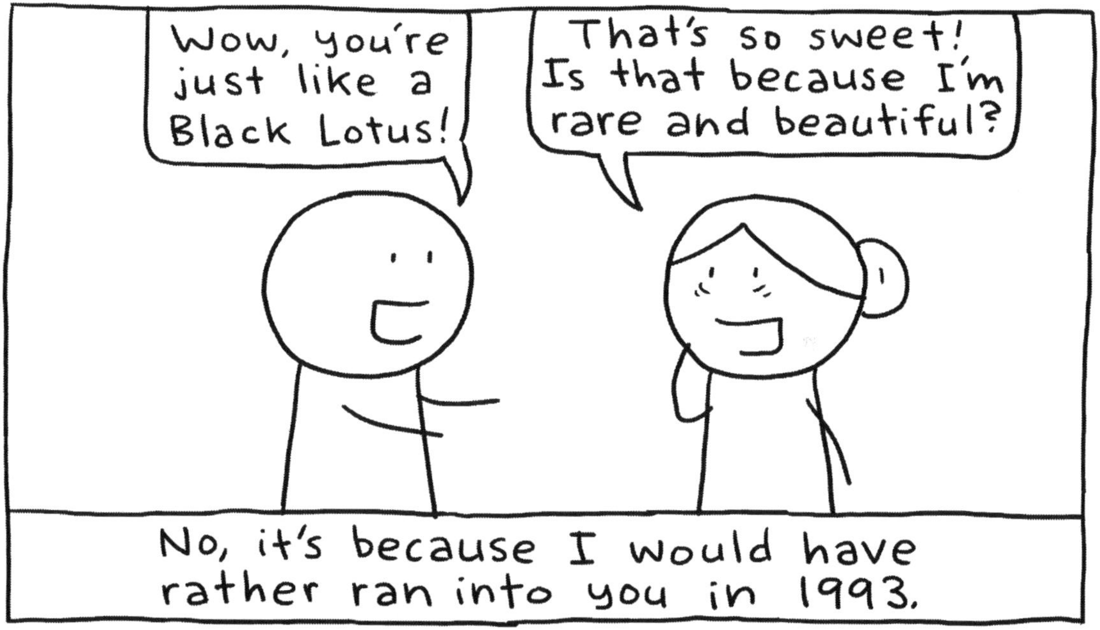
Wow, you're just like a Black Lotus!
That's so sweet! Is that because I'm rare and beautiful?
No, it's because I would have rather ran into you in 1993.

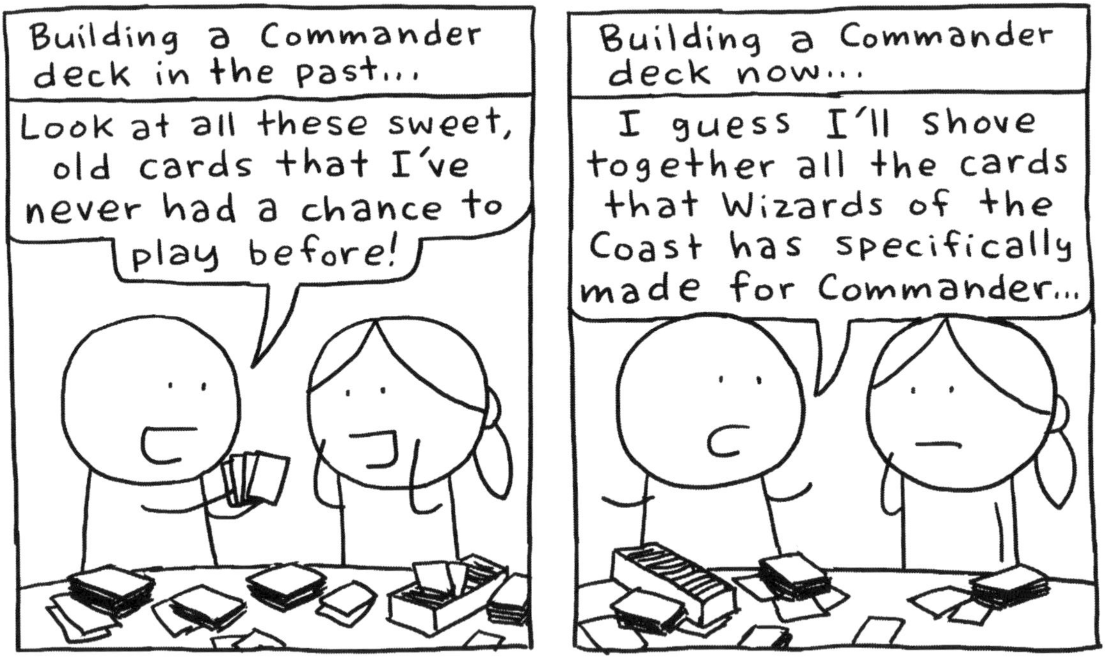
Building a Commander deck in the past...
Look at all these sweet, old cards that I've never had a chance to play before!
Building a Commander deck now...
I guess I'll shove together all the cards that Wizards of the Coast has specifically made for Commander...

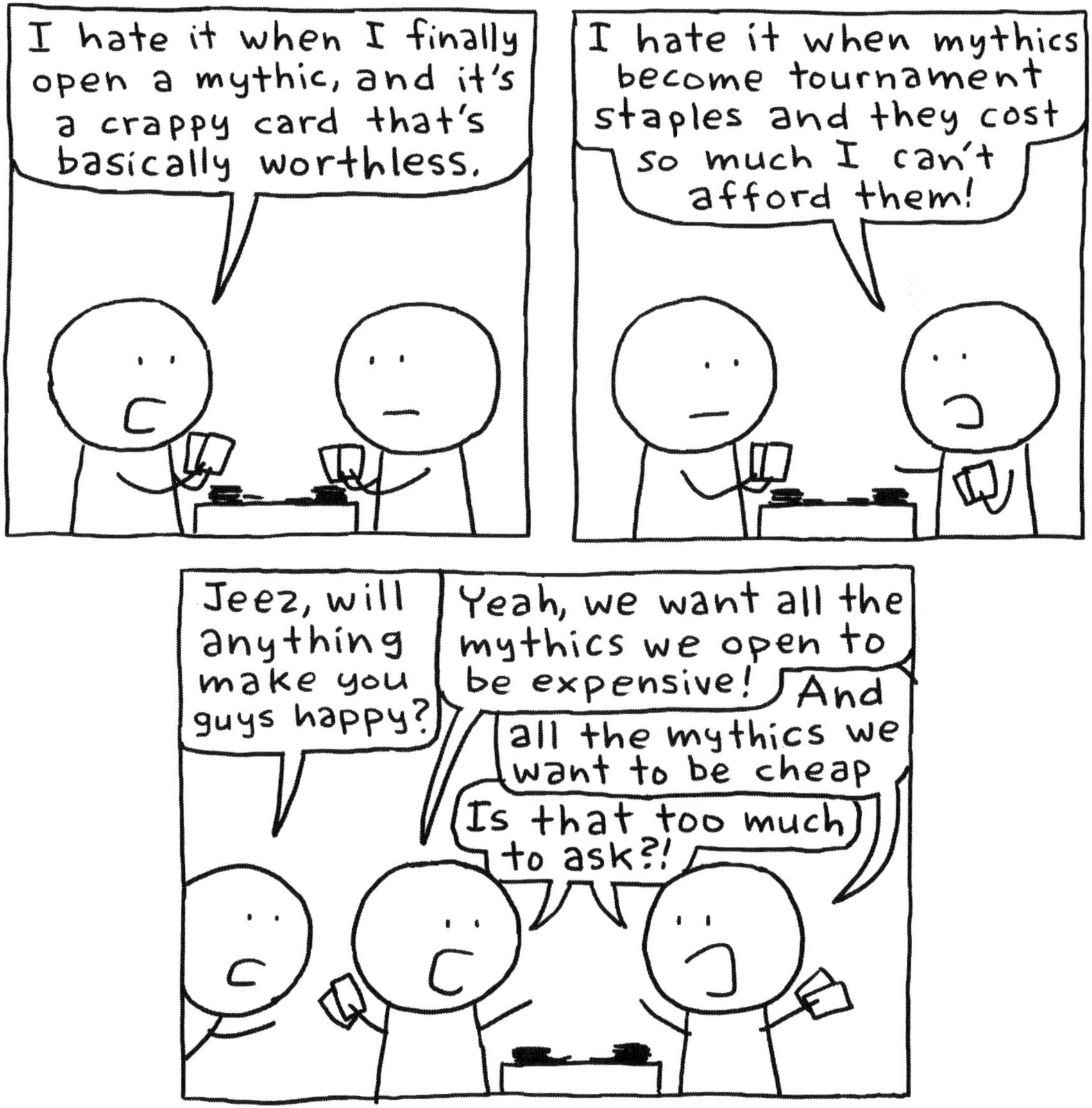
I hate it when I finally open a mythic, and it's a crappy card that's basically worthless.
I hate it when mythics become tournament staples and they cost so much I can't afford them!
Jeez, will anything make you guys happy?
Yeah, we want all the mythics we open to be expensive!
And all the mythics we want to be cheap
Is that too much to ask?!

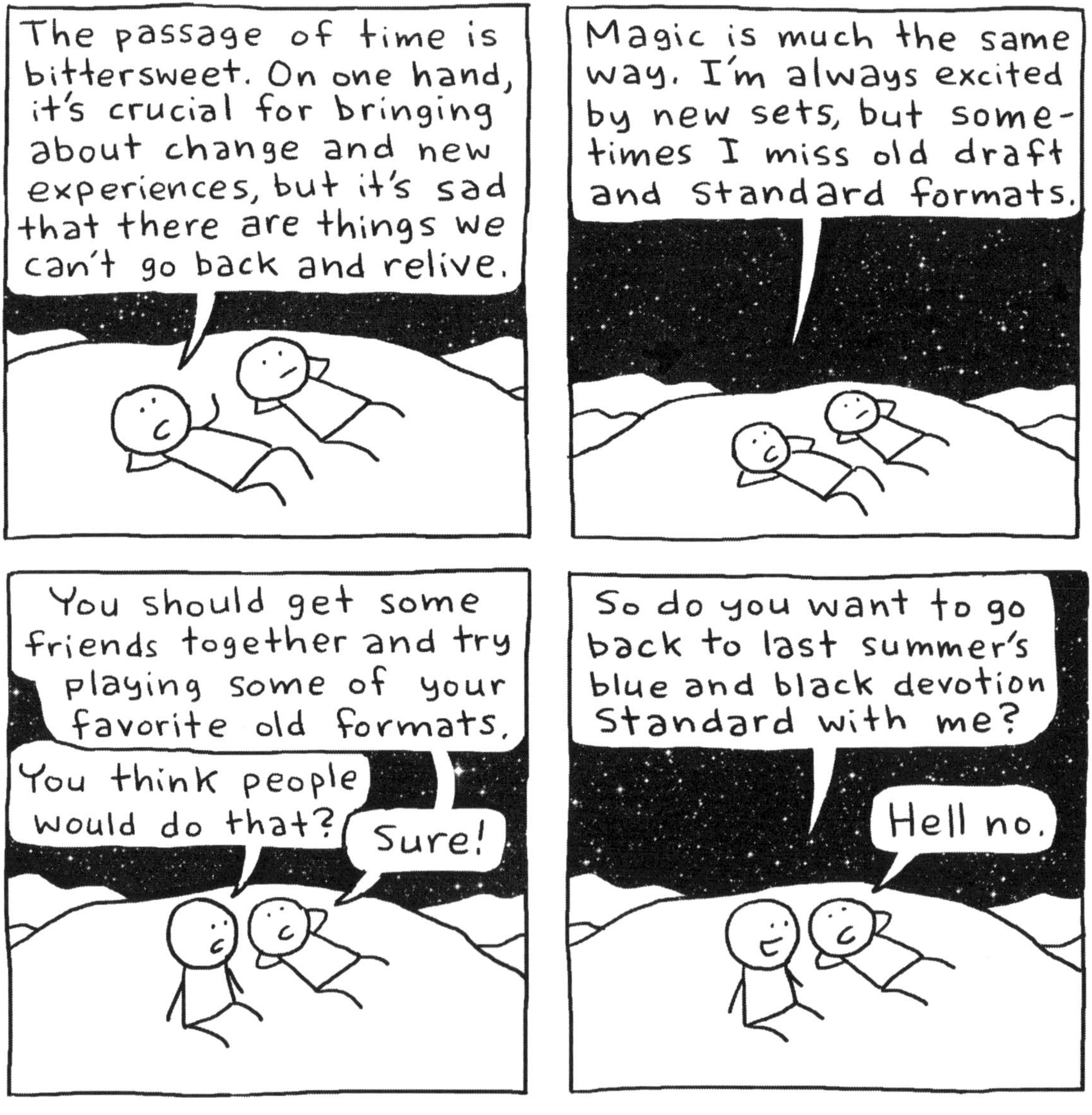

The passage of time is bittersweet. On one hand, it's crucial for bringing about change and new experiences, but it's sad that there are things we can't go back and relive.
Magic is much the same way. I'm always excited by new sets, but some-times I miss old draft and Standard formats.
You should get some friends together and try playing some of your favorite old formats.
You think people would do that?
Sure!
So do you want to go back to last summer's blue and black devotion Standard with me?
Hell no.

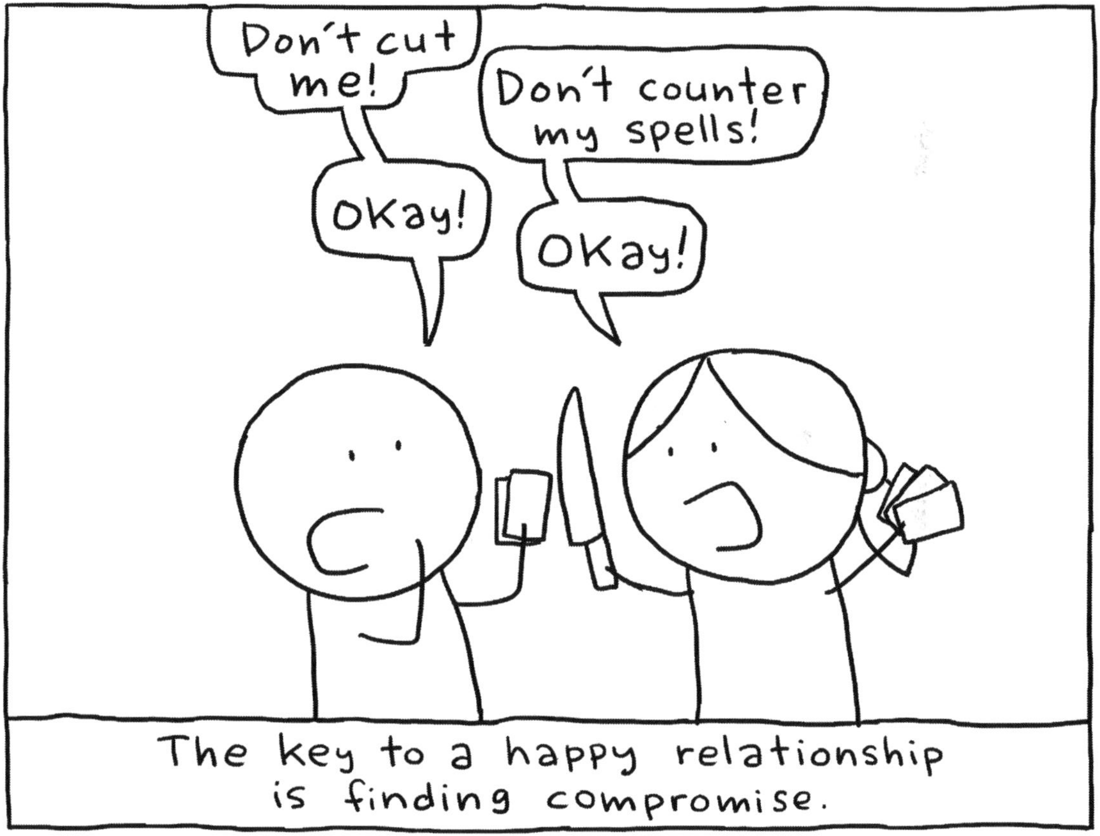
Don't cut me!
Okay!
Don't counter my spells!
Okay!
The key to a happy relationship is finding compromise.

I can't believe some Magic cards are worth so much! They're basically just printed paper!
Couldn't you say the same thing about money?

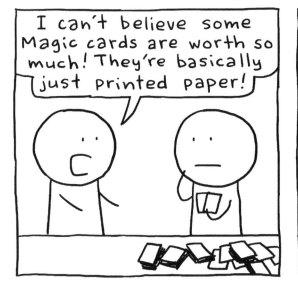

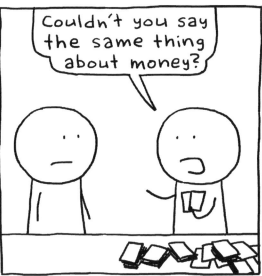

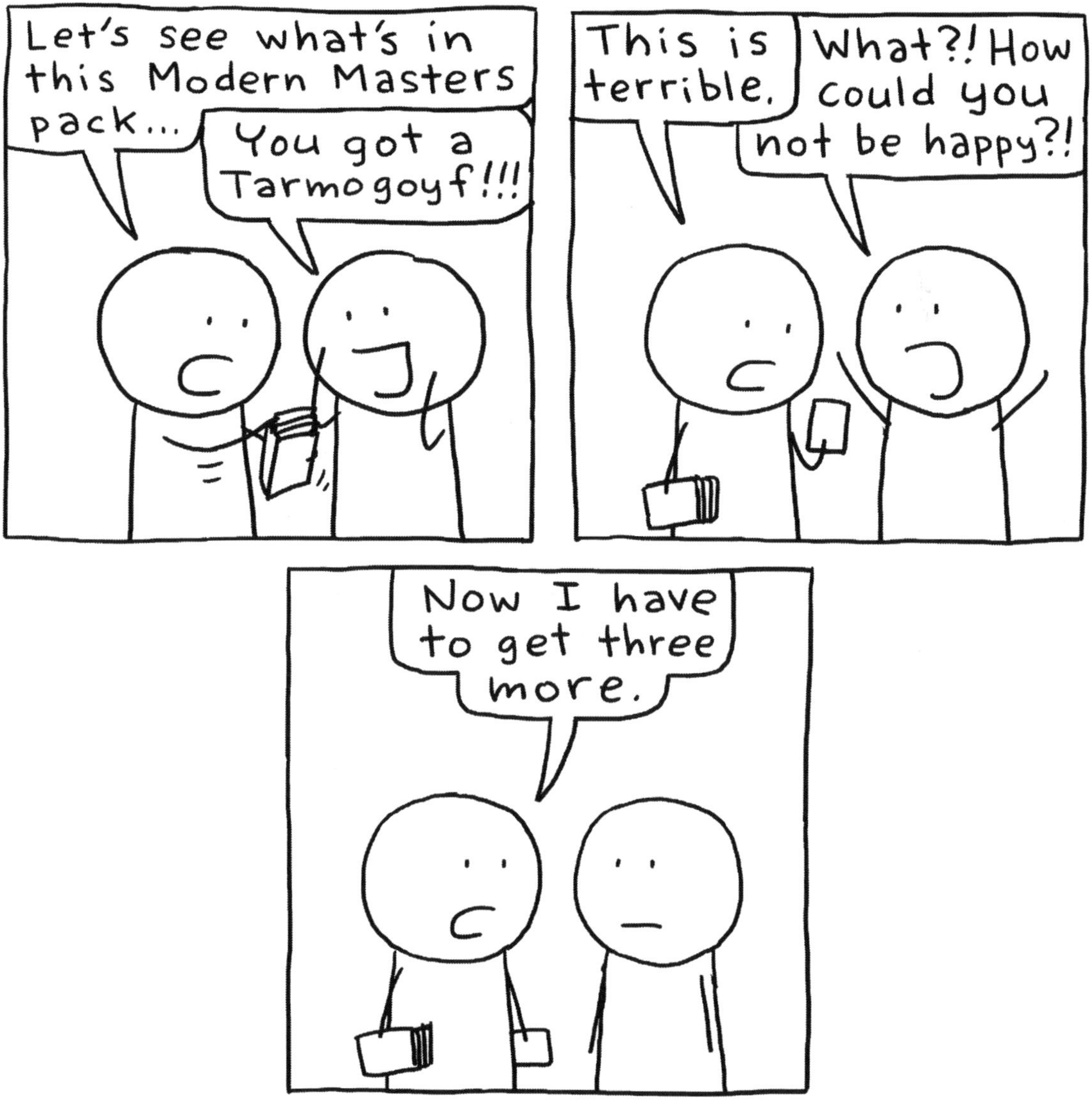
Let's see what's in this Modern Masters pack...
You got a Tarmogoyf!!!
This is terrible.
What?! How could you not be happy?!
Now I have to get three more.

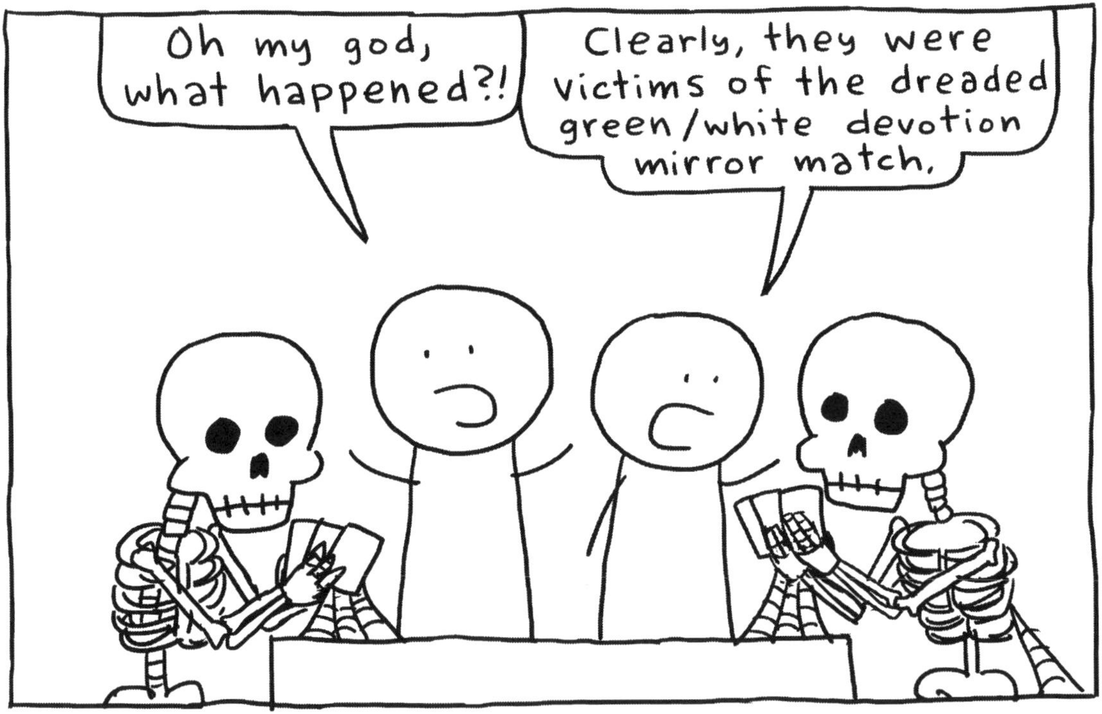
Oh my god, what happened?!
Clearly, they were victims of the dreaded green/white devotion mirror match.

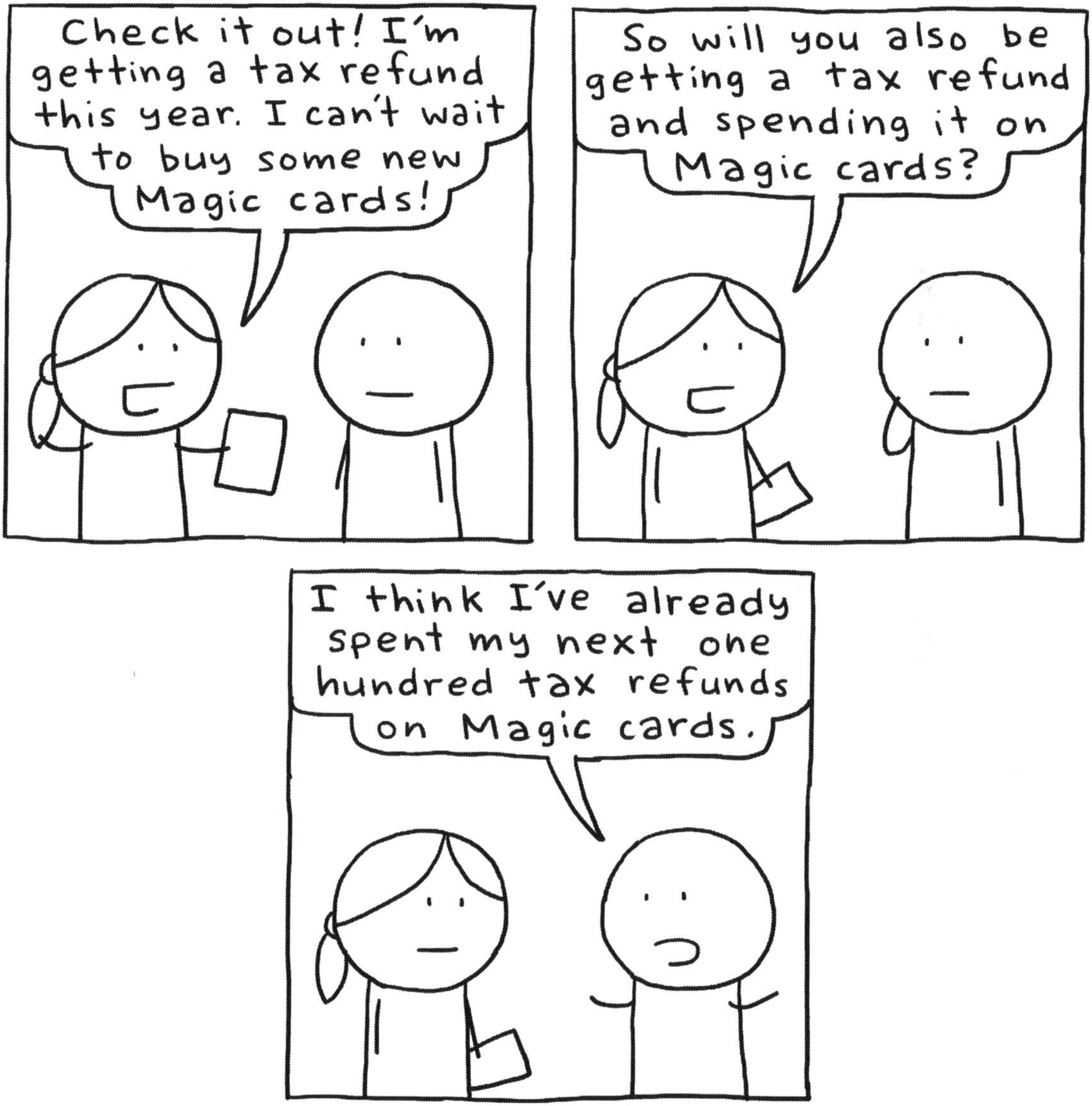
Check it out! I'm getting a tax refund this year. I can't wait to buy some new Magic cards!
So will you also be getting a tax refund and spending it on Magic cards?
I think I've already spent my next one hundred tax refunds on Magic cards.

Someday I want to be as good as Luis Scott-Vargas.
You'll have to practice really hard, but maybe one day you can be good at Magic like LSV.
Magic?! No, I want to be good at puns like LSV!
Don't even bother trying.

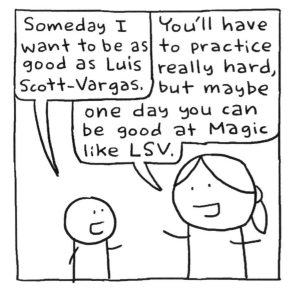

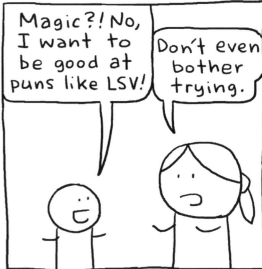

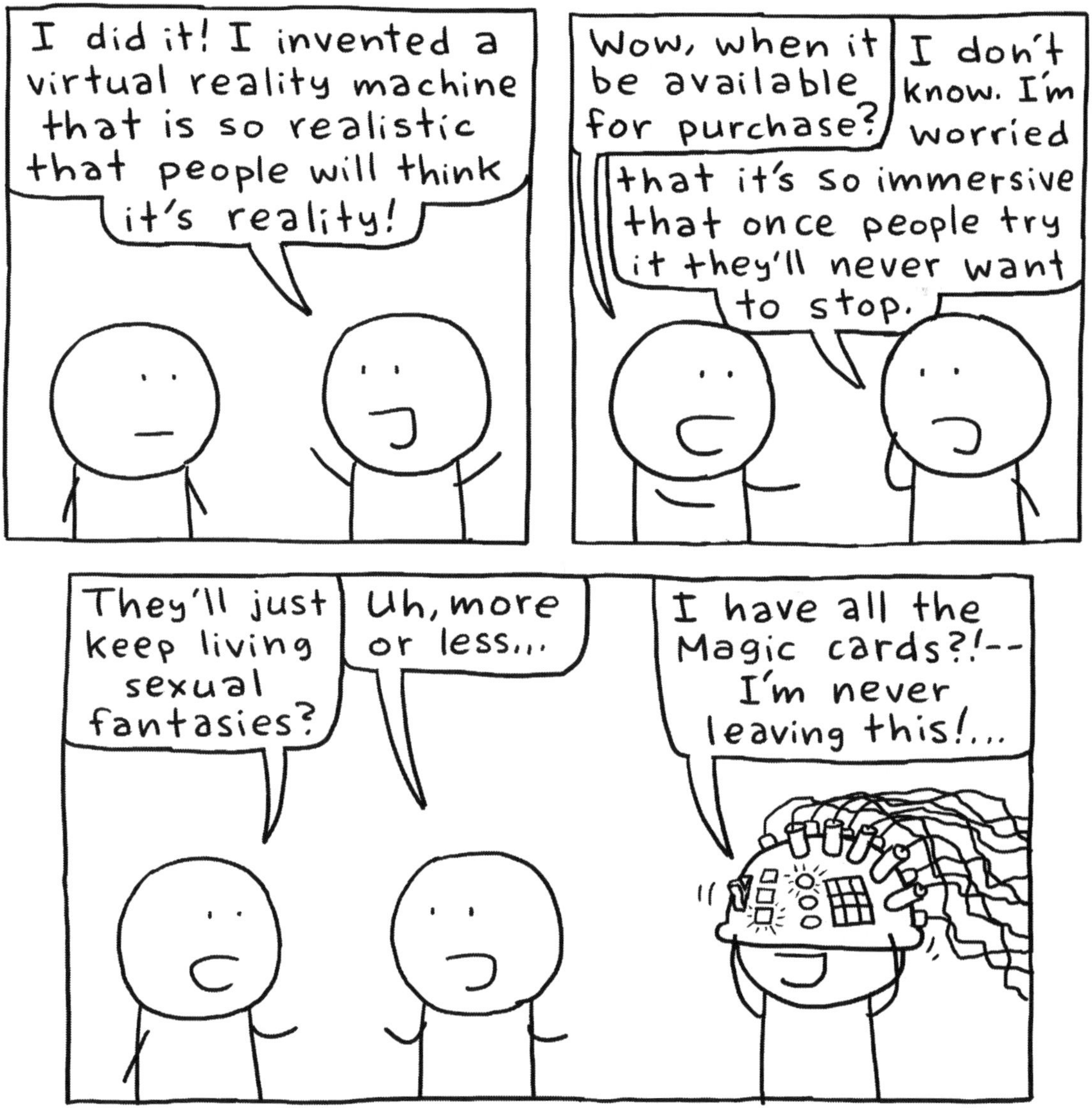
I did it! I invented a virtual reality machine that is so realistic that people will think it's reality!
Wow, when it be available for purchase?
I don't know. I'm worried that it's so immersive that once people try it they'll never want to stop.
They'll just keep living sexual fantasies?
Uh, more or less...
I have all the Magic cards?!-- I'm never leaving this!...

Cardboard Crack has been online since 2013, featuring comics exclusively about the world's most addictive game, Magic: The Gathering. Since that time, the Cardboard Crack website has gained many thousands of followers and many millions of page views. It has received links from a wide variety of prominent personalities in the Magic community, from Aaron Forsythe (current director of Magic: The Gathering R&D) to Jon Finkel (widely regarded as one of the greatest Magic players of all-time). Cardboard Crack is also featured in the weekly newsletter of StarCityGames.com (the world's largest Magic store).

New comics can be found regularly at:
cardboard-crack.com
facebook.com/CardboardCrack

Check out these other Cardboard Crack books:
Cardboard Crack
I will never quit Cardboad Crack
Cardboard Crack anytime, anywhere
Cardboard Crack until the day I die
I'm always thinking about Cardboard Crack

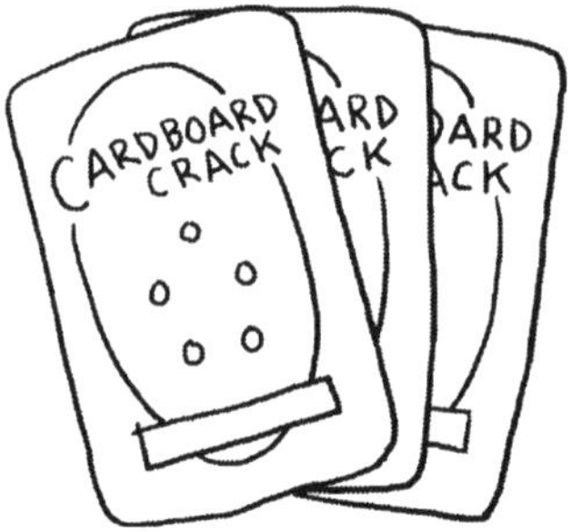
CARDBOARD CRACK

Made in the USA
Middletown, DE
08 May 2016